EXPLORATION OF INTERNATIONAL RELATIONS DATA

AN OBJECT-ORIENTED APPROACH

Sigrid Unseld

IEEE Computer Society Press
Los Alamitos, California

Washington • Brussels • Tokyo

Library of Congress Cataloging-in-Publication Data

Unseld, Sigrid.
Exploration of international relations data: an object-oriented approach / Sigrid Unseld.
p. cm.
Includes bibliographical references and index.
ISBN 0-8186-7095-9.
1. Object-oriented programming (Computer science).
2. International relations—Data bases I. Title.
QA76.64.U57 1997
327' .0285'74—dc20

95-8108
CIP

IEEE Computer Society Press
10662 Los Vaqueros Circle
P.O. Box 3014
Los Alamitos, CA 90720-1314

IEEE Computer Society Press Order Number BP07095
Library of Congress Number 95-8108
ISBN 0-8186-7095-9

Additional copies may be ordered from:

IEEE Computer Society Press
Customer Service Center
10662 Los Vaqueros Circle
P.O. Box 3014
Los Alamitos, CA 90720-1314
Tel: +1-714-821-8380
Fax: +1-714-821-4641
Email: cs.books@computer.org

IEEE Service Center
445 Hoes Lane
P.O. Box 1331
Piscataway, NJ 08855-1331
Tel: +1-908-981-1393
Fax: +1-908-981-9667
mis.custserv@computer.org

IEEE Computer Society
13, Avenue de l'Aquilon
B-1200 Brussels
BELGIUM
Tel: +32-2-770-2198
Fax: +32-2-770-8505
euro.ofc@computer.org

IEEE Computer Society
Ooshima Building
2-19-1 Minami-Aoyama
Minato-ku, Tokyo 107
JAPAN
Tel: +81-3-3408-3118
Fax: +81-3-3408-3553
tokyo.ofc@computer.org

Publisher: Matt Loeb
Acquisitions Editor: Bill Sanders
Developmental Editor: Cheryl Smith
Advertising/Promotions: Tom Fink
Production Editor: Lisa O'Conner
Printed in the United States of America by BookCrafters

The Institute of Electrical and Electronics Engineers, Inc

PREFACE

As the complexity of the world increases, so too does the volume of information available in all fields of research. International relations is no exception. Information converted to structured data and collected into large datasets is available on phenomena such as crises, conflicts, countries, leaders, and on socioeconomic and ecological issues. A mass of unstructured data, written text on current and past events together with interpretations and possible explanations, is produced in the form of books, reports, and articles. In addition, on-line news sources such as Reuters provide daily coverage of worldwide events. Computer technology was an obvious choice as a means of coping with the mass of information that has become available. Numerous computer programs and systems have been developed to facilitate data collection, storage, and processing. Clearly, the greater density of information and its ready availability to political decision makers and analysts have had considerable influence on the way both national and foreign policy are currently decided.

The increase in computer-readable data on information that is relevant to politics, together with new, more powerful computational techniques that operate on this data, have also had an impact on the sector of the international relations research community that favors computational approaches. Numerous systems have emerged, embodying different programming paradigms and using various representation, learning, and reasoning techniques to study the phenomena of international relations. The potential of artificial intelligence for symbolic modeling, and the awareness of the limitations of purely quantitative analyses, inspired many computationally oriented political science scholars to seek new ways of approaching their research topics. The majority of their work has focused on conceptualizing and implementing various domain theories that model, for example, the processes involved in political decision making and simulate the interactions of parties in cooperative or conflict situations.

While many of the present computational efforts in the field are valid in the sense that they experiment with new techniques and procure new perspectives for the study of political phenomena, the following issues have not received much attention:

Exploration of data Largely absent in the computational branch of international relations are systems that use modern software engineering technology and provide various techniques and methods to analyze politically relevant data and to help synthesize the information conveyed in large datasets. The work by Young (1970) on exploratory analysis and Andriole and Young's project of a user-oriented crisis-warning system (Andriole and Young, 1976) stand out as notable exceptions, although they lack the capability of today's hardware and software technology. More recently, Schrodt (1984a, 1987a, 1987b, 1989) has used different algorithms from artificial intelligence and machine learning for the purpose of analyzing and exploring international relations data.

Working with different datasets Most systems developed in international relations are customized to one particular set of data. They are too specific to operate on different, often incompatible representations of existing datasets. However, this does not apply to Mallery's Feature Vector Editor, which offers general editing facilities for a variety of codebooks and datasets (Mallery, 1988b). Equally, the algorithms developed by Schrodt (1984a, 1987a, 1987b, 1989) are not confined to a particular dataset but are applicable to different datasets in international relations as well as to datasets in other domains.

Influence of a particular computational approach Although computational models in international relations are at the crossroads of two disciplines, the focus has usually been on the problems to be solved rather than on the software engineering techniques and the programming paradigms that are used in the process. Thus, the influence of a particular computational approach on the kind of problem solving that is undertaken is rarely investigated. However, the work of Sylvan, Goel, and Chandrasekaran, which, while modeling aspects of Japanese energy supply decision making, investigated the usefulness of information processing as a potentially useful way of understanding political decision making (Sylvan et al., 1991a).

Obviously, these issues are different in nature. While the first and the second concern problems that are relevant to scholars of international relations, the third is of particular relevance to the computer science community. This study addresses this last issue while presenting a solution to the domain-specific problems mentioned in the other issues.

The Topic of this Study

The lack of appropriate computational assistance in the systematic analysis of phenomenological data and in the work on different data collections has frequently prevented scholars of international relations from making full use of the information potentially available to them. As a result, large quantities of carefully collected data are lying idle, instead of being used as a valuable source for investigating phenomena within international relations. Even if the usefulness of such data collections for research in international relations has to be carefully assessed, scholars and analysts should at least have the means to explore this data in the way they consider appropriate and to the degree they require. What is needed is a system that assists researchers in making use of the data they and others have collected. Rather than modeling a particular theory, the system should provide a set of methods and techniques, including knowledge-based techniques, which help inspect, analyze, and synthesize the data and gather new findings. In addition, the system must be capable of operating on different datasets in order to allow users to work with the data they are most interested in, as well as to explore further across different data collections.

Developing such a system is an interdisciplinary project that involves both international relations and computer science. The techniques of the former are used to address the problems of the latter. Yet rather than concentrate exclusively on the final product, it is crucial to focus equally on the problem-solving process and to evaluate the impact of the techniques that are applied. On the one hand, the potential of those techniques with respect to domain-specific demands has to be exploited and their possibilities and limitations exposed. On the other hand, and bearing in mind the analogy of the hammer to which everything appears to be a nail,[1] their influence in shaping the way in which a domain problem is approached has to be acknowledged.

This study uses object-oriented programming and modern software engineering techniques to develop and, later, extend a prototype

[1] Kaplan's "law of the instrument." In Abraham Kaplan, *The Conduct of Inquiry: Methodology for Behavioral Science*, Chandler, Scranton, Pa., 1964.

system for data exploration. The domain-specific objective is to bridge the gap between large bodies of data and the researchers who wish to use and analyze them. From the perspective of the international relations community, the project is promising on several grounds:

Extracting information from data Simple but effective facilities for browsing, inspecting, and comparing data mean that many interesting characteristics of a dataset can be explored more reliably, faster, and more easily than would be possible with a manual search. Other, more sophisticated analysis tools can complement surface findings by yielding inferential and condensed information based on the data examined. Given the opportunities these tools provide, large collections of data can easily be used for reviewing existing hypotheses and generating new ones. This bottom-up approach to studying different aspects of the phenomena might prove to be more productive than the more frequently adopted top-down approaches based on *a priori* assumptions about "the primary mechanisms" in political behavior and decision making.

Working with different datasets Data exploration across different data sets on the same phenomenon (for example, international conflicts) permits a comparison of different findings and allows the user to search for the causes of any divergence. Some findings may also hint at new lines of inquiry or indicate where richer data would be needed to address a given research problem. Exploration of data on different phenomena (for example, data on national profiles, economic developments, international organizations) on the other hand, helps to shed light on the interdependence of political, socioeconomic, and ecological factors. Having a system operate on different datasets rather than being customized to one in particular allows scholars to pursue many interesting research questions.

Matching data and analysis Limited interchangeability and doubtful reliability across datasets, as implied, for example, by comparative studies of the WEIS and the COPDAB datasets (Howell, 1983; Vincent, 1983; McClelland, 1983), suggest that the circumstances under which a dataset may be used should be carefully considered. A system that provides tools for examining the coding categories as well as their proportions and patterns helps the user to decide what weight these categories should be given in a particular analysis, or which of them should be included, or excluded.

Assessing technical and/or methodological feasibility Few of the international relations researchers who favor computational approaches engage in careful evaluation of the feasibility of the available techniques or systems, and thus often either underestimate or overestimate the potential at hand. An example of the latter is the processing of unrestricted text. Although there is a growing number of natural language systems, they have yet to live up to what some international relations scholars believe them capable of—for example, the automatic parsing of huge bodies of politically relevant texts (books, interviews, historical records) or automatic processing of daily news agency reports. Other scholars, inspired by what human experts can do, and thus satisfied with nothing less, often fail to acknowledge the usefulness of computational systems or concepts for specific tasks. Discussing the kind of problem that can be mastered and showing how they are tackled by techniques such as object-oriented programming techniques help scholars of international relations to size up the possibilities and limitations of these techniques.

From a computer science point of view, the challenge is to develop a system that effectively addresses these domain-relevant issues. Evidently, this is not a trivial undertaking since there is no readily available design that could be implemented. Rather, an object-oriented approach to data exploration is a research issue that suggests a prototyping-oriented, stepwise refinement process: the first step involves the design and implementation of a particular operational system. Successive steps extend the original system, thereby defining components that can be used for the development of other data-exploration systems.

Moving from specific to more general considerations, this study on data exploration is divided into two parts.

Part I: A Prototype System for Data Exploration

Part I describes the development of a prototype system that aims to assist users in exploring domain-specific data. The domain that has been chosen is international relations, but any domain for which systematic data exploration is crucial could be used. The prototype, called CrisView (an abbreviated form for view or review of crises), operates on publicly available datasets that describe international conflicts and country profiles. The datasets contain highly structured coded data—that is, factual data that has been hand-compiled into feature vector format. Although desirable, the use of textual information such as news agency reports and summaries of crises and conflicts, which are sometimes referred to as "narrative data," is beyond the scope of the prototype.

A high-level object-oriented approach has been chosen with the additional goal of investigating object-oriented claims for modular software engineering design. The implementation language is CLOS (Common LISP Object System), which in 1994 became the first ANSI standard object-oriented programming language. The prototype is fully object oriented. All data items that are imported from domain-specific datasets are represented as instances of object classes and can thus be manipulated in a flexible way. As will be shown, data representation in the form of objects has distinct advantages over other forms of representation (for example, the tables and tuples in relational databases). An entire dataset corresponds to a document. Documents are the main entities managed by the prototype. The concept of documents, which follows a design principle that has been popularized primarily by Apple Computer, enables the user to work conveniently with his or her choice of dataset, having to worry neither about loading data into the system nor about the internal representation of the data. The prototype supports several analysis techniques, ranging from simple browsing, filtering, and retrieval mechanisms to more sophisticated and complex learning and reasoning algorithms. The usefulness and limitations of these techniques with respect to data exploration are discussed and illustrated.

Much emphasis is placed on the role of object-oriented programming in addressing the technical problems that evolve around data representation and data analyses (for example, dealing with different data structures across datasets, defining efficient operations for different types and aggregations of data, matching data format with the data requirements of analysis techniques, providing a convenient and easy-to-use interface to the data, and so forth). General design considerations are followed by a detailed description of the various aspects of the development process. The feasibility of particular design decisions and their consequences is further investigated in Part II.

Part II: A Protocol for Data Exploration Systems

Extensibility is a problem that seriously challenges most applications in computer science and artificial intelligence. Computational models in international relations are a case in point. They are usually too specific to operate on data other than those for which they were originally designed. Moreover, they are too rigid to incorporate already existing analysis algorithms, requiring instead that they be built up from scratch. The object-oriented approach presented in this study breaks with the "one dataset, one system" approach, which prevails in computational models of international relations. While the prototype developed in Part I deals explicitly with accommodating the data from two different data collections, Part II goes on to investigate the potential of an object-oriented approach with respect to data handling and analysis extensibility. In particular, this part explores the possibilities and limitations of metaobject programming, a topic that is receiving widespread attention in current object-oriented software design.

Based on the concept of metaobject protocols for object-oriented languages, Part II proposes a specific protocol for data exploration systems. Metaobject protocols are interfaces to a language that enable a user to modify the language's behavior and implementation and to adjust it to new requirements. The main objective of a protocol for data exploration systems is to facilitate the modification and extension of an existing data exploration system and to enable a user to build new systems tailored to his or her needs. The protocol contains four components. The first component embraces the classes of the CrisView prototype developed in Part I. On the basis of the prototype, three additional components will be defined. They provide functionality that is generally required in a data exploration system, functionality that supports specialized behavior for new versions of data exploration systems, and functionality that yields introspective access to the elements of the prototype and the new classes of the protocol. These additional components, dedicated as they are to data exploration, constitute a framework for developing a variety of new data exploration systems. Since system design in general is an activity for which little guidance is available, there is not usually one best solution. Consequently, the solutions offered in Part II are but a specific subset of many.

The motivation for designing and implementing a system that supports systematic data exploration has been a domain-specific one: to assist domain experts in making full use of the information in carefully collected data. Developing a prototype system and the step-by-step procedure involved in extending it in order to meet different data requirements and different user needs are challenges that face the computer scientist. Since this study addresses different research communities, it is perhaps appropriate to conclude this preface with some comments on interdisciplinary work.

INTERDISCIPLINARY WORK

Working in an interdisciplinary field is a constant struggle to satisfy the expectations of both sides. The interdisciplinary nature of the work here arises from the combination of object-oriented programming techniques and methods of artificial intelligence with theories and data from international relations. The challenges are twofold. On the one hand, the engineering aspects of a computer-based system should reflect the latest improvements in programming paradigms, shed light on the relevance of particular features of those paradigms for solving specific problems, and, furthermore, explore new scientific ground. It is not uncommon for computer scientists to sing the praises of highly sophisticated or elegant solutions to technical problems, with no direct relevance to applications, rather than praise more practical applications that serve a specific purpose. On the other hand, social science researchers, and here we will concentrate on international relations scholars, expect practical results, answers to specific questions, and new insights into domain-relevant problems. In addition, policy makers wish to be meaningfully assisted in a number of ways, ranging from simple time-saving tasks to sophisticated and often domain-specific analyses of the material concerned. The techniques that underlie a given application are of minor interest to both the international relations scholar and the policy maker, and their level of sophistication is of even smaller interest. Given the almost exclusive interests of the different research communities and the little empathy between them, it is clearly advisable to make a statement about what the interdisciplinary work attempts to accomplish and to clarify the way in which these aims relate to one or the other community.

Research work that involves two disciplines comes in many different forms. Often it is a type of work in which the models and theories of one discipline are extended by using the modeling potential of another discipline. A case in point is computational linguistics, where computational models have dynamically and quantitatively extended linguistic theories over the past few years. Researchers engaging in this type of work require not only a good understanding of the application domain and its problems, but they also need to be highly effective in their use of modeling techniques. In some disciplines, however, views on how to structure and categorize phenomena diverge considerably, and no unifying theory exists. As a result, the computational models reflect but one specific domain theory and, thus, often have little bearing on the discipline as a whole. Many computer-based models in international relations have been developed along this line.

Moreover it is mostly the scholar of the application domain who builds the models, rather than the computer scientist. This may account for the fact that few models live up to the standards of current computer science engineering.

A second type of merging different disciplines consists in the application of techniques and methods of one discipline to analyze the data of the other discipline. Both those who carry out computationally oriented research in international relations and application-oriented computer scientists have participated in this kind of work. Depending on the interests of those involved, the research tends to lean either toward the development of sophisticated algorithms for highly specific data or toward substantive results with "off-the-shelf" programs. In both cases, there is usually little communication between the two disciplines.

Finally, a third type of work between different disciplines may be located somewhere between the two types just mentioned. It is intended neither to extend or model the theories of a discipline, nor is it confined to the development or use of algorithms to analyze phenomenal data. Rather, it involves the investigation of the potential of one discipline to meet domain-specific needs of the other discipline. In both computer science and international relations, this type of interdisciplinary work has been largely ignored, despite the fact that both disciplines could benefit from the process. On the one hand, it contributes to research in computer science by exhibiting the possibilities of current research paradigms for solving the specific problems of a domain. On the other hand, it contributes to advances in the field of international relations by providing not only a useful application but also an insight into the feasibility of available computational techniques and their impact on further research projects.

ACKNOWLEDGEMENTS

I thank all those who helped me to write this book. At the time I was a postdoc fellow at the Massachusetts Institute of Technology and supported by a grant from the Swiss National Science Foundation. I am grateful to Prof. Pierre Allan who evaluated my NFS proposal and suggested I should go to MIT. A number of people from both the Political Science Department and the Artificial Intelligence Laboratory contributed to this book. In particular, thanks are due to Prof. Hayward Alker for introducing me to the domain of international relations and the artificial intelligence/international relations community. His comments and constructive criticism on the manuscript were most appreciated; Frank Sherman for being kind enough to permit the use of his comprehensive dataset; John Mallery for working together with me on the inductive algorithm; Ian Horswill for useful suggestions and many stimulating discussions.

I thank Prof. Kurt Bauknecht, head of the Computer Science Department at the University of Zurich, for generously supporting the work reported in this book. I also express my thanks to Prof. Robert Trappl, director of the Austrian Research Institute for Artificial Intelligence in Vienna, for his support and motivation over many years and for his helpful review of the manuscript.

I would like to express my gratitude to Allan Neil for the proofreading and editors Matt Loeb and Lisa O'Conner from the IEEE Computer Society for putting the manuscript into its final shape.

My special thanks go to Marc Domenig who not only gave the CrisView prototype its name but also encouraged me to write this book. I thank Marc for his patience during my long absence from home.

Zurich, Oct. 1996

CONTENTS

Part I
A Prototype System for Data Exploration

This part will describe the development of a prototype system for data exploration. The development of such a prototype is the first step in a process that aims to contribute to advances in the field of international relations by offering an alternative for those who search for computational assistance in analyzing and exploring their carefully coded data, those who spend their time implementing a technique to analyze one particular dataset, and those who are involved in preparing data in order to adjust them to the assumptions of a particular system. Considering the costs and development time involved, it seems inappropriate to build numerous customized systems for either specific datasets or specific analysis tasks. The alternative would be to develop a system that adapts to various data and model assumptions, and which can easily be extended to meet new requirements.

Supporting data and modeling needs of users, avoiding duplication of effort, and fostering collaboration and exchange between research communities, are the domain-specific objectives of this study. From a computer science point of view, what motivates this research is the investigation of object-oriented programming techniques for addressing domain-specific problems, the discovery of essential abstractions, and the definition of appropriate interfaces to data and algorithms. Brought together, these objectives define an interdisciplinary approach that neither in substance nor in methodology has received much attention in the computational branch of the international relations research community. The first part of this study reflects the orientation across disciplines: identification of domain-specific problems and task specifications is followed by the design and implementation of a prototype system.

While a prototype has to meet the objectives that lie at the heart of the research project as a whole, it is necessarily restricted in scope and volume. The prototype's major restriction is in the type of phenomenological data it operates on.

Chapter 1
THE DATA TO BE EXPLORED

Collecting data on political phenomena such as crises and conflicts has been a major preoccupation of many scholars in the field of international relations. Various traditions and coding practices have evolved over the years (Sherman, 1987b), generating numerous highly structured datasets amenable to formal, computational, and noncomputational analyses. Some of the better known projects/datasets in the United States include the Comparative Research on the Events of Nations (CREON) project at the Ohio State University (Hermann et al., 1973); the World Event/Interaction Survey (WEIS) project at the University of Southern California (McClelland, 1976); the Conflict and Peace Databank (COPDAB) project at the University of North Carolina (Azar, 1980); the University of Michigan Correlates of War (COW) project (Small and Singer, 1982) and its extensions, the Militarized Interstate Disputes (Gochman and Maoz, 1984) and the Behavioral Correlates of War (BCOW) data project (Leng, 1987); the study of conflict management initiated by Haas (1986), continued by Haas, Butterworth, and Nye (1972), and later by Butterworth (1976), which led to the FACS project at MIT (Farris et al., 1980; Alker and Sherman, 1982) and its extension, the SHERFACS project (Sherman, 1987a). Among the more prominent projects conducted in Europe are the Wars of Ten Years project by Kende (1978) and the project by Ganzel and Meyer-Stamer (1986). For an overview of projects and datasets in international relations, see Cioffi-Revilla (1990).

In response to the growing need of researchers for richer and more comprehensive descriptions of their domains' phenomena, attempts have been made to bridge the gap between in-depth descriptive analyses of selected historical episodes (episodic narratives), and comprehensive long-term interaction chronologies with pre-coded telegraphic event descriptions (Davies and McDaniel, 1991). Moreover, the availability of on-line information on national and international events has given rise to a search for a more integrated and comprehensive approach to data collection. The current DDIR[1] events data project GEDS (Global Events Data System) at the University of Maryland (see section 2.4.2) is a case in point (Davies, 1991). As a result of both previous and more recent data-collecting efforts, large bodies of data are readily available in computer-readable form to international relations analysts. Three types of data can be distinguished: unstructured textual (natural language) data, structured or tagged textual data, and structured coded data.

1.1 DIFFERENT TYPES OF PHENOMENOLOGICAL DATA

Textual accounts of politically relevant content make up the bulk of information available to researchers (for example, yearbooks, archives, newspapers, on-line news-agency services). However, the automatic semantic processing of such *unstructured textual data* remains an unsolved problem, despite recent progress in research areas such as computational linguistics and artificial intelligence (Gazdar and Mellish, 1989) and despite their respective claims, particularly the latter's. A second source of information for international relations research is *structured textual data*—that is, text that is structured into semantic units by inserting special symbols. These symbols, called tags, facilitate search and retrieval operations. Often, some of them are also employed for layout purposes, thus reflecting the partial overlap of information between visual layout and semantic structuring. Structured textual data are used primarily for archiving (for example, newspapers) but also for representing encyclopedic and dictionary information. A third source, and from a computational point of view the most convenient, consists of what may be called *structured coded data*. As the name suggests, the radical difference between this type of data and textual data is that the original information is translated into a highly structured format. The original information is coded, and the coded values are assigned to a limited set of predefined categories according to an arbitrary but fixed coding scheme.

In data collecting and coding parlance, the term *category* is frequently used in the sense of a variable, but can also denote a group of variables that have some characteristic or quality in common (for example, the category "people" in the World Facts dataset includes population, birth rate, death rate, net migration rate, infant mortality rate, life expectancy, and total fertility rate). The literature on data collections and data collecting is not always consistent when it comes to the use of terms such as *categories, variables, factors,* and so on. It would, therefore, be useful at this point to introduce the terminology that will be used in this study.

Terminology

Variable A ***variable*** is a symbol that names a single property of a phenomenon (for example, intensity of a conflict, membership in an international organization). A variable has a specific value or a set of values but does not contain other variables.

Substructure A ***substructure*** is a part of an individual phenomenon in a dataset. As the name suggests, a substructure denotes a compound description of some aspect of the phenomenon that can be further disaggregated. Frequently, a substructure is composed of a set of variables, but it may also be composed of other substructures. In the former case, a common way to represent the data of a substructure is a feature vector.

Feature vector A ***feature vector*** is a sequence of variable value pairs, or features. It can also be viewed as a list of properties with associated values, or a frame with slot and values (Mallery, 1988b, 4). The values of the variables in feature vectors do not represent other feature vectors. Feature vectors are often used in international relations datasets to represent the data that describe an individual phenomenon.

Unit A ***unit*** denotes the individual real-world phenomenon for which data has been collected in a dataset. In the SHERFACS dataset, the unit is an international conflict, in the CIA World Facts dataset, the unit is a country. A unit may be composed of a set of variables, or—if its description is more complex—the unit may be composed of several possibly different types of substructures.

Logical entity In this study the term *logical entity* refers to all the elements in a dataset, the units, their substructures and the variables that have been used to describe the properties of a unit. There are two types of logical entities in the World Facts dataset: the units or individual countries, and the variables that describe the properties of each country. The SHERFACS dataset contains three types of logical entities: the units or international conflicts, five types of feature vectors, and the variables in each feature vector.

1.1.1 Three Criteria

The three types of data mentioned earlier will score differently for criteria such as human effort involved, loss of information, and computer feasibility. The following paragraphs discuss each type of data with respect to these criteria.

Human Effort Involved

When estimating how much human effort is required to store each type of data into its appropriate format, it is evident that unstructured textual data is best. Given today's scanning facilities, no additional work has to be done because the original format and the stored format are the same. In contrast, structured textual data as well as structured coded data are the results of a manual process. For the former, the effort that is needed to produce the desired format depends on the number of different semantic units that are being tagged explicitly. Yet, this is usually less than the effort required for the latter. Producing structured coded data is expensive because it requires the systematic replacing of the data's old format with a new one.

Loss of Information

Unstructured and structured textual data preserve the original amount of information when stored into their respective format (it should be noted that the original form is written text, and not, for example, spoken text). Structured coded data, however, lose part of the original information during the process of coding. The coding scheme that is used provides only a limited number of categories to encode the information. Commitments to a single category might not capture the meaning that was conveyed by a particular piece of information, nor the significance that was attributed to it under different circumstances. In addition, these coding practices inherently rectify the categories because there is no mechanism for representing alternative category systems (Mallery, 1988a, 56). A number of researchers in the field of international relations have thus argued that coded data are of limited use for modeling political phenomena because they fail to capture, consciously or unconsciously, the internationalized, interpretive character of political actions and theories (Alker, 1975). The gravity of this concern, however, depends on the purpose for which the data are used; especially, if the goal is to explore the data rather than to use them for modeling, the concerns are less relevant. Furthermore, in data exploration the categories of a coding scheme might themselves be subjected to investigation.

Computational Feasibility

Approaches to automatic processing of unstructured textual data (or natural language) can roughly be divided into two groups: content-analytic approaches and semantic approaches. Content analyses (Weber, 1985) make use of string or keyword searches to find frequencies and correlations of words, thereby providing information about particular value orientations expressed in textual data (Mallery, 1988a, 47). They analyze neither syntactic structures nor the semantic content of the data and thus avoid many of the problems involved in understanding natural language. Semantic approaches are more ambitious in that they seek to capture the meaning of textual accounts.[2] Since technical and language-inherent difficulties abound, semantic analyses of unrestricted textual accounts are far from being applicable outside the laboratories (Duffy, 1987).

Although statistical methodologies are used extensively for processing textual data,[3] Salton notes that the statistical component provides little information when the full scope of automatic text processing is considered (Salton, 1990, 111). Text processing and analysis become more feasible and productive if structural and semantic considerations are also taken into account. In structured textual data, subdomains that have been demarcated by inserted tags can be retrieved with the use of Boolean operators. The retrieved subdomains can then be subjected to string or keyword search (an extensive overview of keyword search methods, keyword construction, and indexing for the purpose of text retrieval and analysis is given in Salton, 1990). Once these searches are limited to narrow, semantically defined subsets, the quality of the results and the effectiveness of search algorithms are enhanced. Promising applications have triggered efforts to standardize the tagging procedures involved in structuring textual data (for example, Standardized Generalized Markup Language, SGML, ISO-8879, 1986).

Structured coded data carry the greatest potential with regard to computational processing and analyzing. Coded data on domain-specific phenomena are easy to read by computer programs and thus, at least theoretically, can be analyzed by various formal methods, including statistical methods and methods developed in artificial intelligence (AI) and machine learning. Although methods in AI have been applied to unstructured textual data, many of the problems that generally haunt AI systems and AI research paradigms disappear or can be addressed effectively when structured coded data are used. An example is scalability: systems that operate on structured data scale up more easily, that is, they do not "break" when the amount of data multiplies, though their performance might slow down. In contrast, many systems that aim to analyze unstructured textual data work either in a micro world for which complete knowledge is built into the system or are limited to a few carefully prepared texts. A case in point are the top-down or expectation-driven systems in the Yale tradition (Schank and Abelson, 1977; Kolodner, 1983; Schank and Childers, 1984; Alvarado, 1990). Extending the systems' capacity requires considerable manual coding effort, either to update the systems' knowledge base such that additional textual data can be analyzed or to prepare (select, and literally and explicitly express) new textual data.

These criteria highlight some of the differences among the three types of data. Of course, there may be other criteria (for instance, expense). The relevance of a criterion, however, depends on the purpose for which the data will be used.

1.1.2 The Choice of Data

Since one of the goals of this study is to develop an operational prototype for data exploration, computer feasibility is crucial, and thus the use of structured coded data is preferred to other types of data. There are several other reasons for choosing structured coded data.

Explicitness

Any account of domain-specific phenomena (for example, a summary or a report on a current event) abstracts the observed by using some kind of coding. In the social sciences, the coding schema that are applied to generate textual abstraction are mostly implicit and so are the theories about the domain's phenomena that underlie the choice of a particular scheme. Moreover, the use of modal terms in textual accounts is acceptable or even desirable whenever exact definitions cannot be provided. In contrast, the creation of structured coded data requires the coder to make commitments to a specific model or theory that explains the structure, behavior, and interactions of the domain's phenomena. On the one hand, this process makes scholars more aware of the incompleteness of and inconsistencies in their own and other's theories and, hence, urges them to clarify and refine. On the other hand, it facilitates the use of computer-based tools and formal methods in the systematic investigation of the data.

Unused Potential

Structured coded data offer excellent opportunities for gaining additional or new insights into the domain's phenomena because they have generally been constructed for highly dedicated applications but have rarely been subjected to comparison across datasets or investigated for different purposes. Although some of the large collection of events data such as COPDAB, the Conflict and Peace Databank (Azar, 1980),

WEIS, the World Event Interaction Survey (McClelland et al., 1971), or WHPSI, the World Handbook of Political and Social Indicators (Taylor and Joice, 1983) have been used in a variety of studies, the investigations were usually tailored to one particular dataset, and they rarely employed more than one type of technique. Other datasets have received less attention, in particularly those whose data organization exceeds in complexity the flat feature vector structure (see section 3.2.2) commonly used in collections of events data. To illustrate, an example of an entry in COPDAB reads:

900808 645 690 94 ANNEX 37 13 Following AUG 2 INVASION

denoting the date (year/month/day), actor code (Iraq), target code (Kuwait), news source code (Reuters), a one-word action description, the issue type (military/strategic, political/legal), a 15-point international cooperation-conflict scale value, and an event summary of at most 80 characters (example from Davies, 1991). In contrast, the entries in the SHERFACS International Conflict Management dataset (Sherman, 1987a, 1988) are structured in a complex and irregularly shaped manner. SHERFACS is a case in point where the potential of a dataset for providing insight into the structuring of conflict, and conflict behavior—based on its coded data—has not yet been fully exhausted (an extended inductive analysis technique has been applied to the SHERFACS data [Unseld and Mallery, 1992] and will be described in Chapter 4).

Fall-back on Coded Data

Although researchers in the field of international relations are eager to use computational techniques that would allow them to analyze unstructured textual data, such techniques are not yet available. As a result, the interface between unstructured information and the techniques for analyzing and synthesizing the data is still a human coder who spends weeks and even months converting the incoming information into a structure that is acceptable by computational algorithms and procedures. The aforementioned GEDS project is a good example. Its approach to processing articles from the Reuters news agency involves tagging and/or coding the reported events according to the practices defined in GEDS. Although assisted by the system, it is still largely the human coder who is responsible for producing structured textual data amenable to string search within well-defined semantic units or structured coded data that can be used to update existing data collections.

Similarly, many concepts for modeling international political behavior involve the use of textual information. However, when operational models are presented along with these concepts, those models frequently work on data that has been carefully coded in order to meet the requirements of the algorithms they incorporate (see, for example, Sylvan and Majeski, 1992). This "fall-back" on structured coded data as the predominant strategy for dealing with information on political phenomena suggests that closer attention should be paid to how this type of data could be used more effectively by the international relations community as a whole. The efforts spent on data coding could be channeled by developing generally accepted coding schemes that incorporate essential characteristics of the phenomena. Scholars could then use this data as input for their specific models, instead of engaging themselves in the laborious and time-consuming process of constructing the necessary data. In addition, by enabling researchers to exploit fully the information that is cast in coded form, existing datasets stand a better chance of actually being used for research.

The feasibility of structured coded data for computational analysis, the fact that numerous interesting datasets are publicly available and distributed, for example, by ICPSR, the Inter-University Consortium for Political Science and Social Research,[4] and the reasons discussed in the previous paragraphs consolidate the argument for focusing on this type of data. In particular, CrisView, the prototype that will be developed here, operates on data from the SHERFACS dataset,[5] a collection of data on international conflicts and conflict management actions, as well as on subsets of the CIA World Facts Handbook,[6] featuring data on country profiles. The prototype, however, is not limited to these particular datasets.

1.2 Outline of Part I

While this chapter presents the arguments for restricting data exploration to structured coded data, Chapter 2 introduces the purpose and scope of data exploration. It starts by identifying a number of domain-specific problems that have challenged the systematic analysis of phenomenological data and their comparison across datasets. These problems call for a system that is capable of handling differently structured datasets, thereby eliminating the need to build single systems that are customized to a specific dataset. While the development of such a system is the topic of Chapter 3, Chapter 2 will define the concept of data exploration, state the computationally relevant goals with regard to system development, and discuss domain-specific benefits. A brief summary of formal approaches in international relations research will be followed by the comparison between the prototype developed here and existing or projected systems that are related to or share some common ground with the concept of data exploration. The concluding paragraphs will stress the difference between data exploration and information retrieval on the one hand, and hypertext on the other.

Chapter 3 provides a number of strong arguments for choosing an object approach to data exploration. The remaining part of the chapter describes the CrisView prototype. CrisView comprises two conceptual components: data management and data exploration. The data management component embraces all the classes and method interfaces for representing and manipulating the data. The main entity managed by CrisView is the document. A document corresponds to a collection of phenomenological data. Several operations are defined on documents, including the import and export of data (which are crucial for a data exploration system). A major advantage of using documents is the convenience and ease with which users can work with the data they are interested in. All logical entities of a dataset as well as the document itself will be defined as instances of object classes. This characteristic provides great flexibility in exploring the data. The data exploration component presents a hierarchy of windows that enable the user to carry out various exploration tasks. CrisView offers some surface analyses techniques (browsing and inspecting, filtering and retrieval, inquiries, and comparison) as well as knowledge-based analysis techniques. Knowledge-based analysis techniques will be treated separately in Chapter 4.

Chapter 4 presents two knowledge-based analyses techniques supported by CrisView: induction and precedent-based reasoning. Both are believed to be essential for data exploration, and both are sufficiently robust with regard to the characteristics of the domain (international relations) and its data. Induction and precedent-based reasoning form complementary analysis techniques. When the two are combined, the resulting analysis benefits from their respective strengths. The inductive technique incorporated in CrisView extends traditional induction techniques in that it can operate on arbitrarily structured datasets. The precedent-based reasoning capability of CrisView integrates many of the analysis techniques that have been introduced in the third chapter (for example, inquiries, comparison, induction). Instead of being employed in isolation, here they are used in tandem to search for and evaluate relevant precedents. The last section of Chapter 4 addresses some of the challenges involved in exploring and analyzing real-world datasets, touching upon technical as well as methodological problems.

Chapter 5 concludes the first part of this study. The main characteristic of the prototype and of the object-oriented approach to data exploration will be summarized and considerations concerning possible extensions of the prototype will lead into the second part of this study.

ENDNOTES

1. Data Development for International Relations.
2. For a survey of different semantic modeling approaches to natural language, critical discussion of their limitations, and references to particular models and theories, see Mallery, 1988a.
3. Examples include the statistics of word occurrences for setting the coefficient of linear discriminant functions (Salton, 1986), or entropy measurements, which are used to find the words that contribute the most (have the highest entropy) to the characteristics of individual texts (Salton, 1990).
4. ICPSR is a central repository and dissemination service for machine-readable social science data. Currently their archive comprises 28,000 files for nearly 2,300 study titles (annual growth about 200).
5. With the permission of its author, Frank Sherman.
6. This dataset is commercially available on CD-ROM (Bureau of Electronic Publishing).

Chapter 2
DATA EXPLORATION

Increasingly, attempts are made to develop computer programs that will automate, at least partially, the otherwise costly and time-consuming manual task of converting full text information into some structured form. Both the GEDS project (described in greater detail in section 2.4.2) as well as a similar, although much smaller, project called KEDS, Kansas Events Data System (Schrodt et al., 1992), are attempts of this kind. GEDS seeks to automate partially and to assist coders effectively in updating and expanding some of the earlier, more specialized datasets on international crises and conflicts. KEDS generates events data from text provided by the NEXIS data service, working with the WEIS data coding scheme (McClelland et al., 1971). Although neither GEDS nor KEDS equals human coders (experiments with KEDS indicate an 80 to 85 percent agreement with a single human coder within a single source), they are likely to speed up the production of new structured data and the updating of already existing datasets.

However, the question remains as to what the purpose of these efforts should be, whom the updated or new data collections should serve, and, most importantly, how the data can be used.

2.1 Identifying the Problem

The exploration of coded structured data does not figure prominently in the research agenda of those researchers in international relations who favor computer methods. It may be that this issue is not considered spectacular enough or is not regarded as worthwhile in view of immediate research interests; either way little has been done to make use of the information conveyed in existing datasets. Instead, most computational approaches to political phenomena (see section 2.4) have focused on political decision making and models of political behavior, and rather than use existing data collections, the scholars have experimented with their own data, converted into a form their system could manage. This is unfortunate, because many datasets, and particularly those with a rich and detailed description of political phenomena, can yield new insights and possibly new answers to domain-relevant questions.

Due to the advent of systems that accelerate the production of new and updated structured datasets, the gap that already existed between the amount of available data and their usefulness for international relations research is widening. There are at least two reasons that account for the insufficient exploration of many of these datasets, and these will be discussed in the following sections.

2.1.1 Heterogeneous Data Models

International relations datasets organize and represent their data in different ways. The units depicted in these datasets may be described by a set of variables and values, represented in the form of a single feature vector, or they may be composed of several substructures that can further be disaggregated into substructures or variables and values. The organization of the data that have been collected for a unit is characterized by the unit's *data model.* Datasets are frequently biased toward some particular type of data model, reflecting in one way or another the specific—and often limited—research purpose behind the collection effort. Events data, for example, the COPDAB data (Azar, 1980), are a case in point. Breaking down historical connections into "atomistic" actor-action sequences is an analytical move characteristic of the events data coding tradition (Alker, 1985a). The dissection allows comparisons and generalizations to be made across instances of phenomena, thereby serving the specific purpose for which the data were collected.

Although many international relations datasets represent their data in the form of feature vectors, the data models of the units in the datasets vary considerably. There has been no standard for organizing and representing the data in a dataset and no commitment to a particular type of data model. Consequently, existing datasets are often incompatible. The incompatibility here refers to the data models and not to the heterogeneous, often semantically incompatible categories found across different datasets. Concerns with incompatible categories are beyond the scope of this study (see the comments on integrating data from different datasets in section 2.2).

The presence of different data models has often prevented scholars of international relations from extending their analyses to more than one dataset. Facing problems of dataset incompatibility, they felt forced to select one particular dataset and to build computational systems that satisfied the specific organization of the data in a dataset. Or else, they side-stepped the issue altogether by collecting their own data and organizing them according to their needs (for example, Sylvan et al., 1991b). It is not uncommon for the analysis mechanisms of some systems to be rigidly tied to some data. Consequently, these systems can neither operate on new datasets (they might provide an editing facility for manually entering new data) nor be easily extended to provide additional functionality.

2.1.2 Data Assumptions of Algorithms

In the search for techniques that support not only quantitative but also qualitative analyses, computationally oriented scholars of international relations have turned toward artificial intelligence and machine learning. However, although many of the techniques developed in these domains offer new ways for exploring the data, they are not always readily applicable to the data at hand. The reason is the incongruence between the data assumption of the techniques' algorithm and the organization of the data in the datasets. Many of the algorithms developed in artificial intelligence or machine learning assume a uniform data organization. In machine learning, for example, the predominant data organization is a fixed-length feature vector (Quinlan, 1979; Kononenko et al., 1984). Not all datasets in international relations are compatible with this type of data organization. Coercing the data into the required format, in order to fit the data to the algorithms, is a step that might not always succeed. Furthermore, such an approach may be accused of placing method before substance and thus of oversimplifying the research problem by possibly neglecting theoretically important variables. An even more serious consequence of the incongruence between the data model and a technique's data assumption is that those datasets that are not readily susceptible to analysis are left aside altogether, although their data may convey valuable information to politically relevant research issues.

Both problems arise from the lack of appropriate interfaces between the data and the user—more specifically, between the data and analysis techniques. Apparently, data access and modeling requirements in international relations have been affected by the availability of more and richer data as well as new techniques to analyze them. Yet little effort has been put into developing systems that are capable of addressing the problems that have been mentioned or of supporting analysis techniques that operate effectively on existing and new datasets. Before discussing the characteristics of what will be called a data exploration system, the concept of data exploration has to be elaborated.

2.2 THE CONCEPT OF DATA EXPLORATION

Data exploration in this study is considered a process of inspecting, analyzing, and synthesizing highly structured data by using the management and exploration facilities of a dedicated system or application. Data exploration does not include data collection; rather, it steps in once the data are collected and converted into some formal representation. Nor does it attempt to model particular domain theories. Instead, data exploration defines a data-driven approach of investigating and providing insight into the characteristics of the phenomena for which data have been collected.

2.2.1 Purpose of Data Exploration

The concept of data exploration covers considerably more than mere browsing through data. Data exploration offers different views of the data by enabling the user to split and recombine the data in various ways. It also facilitates other processes: recognizing salient features or previously unnoticed aspects of the phenomena; finding phenomena that have some properties in common and inducing generalizations; searching for conditions under which specific properties of a phenomenon occur; extracting significant patterns implicit in the possibly complex and detailed descriptions, and analyzing patterns of change. Furthermore, data exploration seeks to increase the awareness of how the different categories by which domain-specific phenomena and their properties have been described influence and sometimes dominate the analyses of the phenomena. It also permits experiments with new categories both for phenomenological instances as well as for their properties. In the process of exploring the data, new phenomenological typologies and appropriate degrees of aggregation can be recognized.

2.2.2 Data Integration

Data exploration touches on the issue of data integration, a topic that merits some comment. Ideally, a system for data exploration should support the simultaneous use of multiple datasets and enable effective cross-dataset analyses. However, since multiple datasets may each contain data that refer to one and the same "real-world" object, a reference framework has to be established between the matching parts in the different datasets. This is primarily a semantic problem and not a technical one. The computational support that can be provided is limited to state-of-the-art retrieval, matching, and viewing techniques that may be helpful in inspecting the data but do not solve the problem. The lack of more powerful tools is a direct consequence of the nature of the domain and its data: in contrast to some artificially generated datasets, most "natural," carefully hand-crafted datasets, and in particular those found in social science domains reflect the different conceptual orientations and phenomenological ontologies in the mind of data collectors and coders. The concept "political actor" in one dataset might be equivalent to the concept of "nation-state" in another dataset. Any attempt to establish reference links between the data for the purpose of merging apparently identical concepts thus requires a semantic understanding of the concepts the data represents, a capacity no computer system has. Moreover, the construction of a single "objective" account of some phenomenological characteristic may not necessarily be considered desirable from the point of view of international relations research, because such an attempt conceals the different perceptions of the phenomena that might themselves be subject to investigation. For these reasons, the system developed in this study does not attempt to integrate the data from different datasets.

2.3 OBJECTIVES

Data exploration, if seen as an interactive process between domain experts and a user-friendly, sophisticated system relies heavily on the appropriate transfer of computational modeling techniques to the application domain. The impact of this transfer concerns the solutions to domain-specific problems as well as the influence of the techniques to address these problems. The goals of data exploration can thus be formulated from two different perspectives: from computer science and from the application domain.

2.3.1 Computational Goals

Considering the kind of problems that have so far prevented scholars of international relations from making full use of the structured data that is available to them, and taking the first step toward developing a system that responds to new data and analyses requirements, the computational approach to data exploration intends the following goal:

> To develop an extensible prototype system for exploring phenomenological data, thereby investigating the feasibility of a fully object-oriented approach to two major tasks: providing access to different datasets and supporting various exploration facilities.

This goal defines an important feature of the prototype system, namely its commitment to modularity and extendibility. All the data items in the prototype will be represented as instances of some object classes. While the number of instances that are created for various data classes may be quite enormous for large datasets, the operational costs of maintaining these instances are compensated for by utmost modularity. This offers new ways for exploring every element in a dataset and provides flexible alternatives for processing the data.

A second characteristic is the development of a small but comprehensive set of operations that can be shared among many of the exploration techniques. Rather than designing and implementing each technique from scratch, the focus is on breaking an exploratory process down into operations that already exist, that is, have been defined elsewhere.

A third characteristic is the integration of knowledge-based techniques. The idea is to combine the potential of knowledge-based techniques for symbolic modeling with the requirement for exploratory, quantitative, and qualitative analysis of rich, complex datasets in international relations. An object-oriented approach fosters the establishment of clearly defined and, at the same time, sufficiently abstracted interaction patterns between the data and the analyses techniques. It furthermore ensures functional extendibility.

Fourth, close attention is paid to facilitating the interactions between the users and the system and to ensure that they can work conveniently with the datasets of their choice. They do not have to worry about loading data or system files, nor do they have to concern themselves with the prototype internal management of the data. Rather, they can concentrate fully on the analysis and the exploration tasks they want to carry out.

Finally, portability of the system as a whole is critical if cooperation among research teams and a wider use of the system's capability are desirable. Portability is facilitated, on the one hand, by developing the system on a personal computer, which is available in a variety of locations, not exclusively in universities. It is also achieved by implementing the system in a standardized computer language that can be run on different platforms.

2.3.2 Task-related Requirements

The two major tasks that the computational approach to data exploration seeks to address—namely, access to and analysis of data—give rise to a number of requirements that a prototype system has to fulfill.

Data Access

Obviously access to data in a data exploration system calls for more than just a pointer to a large dataset or, for that matter, to several datasets. Access to every piece of information captured in a dataset is required, as well as the means to explore it. Furthermore, if users wish to extend their analyses to a variety of datasets, the system has to provide appropriate operations that can deal with dataset specific idiosyncrasies yet without being customized to one particular dataset. Three types of problems have to be addressed:

Different data models International relations datasets organize their data in various ways employing logical entities of different type and structure. As a result, the interface between the system and the external world (the datasets) has to adapt to these differences.

Different levels of aggregation A phenomenological dataset comprises logical entities on different levels of aggregation. There are, at least, the units (for example, international conflicts, countries) and the variables that describe the properties of a unit (for example, intensity of conflict, land area of a country). An appropriate interface is required to define the necessary operations on the data on different levels of aggregation.

Interaction between data and exploration facilities Exploration mechanisms operate on specific values and thus require access to these values in the dataset. Some of the techniques, particularly domain-independent algorithms of knowledge-based techniques, impose strict assumptions regarding the format of the data. Problems arise when the datasets do not comply with these assumptions.

An essential requirement for a data exploration system is the ability to provide interfaces that manage the interaction between the external world (the domain-specific datasets) and the application, as well as the application-internal interaction between the data and the user or analyses techniques.

Export of Data

While external and internal access to data is an essential part of the functionality of any data exploration system, the capability to export the data or subsets thereof, preferably in different formats, should not be neglected. Such a capacity fosters cooperation among different research teams, who can work on the same data or on some specifically prepared subsets.

Data transfer Other systems may incorporate different and additional analysis mechanisms for data exploration or for a specific type of analysis. If the data can be shared among different research communities, the results drawn from certain types of data exploration experiments can be tested by others and compared to their own findings.

Transferring subsets of data The option to export specific subsets of data serves two purposes. First, other systems may not have the capacity to operate on arbitrary, large datasets. However, they may be useful for working on subsets of data that are limited in size. Second, the subsets may represent a phenomenologically plausible partition of the original dataset; for example, a subset contains the data of international conflicts in a particular area or those that occurred within a specific time period. Working with such partitions enables scholars to focus their investigation on the specific data they are interested in.

Exploration Facilities

A myriad of techniques and methods are useful for exploring data. Although it may in theory be desirable to have at one's disposal whatever method one would like, a prototype system can at least have the potential for achieving such a goal. Namely, it can be based on an architecture that can be easily extended. This gives users the possibility to add the features and techniques they regard as necessary for their exploration and analyses requirements. For the prototype system, the analyses techniques that are readily provided to operate on the internal representation of the data can only comprise a selection of possible techniques. Considering the goals of data exploration mentioned in the previous section, two types of exploration tools are deemed to be important.

Surface analyses techniques Simple but effective facilities for browsing, inspecting, filtering, and retrieving data help to generate a comprehensive picture of the data. With these facilities alone, many interesting characteristics of a dataset are extractable in a way that is easier, faster, and more reliable than the painful manual alternative. If the human effort is lowered, it is likely that a greater number of datasets will be useful to—and used by—those conducting research in international relations.

The capability to create new phenomenological categories, that is, new variables, is a further requirement of a data exploration system. This is viewed as a kind of analysis technique because it enables the user to define new aggregations and different combinations of the data and thus to focus his or her attention on different, previously implicit characteristics of the phenomena. Given the various coding practices and the differences in categories found in the datasets, experimenting with new categories helps test the usefulness of alternative phenomenological descriptions.

Knowledge-based analyses techniques More sophisticated techniques are needed to provide condensed information about the collected phenomena. The bottom-up, data-driven approach of investigating the characteristics of the phenomena, emphasized in the definition of data exploration, suggests that a powerful inductive analysis capability should be included. Inductive techniques generalize from instances and, hence, help detect recurring patterns and possible relevant concepts that are implicitly embedded in the data (for example, the concept of superpower involvement). Induction is particularly important in domains such as international relations, where little is known about the interaction among the various factors that constitute the domain's phenomena.

Complementing the inductive technique, precedent-based reasoning (others prefer to use the more general term *case-based reasoning*) provides another powerful technique to explore the data. Based on the assumption that situations similar in some respects are likely to be similar in other respects, too, this type of reasoning makes use of previous experience in solving new problems or assessing the impact of new situations.

2.3.3 Data Exploration for International Relations Research

The domain-specific goal of data exploration in a domain such as international relations is to assist domain experts in their search for new findings in large bodies of phenomenological data. Users should have easy access to the data they wish to explore without having to worry about the organization of data in different datasets. In addition, a range of analysis mechanisms, from simple surface exploration techniques to more sophisticated knowledge-based techniques, should be available to extract valuable information from the data in various degrees of detail.

To international relations researchers and analysts, systematic data exploration is important for several reasons:

Refining domain hypotheses Data exploration is crucial for domains in which little consensus exists regarding the theories and hypotheses that surround the domain's phenomena. In contrast to domains such as linguistics, in which a rich descriptive structure governs the use of its essential elements, the international relations community recognizes no such structure. The heterogeneity of theories and hypotheses becomes apparent when considering the variety of competing computational and noncomputational models that have been developed over the years. The goal of data exploration, however, is not to find the "correct" theory. Rather, it aims to shed new light on the phenomena by systematically investigating their occurrences and their different features. In a bottom-up approach driven by the data from different datasets, data exploration adds to the knowledge about the phenomena and may be used to broaden the consensus within the field concerning the theories explaining political phenomena.

Learning from historical experience Historical instances of political phenomena are an important source of information in forming judgments about a new situation and in developing an understanding of the dynamics that govern, for example, international conflicts. Data exploration can complement the limited human capability of processing large amounts of data (for example, numerous instances of international conflicts, detailed data on country profiles) and thus serve as an aid to memory and imagination (Bloomfield, 1989), by providing either selected or condensed information about different aspects of politically relevant situations.

Extending scope One of the major benefits of the projected data exploration system is its applicability to different data collections. It extends the scope of data analysis to different phenomena (for example, data on country profiles, economic developments, international organizations). In the process, knowledge about power-political interactions in the international arena can be augmented by including the constraints and opportunities generated by socioeconomic, technological, or environmental conditions. The interdependence of political, socioeconomic, and ecological factors has been the concern of global modeling efforts (see Alker, 1985b, for a review; Onishi, 1986).

2.4 Comparison to Other Approaches

Formal models and techniques have been widely used in international relations research for many decades and are divided into three broad categories (Schrodt, 1984b): statistical studies, dynamic models (differential equations, simulations, and stochastic processes), and rational models (game theory, expected utility, and optimal-behavior models). For an overview of political statistics (polimetrics) and a categorization of statistical procedures in terms of practical decision, scientific inference, and data analyses, see Alker (1975). A fourth, more recent category are systems that employ techniques from artificial intelligence. These systems have emerged largely due to limitations of each of the other formal approaches to the study of international relations (for a critical review of the different formal approaches, see, for example, Morgan and Sonquist, 1963; Schrodt, 1984a, 1984b; Smoker, 1985; Mallery, 1988a). Interest in artificial intelligence has created a new branch within that sector of international relations research that is oriented toward formal modeling, often referred to as artificial intelligence/international relations (AI/IR) community.

2.4.1 Systems That Implement A Domain Theory

Among the more recent computational systems that embed artificial intelligence techniques, models on foreign policy decision making figure prominently (for example, Thorson and Sylvan, 1982; Job and Johnson, 1991). Some involve the modeling of political argument and discourse (for example, Sylvan et al., 1991b; Boynton and Dozark, 1992). Another large group of models addresses the behavior and policy of nations (Tanaka, 1984; Bobrow and Sylvan, 1988) or organizations (Alker and Greenberg, 1971, 1977; Alker and Christensen, 1972; Alker et al., 1980). Modeling organizational learning is a third major area that has received attention. Typically, these systems employ precedent-based or analogy-based learning mechanisms (Tanaka, 1984; Mefford, 1984; Schrodt, 1985).

Given research issues such as political cognition and reasoning, together with the potential of artificial intelligence techniques for symbolic modeling and qualitative analysis, it is not surprising that the majority of computational systems in the field are theory driven rather than data driven. Scholars formalize their theories and then seek to test them with phenomenological data that they either collect themselves or, in fewer cases, take from existing datasets (for collections of recent papers, see Sylvan and Chan, 1984; Cimbala, 1987; Hudson, 1991). Only a few systems incorporate domain independent knowledge-based algorithms to analyze phenomenological data (Schrodt, 1984a, 1987a), and they have usually been customized to a particular dataset. There is a general lack of systems that are neither theory specific nor data specific but that support rather systematic data exploration in a bottom-up, data-driven manner, including the use of knowledge-based techniques.

2.4.2 Related Approaches

There are two systems that bear some similarity to the approach described in this study: Bloomfield's CASCON system and Mallery's Feature Vector Editor. While they do not conform to the concept of data exploration as defined in section 2.2, they both share some of the properties that are considered relevant to data exploration and will thus be discussed in more detail later. A third system, the Global Events Data System (GEDS) mentioned earlier, will also be included. The GEDS project intends to support data analysis techniques, although its primary objective is to provide access to on-line data.

CASCON

CASCON (computer-aided system for analysis of local conflicts) was conceived as a decision-support system for analysts and international relations scholars (Bloomfield and Beattie, 1971). It was later revised (CASCON II, III) and currently runs on IBM-compatible personal computers (Panagos, 1985; Bloomfield and Moulton, 1989). CASCON's goal is twofold: first, it aids the memory of the analyst with an inventory of historical facts that might be relevant to an incipient or exploding conflict; second, it aids the imagination by supplying clues to the identification of recurring patterns and thus takes the role of an adjunct to decision making.

CASCON's database CASCON's database of "factors" (500 variable value pairs accounting for specific properties of a conflict) comes directly from the factual statements historians came up with in describing their cases. As later adopted by FACS and SHERFACS (Alker and Sherman, 1982; Sherman, 1987a, 1988), a case is divided into several phases. In CASCON these phases include a dispute phase (a quarrel over something), a conflict phase (conflictual parties start arming), and a hostility phase (organized warfare). The database currently contains the description of 66 conflict cases.

Tasks supported in CASCON Although CASCON cannot operate on datasets that have been generated on other platforms, information about a new conflict case can be entered manually into the system and stored there for further use. Furthermore, cases can be updated when new information arises. Several operations allow the user to retrieve relevant information about the stored cases; that is, the factors whose values are coded as "no information," used as a checklist for generating additional intelligence requirements, the factors whose effect has been estimated as a move toward or away from violence, and full-text précis that are associated with each case. CASCON's main analysis mechanism compares new cases with those stored in the dataset, thereby offering a kind of precedent-based reasoning mechanism. Using similarity measurements, the compare mechanism generates a rank-ordered list of "similar" cases. It can also be used to find the common features of a new case and some or all cases in the dataset.

The CASCON system has been used for academic purposes (Bloomfield and Leiss, 1969; Choucri, 1974) and has found practical application within, for example, the United Nations. Because it is now available on a personal computer, its potential use for research, education, and government has increased. CASCON differs in several ways from the data exploration prototype system that this study envisages. First, CASCON is customized to a particular dataset, and new data has to be entered manually, conforming to the requirements of the database. Second, CASCON's capacity for data analysis is limited and new functionality cannot easily be incorporated. Third, because CASCON's objectives are exclusively domain oriented, the focus is on practical solutions rather than on computational issues.

The Feature Vector Editor

The Feature Vector Editor (Mallery, 1988b, 1994) is a general tool for editing, browsing, and filtering structured coded data. It accepts datasets in feature vector format and has been applied to the SHERFACS dataset. The Feature Vector Editor has emerged as an independent tool in the context of the RELATUS project, a system that operates on relational graphs constructed from natural language sentences (Duffy and Mallery, 1986; Mallery, 1988b; Duffy, 1987). The Feature Vector Editor is quite unique in a domain such as international relations as it employs modern software engineering techniques that facilitate the editing and modifying of structured coded data. It uses a declaratively specified codebook to interpret the variables for a particular dataset. Users are provided with the full-text information of the codebook and a mouse-sensitive multiple-choice questionnaire that does away with the need to remember internal codes. Several mechanisms for browsing, filtering, and sorting of structured coded data are supported. Time-based or temporal filtering of the data is provided by an interval-time indexation system (Duffy, 1987, 1991).

What both a prototype system for data exploration and the Feature Vector Editor share is the focus on generic interfaces that enable the systems to operate on different data formats rather than being limited to a particular dataset. What this implies is the commitment to operator and data abstraction, modularity, and extendibility and thus the use of LISP and object-oriented programming. However, the primary objective of the Feature Vector Editor is to edit and manipulate structured coded data. An inductive analyses system has been interfaced to the editor (Unseld and Mallery, 1992) to extend its functionality. In contrast, a data exploration system aims to support systematic data analyses by providing easy access to every piece of information conveyed in the data and a variety of techniques, including knowledge-based techniques, to carry out more sophisticated types of analyses. Furthermore, the computational techniques employed are themselves subject to investigation, with the prototype conceived as the first step in the process of developing a framework for data exploration systems (Part II of this study).

The Global Events Data System (GEDS)

The GEDS project is first and foremost an effort to offer analysts comprehensive international relations data, and hence it can be viewed as a "front end" to a data exploration system. GEDS uses the NEXIS data service, which supplies daily information on international and domestic events, as reported, for example, by Reuters and other sources. GEDS aims to provide computer-assisted identification, abstraction, and reporting of daily news. A single data stream is to be produced from which different datasets can be developed, expanded, and updated. GEDS should also help to develop new coding schemes that sacrifice neither the comprehensiveness and analytical strength of global coding efforts nor the depth, complexity, and diversity of coverage of the episodic coding projects (Davies, 1991). The COPDAB data (Azar, 1980) and an extended version of its coding scheme serve as the basis for coding new events.

As indicated in the project description, GEDS will also incorporate various analyses mechanisms in order to enable researchers to extract valuable information from the new or updated accounts of political phenomena. Whether flexible data exploration components will emerge, whether they will be capable of accepting different datasets, or whether the analyses facilities will be customized to GEDS' internal requirements and to the enlarged COPDAB dataset remains to be seen.

2.4.3 Information Retrieval and Hypertext

This chapter concludes with a comparison of a different kind. In the previous paragraphs, data exploration, the concept and the prototype system, was compared with other systems developed in the computationally oriented sector of international relations. This section contrasts data exploration with information retrieval and hypertext. Both represent well-known and widely applied approaches to the organization, representation, and selection of data. Operational systems have found applications in a number of different domains, including international relations.

Information retrieval and hypertext systems share some common characteristics with data exploration systems. However, there are some fundamental differences that should be noted.

Information Retrieval Systems

Information retrieval systems typically work with vast amounts of rudimentary structured or unstructured data. The focus of these systems is to provide efficient and convenient retrieval operations rather than effective data management facilities for storage and updating.

The data The major difference between information retrieval systems and data exploration systems is the nature of the data treated: in general, it is poorly structured in an information retrieval system but well-structured and carefully handcoded in a data exploration system.

Functionality While a data exploration system supports the filtering and retrieving of data—the respective mechanisms make use of the structure in the data and thus differ significantly from those applied in information retrieval systems—the main emphasis lies on data analysis and on the provision of suitable analysis techniques.

Hypertext Systems

Hypertext systems operate on data that range from written text to pictures and even sound and video clips, a case where the term *hypermedia system* is more accurate. These systems could be viewed as a particular implementation of an information retrieval system provided that the information retrieved is not necessarily restricted to text. The difference lies in the way in which the two are implemented.

The data If hypertext systems are viewed as a subset of an information retrieval system, the significant difference between them and data exploration systems, as has been noted earlier, is the kind of data they operate on, namely unstructured rather than structured data.

Functionality Hypertext systems, in general, return pieces of what is explicitly contained in the original data, although those pieces might be differently grouped and ordered. A data exploration system yields information that was only implicitly in the data. It can provide condensed information and new concepts, which are "learned" from the data. Obviously, some of the functionality of a data exploration system can and has been provided in hypertext systems. However, the nature of the data in these systems limits the applicability of complex exploration mechanisms.

Chapter 3
THE PROTOTYPE

Chapter 2 introduced the reasons and intentions behind the development of a data exploration prototype. In the process, a major distinction was made between the objectives of the present approach and most of the work described in the AI/IR literature; the latter group attempts to model and test domain-specific hypotheses and theories by employing various quantitative and qualitative techniques, while this approach reverses the perspective by shifting the focus from the application domain to the modeling domain. It puts the main stress on the computational modeling techniques themselves and their usefulness for tackling application-specific problems.

In Chapter 2, the mandatory as well as some of the desirable features of a prospective prototype for data exploration were identified. This chapter elaborates on the conceptual and technical considerations that went into the development of the prototype. Each of the prototype's components is described in detail, illustrating the way in which the particular problems are addressed by object-oriented programming techniques. Yet, before going into the details, it would be helpful to make some comments on the implementation language and present arguments for choosing an object-oriented approach to data exploration.

3.1 Object-oriented Data Exploration

The language for implementing the CrisView prototype is CLOS, Common LISP Object System (Steele, 1990; Keene, 1989), which in 1994 became the first ANSI standard object-oriented programming language. CLOS has been chosen in preference to other object-oriented extensions to Common LISP (for example, Flavors), because it is a standard. Furthermore, CLOS runs on personal computers such as Macintosh and PowerPC. While the use of a standardized language enhances code sharing and widens the applicability of a system, the common availability of the hardware on which the system can run ensures independence from highly exclusive and often sparsely available computer systems (for example, LISP machines) and thus increases the number of potential users. Another reason for choosing CLOS is that it supports metaobject protocols (Kiczales et al., 1991), that is, language interfaces that enable the user to modify incrementally the language's behavior. Although metaobject protocols are not exploited in the first part of this study, it is the second part that draws heavily on the concept of metaobject protocols for extending the CrisView prototype. The features that are available in CLOS but not in other object-oriented languages are crucial for the design considerations addressed in Part II.

There is no shortage of books, technical reports, and working papers on the theoretical and practical aspects of object-oriented modeling and programming, and so this section refrains from repeating what has been mentioned in detail elsewhere. Good accounts of object-oriented modeling (object-oriented analysis and design) are given in Wirfs-Brock et al. (1990), Rumbaugh et al. (1991), Jacobson et al. (1992), Booch (1994), Gamma et al. (1995). Object-oriented programming, in general or in the context of a particular object-oriented programming language, has been described, for instance, in Shriver and Wegner (1987), Meyer (1988), Budd (1991), Norvig (1992, 434–459).

3.1.1 Reasons for An Object-oriented Approach

There are strong arguments for choosing an object-oriented approach to data exploration. The arguments relate to the kind of data that is being represented and managed in a system such as CrisView as well as to the requirements of data exploration and analysis in the field of international relations. The choice of an object-oriented approach is not only based on considerations about software development, which place demands on the flexibility and extensibility of the system to be built as well as on the capability of the implementation language and the concepts it allows the developer to use. It also has an impact on what a user can do and how well he or she is assisted by the system when carrying out some research tasks.

Representation of The Data

Datasets in international relations present a heavily abstracted picture of some real-world phenomena because they use a limited set of predefined categories. When representing these data in a system, the goal must be to preserve the relationships and dependencies between the various pieces of data in order to reflect differences and deviations where they appear and to capture some of the semantics underlying individual data categories or groups thereof. This is especially important for datasets that attempt to give a richly structured account of the phenomena they describe. One of the advantages of an object-oriented approach is that it does not further widen the gap between the phenomena and its corresponding dataset by forcing the data into yet another rigid form when representing it. Rather, it allows the software engineer to model a structured entity such as a SHERFACS conflict or a World Facts country as a part consisting of data and functions that can be performed by it. Such a part may itself be composed of other parts that again comprise data and functions. It differs from the relational approach, which not only separates data and functions but also flattens what is perceived as a richly structured entity into the tuples of one or more relational tables.

Data representation and manipulation may not be an issue for users as long as their queries for specific data items are answered correctly and they do not have to worry about the way queries are handled internally. Indeed, these users may have no preference for either objects or tuples. However, it matters to the system developer or the user who wants to add a new dataset to the prototype or expand its functionality, as discussed in the second part of this study. An object-oriented system is easier to maintain and to extend than a traditional application whose programs operate directly on the tables of a relational database. Moreover, it is better suited for managing heterogeneous complex structured data. (It should be noted that the debate is not about persistent data store; object-oriented systems may well and often do use relational databases as their persistent data store; what is important is whether the application is object-oriented). To offer but a few arguments: in a traditional system operating on a relational database, a complex object is distributed over many different tables and cannot be accessed directly; since tables and tuples are the only descriptors, different relationships between data items cannot be represented other than by introducing additional tables and many foreign keys; the representation of a particular characteristic that holds for only a small subset of the data is a cumbersome task because definitions always apply to entire tables and not to tuples therein.

Object-oriented data representation may also have an impact on future efforts to collect data. Uniformity and simplicity of phenomenological data may be a quality that is imposed in order to match limited data management capabilities rather than an adequate description of a real-world phenomenon whose individual occurrences may be highly heterogeneous. In the face of object-oriented systems, data collectors may be encouraged to produce richer and more valuable datasets by capturing aspects of the real phenomena that heretofore had to be ignored because they did not fit into simple data structures.

Generalizations and Specializations

The desire to work with phenomenological data from different datasets requires flexible data management that is capable of handling different data models. Although datasets in international relations that contain structured coded data are similar, the structural organization of their data varies. Figures 3.3 and 3.4 in section 3.3.2 show the different structuring of the SHERFACS and the World Facts datasets, respectively. Both datasets are similar in that they contain a set of structured elements. Similarities between different datasets can be exploited and differences can be accounted for in a powerful, elegant, and parsimonious manner by defining object hierarchies or composites and using the mechanisms of inheritance and polymorphism in object-oriented languages. Operations on classes (for example, functions applied to or by objects) can be defined at the appropriate level of specification, thereby minimizing code duplication but without sacrificing specificity.

In the process of working with different datasets, a set of general, dataset-independent object classes can be developed and further refined to form, eventually, the kernel of a data exploration system that can be used for any new dataset. Such a kernel facilitates the incorporation of new datasets. The methods defined for the kernel classes can readily be used by dataset-specific subclasses thus reducing the number of methods that have to be specialized to a new dataset. However, as will be shown in Part II, the definition of such a kernel, as well as operations that are at the same time powerful and general, requires some additional consideration.

Data Exploration

Data exploration is conceived as a process in which domain experts and others increase their knowledge of a domain's phenomena by extracting information from collections of phenomenological data. The information is drawn by splitting up and recombining the logical entities of a dataset in various ways and by investigating the data on different levels of aggregation. Crucial to a data exploration system is, thus, its ability to offer multiple views of the data and to factorize what is conveyed by the data according to the user's interests. An object-oriented approach is particularly suited to procuring these abilities: by modeling the logical entities of a dataset as instances of dedicated object classes, methods specialized to these classes can provide exactly those data exploration mechanisms that are of interest when instances of a class are investigated.

In particular, and unlike most other object-oriented languages, the CLOS language provides generic functions[1] that are able to dispatch on multiple arguments and therefore on multiple classes and other identities. As a result, data exploration mechanisms can be applied very selectively and can be specialized on individual object classes as well as on different groupings of classes. They can also be made dependent on the context in which they are invoked, for example, the window from which they are called. New conditional settings can be specified by adding a method with the appropriate arguments to the method set of a generic function. The notion of an operation that takes on different forms depending on the type of objects it is applied to is called polymorphism and is an important concept in object-oriented languages; interestingly, it is also consistent with the way humans address problem-solving tasks. Most object-oriented languages support polymorphism, although not the type of multiple polymorphism (multiple argument dispatch) that is supported in CLOS and greatly facilitates the manipulation of heterogeneous data.

Although elaborated in more detail in Part II, it is worth mentioning here that the object-oriented environment provided by CLOS (in particular, its support of metaobject protocols) offers an excellent opportunity for defining browser and other analysis tools that enable the user to explore not only the phenomenological data represented in the prototype but also the prototype itself. Users can find answers to questions about the behavior of the prototype's classes by inspecting, for example, the hierarchy of object classes and the operations for which they are responsible. By providing convenient access to the elements of a system, browsers remove some of the "black-box" aspects that are frequently, though not exclusively, the source of skepticism about the use of computers for anything that smacks of the type of substantive analysis performed by professionals.

3.1.2 CrisView's Main Components

Considering the tasks that a data exploration system has to perform, we distinguish two major components: data management and data exploration. Figure 3.1 depicts the components of CrisView interfacing domain-specific data and users.

Data management The data management component comprises the hierarchies and composites of object classes that correspond to the logical entities of a dataset. The dataset-specific classes are subclasses of either abstract classes or other classes that serve as superclasses. The core class of this component is the document class whose instances are the main entities managed by CrisView. The concept of documents is elaborated in the next section because of its major impact on all other parts of CrisView as well as on users working with CrisView and their domain data. Operations that manipulate the document and the objects it comprises are defined in the data management component.

Data exploration The data exploration component comprises several windows and graphical user interface widgets. The main window is the document-window controlling the other windows of the exploration environment. All windows are defined as instances of object classes. The windows or parts thereof are associated with one or more of CrisView's exploration techniques. These techniques include the surface analyses techniques that were mentioned earlier as well as the knowledge-based algorithms incorporated in CrisView. The latter are treated in a separate chapter because they play a major role for exploring data in a domain such as international relations.

CrisView distinguishes two modes: An exploration mode for the user and a development mode for the prototype developer—or the user if he or she wishes to change or extend the prototype. A mode is a part of an application that the user has to enter and leave formally (Macintosh, 1985, I-28); it also controls the operations that are available to the user.

Figure 3.1: Components of CrisView.

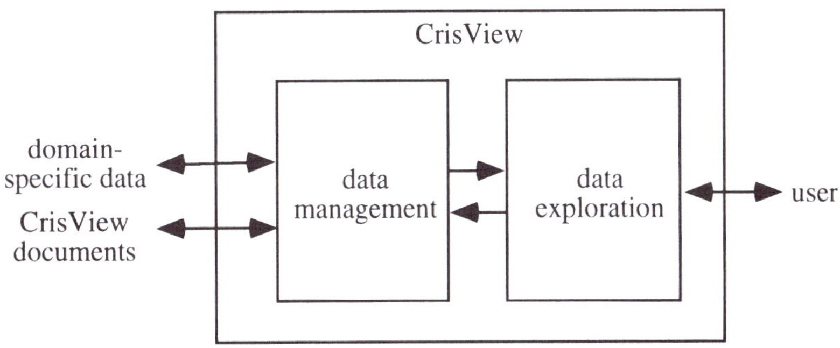

The exploration mode consists of the windows and widgets defined in CrisView's exploration component. From these windows the user invokes the various exploration facilities supported in CrisView. Familiarity with the concepts underlying graphics-oriented, event-driven user interfaces is assumed (Macintosh, 1985, 23–79), including the selection of entities in tables and text-oriented editors, menu-driven selection of commands, and the use of controls such as buttons to invoke further actions.

It would be useful at this point to introduce the dataset that is being used most in this study to illustrate the main concepts of CrisView and the capabilities of its data management and data exploration components. The SHERFACS dataset has been chosen because it provides an excellent opportunity to address the kind of problems that challenge the development of a data exploration prototype. Since it is one of the richest and most complex collections of structured coded data in international relations, a solution that complies with the complex structured SHERFACS data is likely to address the problems generally encountered when dealing with other complex structured datasets.

3.1.3 The SHERFACS Dataset

The SHERFACS International Conflict Management Dataset (Sherman, 1987a, 1988) is one of the most comprehensive datasets in international relations, covering the period from 1945 through the end of 1984. It contains approximately 700 international disputes (conflicts in which parties on both sides are internationally recognized actors) and more than 1,000 domestic quarrels (conflicts in which only one side is an internationally recognized actor). A conflict in SHERFACS is defined as:

> A situation where there exist mutually exclusive sets of competing claims or challenges to sovereignty between at least two actors, one of which must be an internationally recognized political actor. (Sherman, 1988, 6)

Adopting the phase-structured framework (Figure 3.2) from Bloomfield and Leiss (1969) with slight modifications of the terms, the SHERFACS dataset uses phases to describe escalation and de-escalation of a particular conflict case. A conflict may proceed from dispute phase (at least one party claims the issues to be of substantive international political significance), to crisis phase (the use of military force is

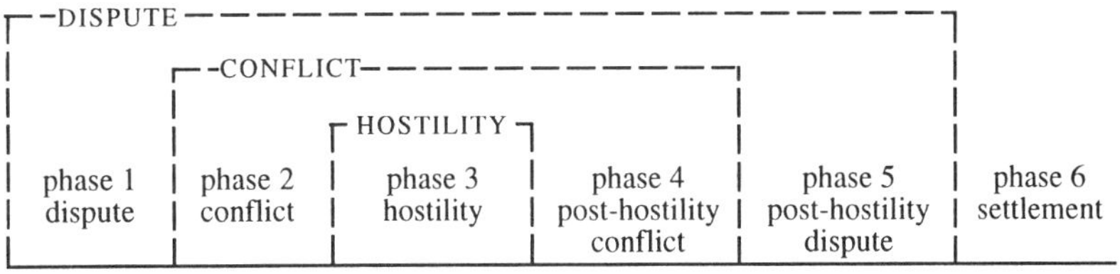

Figure 3.2: Phase-structured framework by Bloomfield and Leiss (1969).

considered as an option), to hostility phase (actual violent conflict and fighting), through post-hostility crisis phase, and post-hostility dispute phase to a settlement phase (where the issue under contention is resolved or the conflict collapses).

In addition to the conflict phase information, the dataset includes information on the nature of actions by the parties to the conflict as well as on referrals of the conflict to management agents and their actions.

As will be shown in section 3.3.2, SHERFACS constitutes a rather irregularly shaped, complex dataset organizing the data about a conflict in different tree-structured data models. It is thus closer in texture to the narrative accounts because certain phases—for example, hostilities—can repeat several times without necessarily leading to the definition of a new conflict case. The SHERFACS dataset also contains expertly crafted narrative accounts for some of the conflicts.

3.2 Documents

The primary entity managed by CrisView is the document. A document corresponds to an arbitrarily sized dataset that has been prepared for data exploration. The user opens and closes documents and, thus, can work conveniently with the dataset of his or her choice. The concept of document follows a design principle that has been popularized primarily by Apple Computer and its guidelines on how to develop applications.

On the level of the operating system, the document is represented as a file. This file contains a printable (ASCII) representation of core data and supplementary data.

A document's core data The *core data* comprise the phenomenological data collected in a dataset. From the logical point of view, the representation of the core data mirrors the semantics expressed in the corresponding dataset, that is, the phenomenological ontology on the basis of which data collectors and coders have generated the dataset. Since datasets in international relations and related domains are bound to differ in the organization of the data, the corresponding documents, that is, their core data, will reflect these differences.

A document's supplementary data Apart from the core data, a document contains what is called *supplementary data*. Supplementary data include the windows associated with the document, the acceleration structures built on top of the core data, user-defined views, and so on. The only way for the user to see the content of a document other than by looking at its printable representation is through a window. The main window of a document is the document-window providing different views (including user-defined views) of the document's core data. The supplementary data are hidden from the user; browsers that help to inspect this data are discussed in Part II.

3.2.1 Document Operators

Documents are linked with and can only be manipulated by the application in which they have been defined. CrisView is thus responsible for managing the documents it has generated. Following standard Macintosh guidelines for application development (Macintosh, 1985, I-55), three basic document operations can be invoked by the user: open, close, and save.

Standard Document Operators

Open The user who issues the "open" command is presented with a list of existing documents. When a document is selected, core and supplementary data of the document are activated, and the user sees the main document-window fitted with the core data (the document-window and the window panels that display different parts of the core data are described in section 3.4.2).

Close The "close" command closes an active document-window. If the user has altered the document—for example, created a new view of the data—then he or she is asked whether these changes should be saved. It should be noted that changes to a CrisView document do not include changes to its core data, because CrisView is conceived as an exploration system not as an editor. Neither the addition of new logical entities nor the manipulation of existing ones is supported. The permissible "changes" to the document (elaborated in section 3.4) only pertain to the user-defined objects that are stored in the slots of the document such as filters, subsets, new variables, and knowledge-based experiments. When changes have been made and the document-window is closed, core data and supplementary data of the document are written to a file in ASCII representation.

Save The "save" command makes permanent any changes to the active document. It leaves the document and the document-window open.

Saving Individually Sized Documents

Rather than saving the entire document that is active in CrisView, the user can save a document that contains only a specific subset of the core data. The data to be exported can be earmarked by using CrisView's selection or filtering operations (section 3.4.3). For example, the user may select a subset of units that represents a phenomenologically cohesive partition or a particular chronological sequence. A special command, the "save-with-data-subset" command triggers an operation that creates a partial copy of the active document. This copy includes the earmarked core data and corresponding supplementary data (for example, the acceleration structure for the selected part of the core data). The newly generated document can be used in later sessions or be transferred to other machines where the prototype has been installed. Reducing the size of a document while at the same time keeping a coherent partition of the data is particularly helpful if the user wishes to work on a machine whose capacity is limited.

3.2.2 Special Data-interface Operators

CrisView differs from other applications in that it does not support editing operations on the data. These operations have been left aside because CrisView is conceived as a data explorer rather than a data editor or generator. Working with different datasets is made possible in CrisView by data import and export operations.

Import of Data

The import of data involves reading phenomenological data from a file into their internal representation in CrisView. It is assumed that the files that store the phenomenological data are available in some import/export format. Currently, the import/export format managed by CrisView is an arbitrarily structured list. This format restriction is suitable for the data models commonly found in international relations datasets. The predominant data model in both of these datasets and collections of structured coded data is the *feature vector data model.* Several types of feature vector data models can be distinguished.

A flat data model Each occurrence of a phenomenon is described by a single feature vector, frequently represented as a vector of values where each value is associated with a particular variable or as a list of variable value pairs. The variable values can be atomic or lists. There is no additional structure among the variables.

A synchronic (or lateral) data model The data model contains an arbitrary number of flat data models each representing an aspect of the phenomenon that occurs repeatedly. The flat data models, the feature vectors, contain the same types of variables, but with different values in each feature vector. This type of data model is often represented in the form of a two-dimensional array in which each row represents a vector of values. Again the ordering of the rows is arbitrary and has no further significance. For example, the coded actions of all the parties involved in a conflict can be represented by this type of data model.

A sequential (longitudinal) data model The data model consists of a sequence rather than a set of flat data models. The difference between the sequential and the lateral data model is thus the particular relationship (for example, a temporal relationship when values have been collected over time) between the flat data models. Again, the feature vectors contain the same variables, instantiated individually for each feature vector.

A hierarchical data model This type of data model contains a number of flat data models ordered according to specialization/generalization or part/whole relationships. A parts list would be a typical example of a hierarchical data model.

A tree-structured data model This is the most general type of data model subsuming all the types just mentioned. An individual occurrence of the phenomenon is described by a collection of feature vectors, the nodes of a tree, which may be related in a variety of ways—for example, laterally, sequentially, or hierarchically, thereby mirroring the observed relations between the aspects they describe. A flat data model can be seen as a special case of a tree-structured data model, namely a degenerated tree with one single node. A "pure" lateral data model can be represented as a tree whose nodes are all on one level. Similarly, a "pure" longitudinal data model is also a tree with all the nodes on one level; however, the nodes form a sequence rather than a set. Finally, a hierarchical data model is a tree in which the branches between the nodes denote specification/generalization or part/whole relationships.

The data in a tree-structured data model can be converted into an arbitrary structured list. Consequently, the CrisView import/export format is general enough to account for all types of data models commonly found in the datasets of the domain. It also accepts feature vector data models whose feature vectors are both fixed-length or variable-length. Fixed-length feature vectors are more common, probably because they have traditionally facilitated the application of many analytic algorithms and formal methods.

The conversion of machine-readable datasets on political phenomena into the desired import/export format, if necessary, is done by programs or tools external to CrisView. The task of these programs and tools is to translate between two syntactic forms: the original form in which the data has been stored onto a file and the result form, which is the syntax of the import/export format. For those files whose format already exhibits a strict, unambiguous syntax, the translation is straightforward. For other files, for example, in string format, tools such as GREP and AWK (Kernighan and Pike, 1984), or Open Text Tools (OTT), can be applied to render explicit the logical entities embedded in the data.

When phenomenological data are imported from a file, an "import" operation is invoked (by the command "import") to perform the mapping of logical entities from the data file into the document. Before data can be imported into a document, the document must already exist. There are two possibilities:

Enlarging the core data of a document An existing document with some core data has been opened and displayed in the document-window. The new data is added to the core data of the document by invoking the import function. Complying with the object-oriented paradigm, each new logical entity encountered in the data file is instantiated as an object of a previously defined object class (object classes and their instances in CrisView are discussed in the next section). When a new instance is created, the import function tests whether this instance is already present in the document in order to avoid duplication. Further testing is performed to detect possible divergences from the dataset's coding scheme. The necessary information is available from the object class that is instantiated. In the case of a variable, for example, the import function checks whether the variable's value is among the permissible values for this variable.

Generating a new document The user can create a new document by issuing a "new" command that invokes the "new" operation. This operation belongs conceptually to the document operations discussed in the previous section (the standard open, close, and save operations, and the additional save-with-data-subset operation). The reason for discussing the new operation within the context of data import rather than together with the other document operations lies in the character of CrisView. CrisView is not meant to support data collectors in their coding of new phenomenological data, but rather to operate on datasets that have been established elsewhere. As a result, the "new" operation is only meaningful in connection with the import of phenomenological data from a file. On its own, the operation creates a document that contains no core data and presents the user with an empty window that—without data—is of little use. As described earlier, the import operation adds data from a file to the core data of the document. Testing for the presence of instances of a phenomenon should never succeed because the imported data is supposed to be redundancy-free, and the document contains no other core data. Consistency with the coding specifications is checked as mentioned earlier.

Data Export

The export of data involves an operation that writes the document's core data or specific subsets thereof to a file. Data export, like data import, is an operation of the interface between CrisView and the operating system. If only a part of the core data is to be exported, it can be earmarked by the same selection and filtering operations as used when saving documents with subsets of the core data. If the data in a document are identical to those in the file from which they have been imported, no export operation needs to be carried out, because the file is already available. Otherwise, if the core data of the document have been enlarged prior to issuing the export command, or if a specific subset of the data has been collected, these data are exported. On the level of the operating system, the exported data are represented as a file in import/export format. Unlike the document files that are linked with CrisView, the file that contains the exported data does not belong to a specific application and can therefore be used by other systems.

The purpose of the export operation is to facilitate the transfer of data between different systems and research teams in other locations. Since arbitrary subsets of phenomenological data are exportable, requests from users for content-specific subsets or modestly sized partitions can be granted. As has been mentioned earlier, the format supported by the export operation in CrisView is an arbitrary structured list. This format meets the requirements of most users and systems because it subsumes the formats commonly found in international relations datasets. However, it is conceivable that some future version of CrisView could choose from among a number of specific export formats. Such an extension would enhance the exchange of data because it does away with the need on the receiver side to adjust the data format to the requirement of particular systems.

Functionality Provided by Import and Export Operations
The import and export operations are crucial for a data exploration system, because they manage the bi-directional communication between the system and the external world. Although CrisView operates on structured coded data, the import and export operations are not limited to this type of data. The functionality achieved by introducing these operations includes:

Making documents The import operation enables the user to create a document that contains a specific collection of politically relevant or interesting data. Once such a document exists, the data are amenable to explorative analyses. Furthermore, the import operation ensures that the imported data are consistent with the specifications in the coding scheme of the dataset from which the data have been imported.

Extending documents The import operation enables the user to enlarge an existing document by gradually adding new data. The newly added data come either from the same or from a different dataset as the data already in the document. In the former case, the resulting document simply represents a larger part of the dataset. In the latter case, two or more subsets of data, which could possibly be very different on the level of content, have been put together—not integrated—and can be explored simultaneously. The incremental import of data enables the user to work with large bodies of data even if the RAM of a computer is limited. Without this incremental capability, importing large amounts of data might exceed the capacity of the machine.

Enhancing data transfer The core data of a document can be partitioned according to some phenomenological plausibilities and written to separate files that are then individually accessible by other users or systems. This export of an arbitrary number of differently sized files in import/export format can provide others with the data they are interested in.

3.2.3 Characteristics of The Document Concept

The major characteristics of the document concept are the ease and convenience that the user experiences when working with documents (the term *document* deliberately draws upon the colloquial notion of document, thereby stressing the association to user-friendliness).

User-friendliness

Users can concentrate fully on employing the functionality provided by CrisView rather than worrying about technical details. On the level of the operating system, each document is a file that the user can select. This selection can be made from within the prototype. Alternatively, and even more conveniently, the user need not start the application but can, instead, simply select a document at the level of the operating system. On the Macintosh computer, a document—due to its linkage—"knows" its application and becomes active within that application and ready for the user to explore.

By importing data from a domain-specific data file, new documents are created, each of which corresponds to a particular collection of data. Since CrisView manages an arbitrary number of documents, the user can build and enlarge his or her collection of documents in a modular and incremental manner. The core data of each document represent either an entire dataset, a subset of a dataset characterizing a meaningful partition, or a mixture of data from different datasets, even though the data are not integrated in the full sense of the term (see section 2.2).

The document approach contrasts significantly with other approaches where different data configurations are built up either by loading multiple files or by saving and restoring a persistent environment. These approaches both have their advantages. However, they have not been chosen due to the following weaknesses: while the "file loading approach" requires the user to know details about the application's data management, the "persistent environment approach" is generally inflexible because the initial data configuration cannot be altered.

Dealing with Domain-specific Information

The use of documents has an impact on how CrisView deals with domain-specific information (that is, the logical entities of a dataset). Whenever new data are imported, CrisView has to "know" what kind of entities are involved and how they are specified. One solution suggests the loading of additional definition files—more specifically, data-specific codebooks that contain the necessary information for each dataset. This rather UNIX-like type of solution violates the concept of documents.

As for solutions compliant with the document approach, two alternatives emerge: the information is either provided at the beginning of a document, or it has to reside within the application. The former causes a bootstrap problem because the core data of a document in CrisView is imported from application-independent files in import/export format, a process that requires that the import operation should already "know" the information concerning the data. One could argue that it would be possible to define an import operation that, by exploiting the syntactic information in the data file, could perform the required task. However, one serious disadvantage of this solution is that it prevents the application from checking the imported data for coding errors, missing values, and other divergences from the underlying coding scheme. As for CrisView, the second alternative has been chosen, which means that data-specific information is part of the prototype. However, it is separated conceptually from other parts of the prototype. The details are given in section 3.3.

3.2.4 Documents in An Object-oriented System

The document concept is particularly suited to an object-oriented application such as CrisView because it suggests a simple and intelligible approach to high-level data structuring: each document can be defined as an instance of document-class (section 3.3.1). The document controls the lower-level objects whose structure reflects the structure of the imported data. The beauty of the approach is its simplicity and extendibility. The data to be stored in a document and its structure can be modified extremely conveniently during the development phase. For example, new classes can be added, without having to worry about the contents and structuring of the data on secondary memory (that is, in the file). The ease with which new classes can be added ensures the flexibility that is required when working with different datasets and their different data models.

The flow of data to and from the files on the operating system is controlled by two processes, called activation and passivation.

Activation Activation denotes the process of reading a CrisView file (an existing document) from the operating system into the prototype, thereby instantiating the printable representation of core data objects and supplementary data objects. The process is invoked when an "open" operation is performed.

Passivation Passivation can be viewed as the inverse of activation. It denotes the process of writing a new version of a document that is currently active in CrisView to a file. This process is invoked when a "save" operation is performed: after importing data into a new document or after making changes to the supplementary data of an existing document. The process is called passivation because instances of object classes are written to a file in their printable representation.

3.3 DATA REPRESENTATION

Following closely the object-oriented paradigm, all logical entities of a domain-specific dataset that is imported into CrisView are represented as objects. This is an important characteristic of CrisView because it enables its operations to manipulate every piece of phenomenological data (for example, single variables) in a flexible way. Although the maintenance of large numbers of objects is expensive compared with other data types, these costs are justified in the context of data exploration where users or analyses tools might require operations to work on the lowest, atomic level of a phenomenon's description. The objects that correspond to the logical entities of a domain-specific dataset are contained in the core data of a document.

3.3.1 Document Class

The definition of the class *document-class* determines the structure (the slots) and the behavior (the methods specialized to this class) of its instances, the individual documents. Because it affects all instances of the class irrespective of the dataset to which a document corresponds or the data models therein, the definition must refrain from making any reference to the idiosyncrasies of a particular dataset.

Structure of The Document-Class

Core data The document-class has a slot called unit-collection that is used to store a document's core data. The value of this slot is an instance of a class called *collection-class*. Collection-class has two slots, one for storing the list of units of a dataset, the individual phenomena, and another one for storing a list of indexes. Each index corresponds to the position of one particular unit in the list. This index is used in other parts of CrisView to access the units. Units contain the logical entities on lower levels (substructures and variables). Consequently, the instance of the collection-class embraces the entire dataset that is imported into CrisView.

Acceleration structures The document-class has two slots whose values are acceleration structures. The acceleration structures in CrisView contain paths from variables to units to help retrieve those units that contain a certain variable value. There are many operations that require this information—for example, the browsing and inspecting operations supported in the document-window (section 3.5). The purpose of establishing acceleration structures is to reduce the time needed to search through the space of data. Time might become a decisive factor once the system has to search through large bodies of data in order to answer a particular query (for example, to access a particular object). CrisView's acceleration structures are described in section 3.3.3.

User-defined data structures Several slots contain data structures that have been defined by the user during data exploration. The values of these slots include instances of filter-class and instances of subset-class. A filter specifies a combination of variables and values and is used to retrieve the units in which this combination occurs. A subset simply contains the indexes of a number of selected units. Both filters and subsets enable the user to store partitions of the core data. These partitions can be recalled whenever the document is activated again. In the case of filters, the user can extract the variable value combination that defines the partition. Filters and subsets are discussed in more detail in section 3.4.3. Other user-defined data structures comprise induction and precedent-based reasoning experiments. When a new induction experiment has been performed, the entire induction-window (section 3.4.7) is added to the list of induction experiments stored in a slot of the document. The same holds for the precedent-based experiments (section 3.4.9).

Windows A number of windows are associated with a document. The document-window is the main window of the user interface. It displays the core data of a document. From within the document-window a number of other windows can be opened and closed. Each provides access to some exploration mechanism or technique. These windows include: filter-window, descriptor-window, new-variable-window, and analyses-window. The analyses-window presents a menu for choosing exploration techniques such as comparison, induction, and precedent-based reasoning. The windows of the CrisView data exploration component are described in section 3.5.

Behavior: The Method Interface of The Document Class

The method interface of the document-class consists of a set of methods that define the class-specific behavior and operations of generic functions (Steele, 1990, 771). The main operations that are available to manipulate CrisView documents have already been discussed in the previous section. They include activating existing documents, passivating new or existing documents, creating new documents, and importing or exporting data.

Activation and passivation are processes that involve most of the objects contained in a document (the core data and parts of the supplementary data). The generic functions underlying these processes are "initialize-activation" and "print-object," respectively. When invoked, both execute a set of methods based on the classes that have been provided as arguments. The method that specializes "initialize-activation" to the document-class makes an instance of the document-class and subsequently binds the document's slots to the values provided in the document file. Similarly, the method that specializes "print-object" produces a printable version of the document's slots content and writes it to a file.

As with the activation and passivation processes, the import and export operations mentioned earlier are defined by generic functions and their methods. The import of data differs from all the other processes because the file that carries the data is not a CrisView document but rather a file in import/export format. The transformation of each logical entity into an instance of the corresponding object class has to be invoked explicitly instead of being handled automatically by the dispatching generic function: when data are imported from a file, the document already exists, and the import specialized to the document class can be called. This method reads the data from the file and creates instances of object classes on the next lower level (units). If the document was previously empty, the method first creates an instance of the collection-class to store the instances to be created in the process. For each new instance it then invokes the import method specialized to the corresponding class. This process is repeated; that is, on each level the methods specialized to the classes on that level create instances of classes on the next lower level and call their methods.

The "export" and "export-subset" operations, on the other hand, make use of the generic function's dispatch capability. The document's methods for exporting the data generate a file and produce an import/export version of the document's core data or a selected subset thereof. In contrast to the passivation process, which involves all the data structures in the slots of the document, the export operations involve only the core data. The classes of the instances in the core data have a method of their own that defines how an instance is printed in import/export format.

There are several other methods that operate on the document-class. Some implement special parts of the processes mentioned earlier. Others, for example, sort or count the core data. Only those methods that generate the acceleration structures will be discussed further.

3.3.2 Core Data

The core data comprise the phenomenological data of the dataset. Since these data are already structured into logical entities on several levels of aggregation, it seems natural to map this structure onto the structure of the internal representation.

Figure 3.3 shows the structure of the SHERFACS dataset. The units in this dataset are international conflicts (called cases) that occurred in the international arena. On the next lower level are the feature vectors. Each feature vector comprises a sequence of variables.

By defining each logical entity as an instance of an object class, the resulting set of object classes will necessarily be dataset specific. Another dataset will comprise other logical entities and thus require another set of object classes. As an illustration of this, Figure 3.4 shows the simpler structured World Facts dataset that contains data on different countries. Each country is described by a sequence of variables and values. There is no intermediary level of data aggregation.

While the definition of dataset-specific object classes is necessary for working with particular datasets, the mechanisms of object-oriented languages help reduce the effort required to define the structure and behavior of these classes. Abstract object classes can be introduced to serve as parents for the more specific object classes.

Abstract Object Classes

Considering the two datasets shown in Figures 3.3 and 3.4, and the logical entities they comprise, the following abstract object classes can be defined:

Figure 3.3: Structure of the SHERFACS dataset

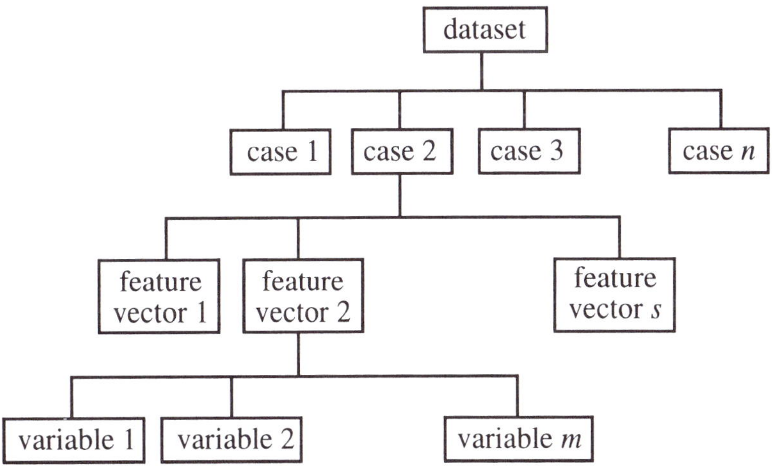

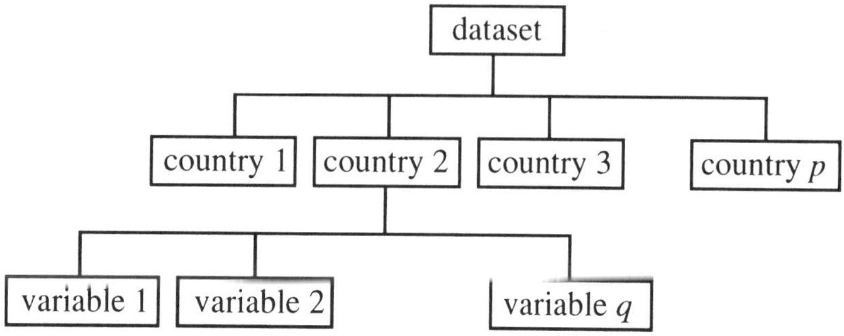

Figure 3.4: Structure of the World Facts dataset

Unit-class The ***unit-class*** is the abstract class for the dataset specific subclasses that correspond to the units of a dataset.

Substructure-class The ***substructure-class*** serves as the abstract class for the subclasses that correspond to the substructures in a dataset. The term ***feature-vector-class*** could have been chosen because most international relations datasets use feature vectors to structure or substructure their data. However, feature vectors are restricted in that they cannot contain other feature vectors. This restriction would unnecessarily limit the kind of substructure or logical entity a particular dataset is allowed to have.

Variable-class The abstract class ***variable-class*** is the class for the subclasses whose instances are the dataset-specific variables in the datasets that are imported into CrisView.

The structure of these abstract classes is simple in order to avoid specificity that fails to hold for all the prospective subclasses. Each class contains a slot called "content." Instances of subclasses of unit-class and substructure-class use this slot to store lower-level objects. Instances of subclasses of variable-class store their value in the content slot. An additional slot called "allowed-content" is defined for unit-class and substructure-class. It stores the names of the classes that correspond to the logical entities on the next lower level. These names are used to check whether a logical entity added to the content slot matches the name of one of the classes defined in the system. This checking is performed by the import operation. Any reference in the remaining part of this chapter to a variable, a substructure, or a unit refers to an instance of a subclass of one of these classes.

Several methods are defined for the abstract object classes. They specify the behavior and operations of the generic functions mentioned earlier, namely initialize-activation, print-object, and import. Extending the range of the generic functions to these classes ensures the flow of data to and from the application, irrespective of the particularities of the document or dataset being processed. The different structuring of the phenomenological data—for example, in the SHERFACS and the World Facts datasets—is dealt with by passing down the control from higher level to lower level objects. Each of the objects involved "knows," by virtue of the method interface of its class, how to initialize, print, and import itself. Only in the process of importing data does the call of the respective methods have to be made explicitly (see the section on the method interface of the document-class).

The mechanisms of inheritance and polymorphism make it possible to draw a clear line between the dataset independent kernel of CrisView consisting of the abstract classes defined earlier and any set of subclasses representing the logical entities of datasets. New datasets can be imported by adding the required subclasses and specifying their behavior without having to change what has already been defined.

Dataset Specific Object Classes

This section discusses the dataset specific object classes of SHERFACS. This dataset comprises the following logical entities: the conflict case, five types of feature vectors, and roughly 270 variables. Figure 3.5 shows the classes that have been defined for these logical entities and their abstract superclasses.

Figure 3.5: SHERFACS dataset specific subclasses

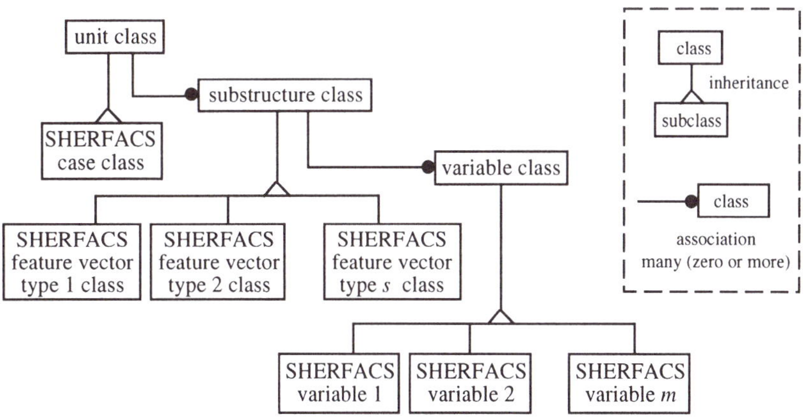

SHERFACS-case-class This class defines the structure and behavior of SHERFACS conflict cases. It is defined as a subclass of the abstract class unit-class and inherits thus the content slot to store the feature vectors with which the case is described. Two new slots are added to the class: a name slot and an identification slot to store the identification number of a case.

SHERFACS-feature-vector-class and subclasses SHERFACS uses five different types of feature vectors: case-overview, phase-structure, party-involvement, agent-action, and agent-referral. Each type of feature vector is defined as a subclass of the class SHERFACS-feature-vector-class that is itself a subclass of substructure-class. From this abstract class they inherit the slot to store the variables that compose the feature vector. A new slot for the name of the feature vector is added. The reason for introducing the SHERFACS-feature-vector-class is that many operations are the same for all types of feature vectors.

SHERFACS variable classes For each variable a separate class is defined as a subclass of the abstract class variable-class. Since variables differ with regard to the values they can accept, these differences are described in the definition of the corresponding classes. Some classes have a slot called value-choices to store the possible values that the variable accepts. The value types differ; they can be numeric, symbolic, or of type string.

Relationships Among Object Classes

Since the data collected in a dataset are structured in one way or another (the complexity of the structuring varies), there are a number of links between the logical entities that denote physical or conceptual connections between them. One type of link has already been introduced, namely the link between unit and substructure, and substructure and variables, respectively. These links represent a kind of "whole-part" relationship between the logical entities involved. They are implicit in the structure of the abstract object classes by virtue of the content slot.

Frequently there are other links between the logical entities in a dataset. In SHERFACS, for example, there are conceptual connections between the different types of feature vectors. The feature vectors form a hierarchy, whose root is the case-overview feature vector. On the next lower level is the phase-structure feature vector. The phase-structure feature vector connects to the remaining feature vectors, namely party-involvement-action, agent-action, and agent-referral. The structure of the feature vector types in SHERFACS is shown in Figure 3.6. For a particular conflict case, the number of individual feature vectors varies.

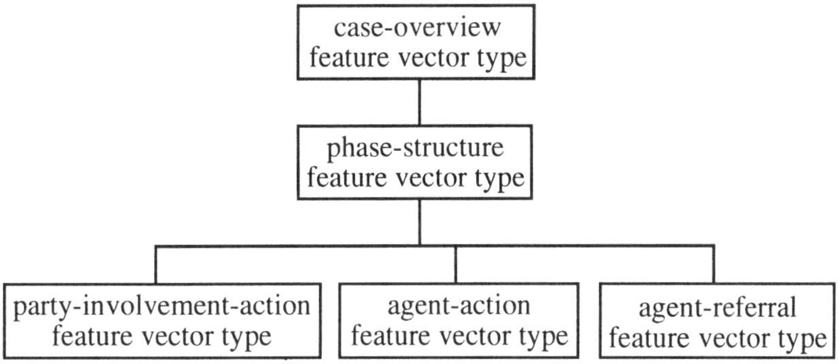

Figure 3.6: Structure of SHERFACS feature vectors

There is only one case-overview feature vector, but depending on the complexity of the conflict case, there may be several phase-structure feature vectors and an even greater number of the remaining types of feature vectors.

While the specific links between logical entities are dataset specific, considerations about how to represent these links—that is, the connections between classes—are not. Because links are not part of either class—they connect but depend on both of the classes involved—some object-oriented modelers argue that links should be modeled explicitly as object classes and subclasses (for example, Rumbaugh et al., 1991). Others concerned with aspects of information hiding (encapsulation) feel that every piece of information should be attached to a single class. No standard design procedure exists, and there is usually no single answer to any design question. Given the hierarchical relationship between the feature vectors in CrisView, the links between them are modeled as "whole-part" relationships. The hierarchy can be traversed by using methods specialized to the feature vector types.

3.3.3 Acceleration Structures

Acceleration structures are established when a new document is created and data is imported into the prototype. As mentioned earlier, the acceleration structures in CrisView provide fast access from variables to units. These structures are used by many exploration tools and help to speed up their performance. Acceleration structures are associated with a document. When the document is saved, acceleration structures are written to a file together with the printable version of the data stored in the document. This ensures that the data are available whenever a document becomes active again.

The content of acceleration structures depends on the requirements of the analyses techniques: how frequently do they need to access what kind of objects? Accessing the instance of a dataset-specific variable when knowing the unit it belongs to, for example, is a straightforward task. The information in the content slot of the latter can be used, recursively if necessary. However, to access a unit when provided with the instance of one of its variables is another matter. Currently, CrisView supports two different acceleration structures. The first lists the names of data specific variables, their values and the indexes into the collection of units. This acceleration structure provides fast access from any variable to the unit in which it occurs. The second acceleration structure is used for documents that contain SHERFACS data. In SHERFACS, a conflict is divided into several conflict phases, each phase being described with an arbitrary number of feature vectors and variables. The multiple occurrence of variables makes it impossible to locate exactly a variable without specifying the phase in which it occurs. As a consequence, the second acceleration structure in CrisView contains sub-lists that consist of a variable name, the variable's value, the phase, and the indexes into the collection of units where this particular variable-value-phase combination occurs.

3.3.4 Reinforcing The Coding Schema

While CrisView itself does not model a particular domain theory, it nevertheless reflects the theories that are implicit in the data that are imported from various datasets. Every dataset—by virtue of its coding scheme—embodies the theory that was used in the process of data collecting and coding. This theory determines the mapping of mostly textual descriptions of phenomena into a set of predefined categories or concepts, thereby producing a view of the real world that is composed of a set of often highly disjunctive logical entities. The treatment of these entities as objects, each with its own set of behavior, further corroborates this view, because the core data of each document exactly mirror the breakdown of real-world phenomena depicted in the datasets, thereby reinforcing what can be seen as an artificial decomposition of the domains' phenomena.

Although intuitively appealing, given that humans tend to perceive the world as composed of objects and their properties, there are two sides to this approach. On the one hand, the locally defined behavior of each logical entity makes it feasible to investigate closely the entity's relation to and effect on other logical entities. Furthermore, the access to each logical entity ensures that the data can be recombined in various ways, thereby rendering relevant information explicit. On the other hand, the user who is working with a particular dataset is limited in his or her explorative analysis to the elements that the theory deemed necessary in the depiction of the phenomena. An object-oriented data representation cannot possibly replace what has been lost in the process of converting textual information into coded structured data. It fosters the kind of critique that generally applies to the use of structured coded data. As will be shown in section 3.4.4, the user may, for example, create new coding categories (variables) that better fit his or her analysis needs, yet the process of creating new categories is basically one of aggregation and does not account for essential information that might be missing in the description of the phenomena.

3.4 Data Exploration

From a user's perspective the main advantage of CrisView are the exploration techniques it supports. In ascending order of complexity and sophistication, the four types of exploration techniques supported in CrisView are browsing and inspection; filtering and retrieval, including the definition of new logical entities; inquiries and comparison; and knowledge-based analysis techniques. Together, they provide a sizable, although far from exhaustive apparatus for exploring and analyzing phenomenological data. The first three types of exploration are called surface analyses techniques, answering simple queries, and offering different views on the data, thereby giving a good account of the structuring and content of various partitions of the data. Deeper insight into the data is provided by inductive and precedent-based reasoning techniques. While the use of the surface techniques does not in general require any familiarity with the data that is being explored, the successful use of the knowledge-based techniques implicitly assumes the setting up of plausible experiments as well as the awareness of the peculiarities in the data.

A particular advantage of CrisView's object-oriented data representation is the ease and parsimony with which the functionality of the system can be extended. Since many of the exploration techniques operate on the same objects, they can profit from generic operations that have been previously defined. The object-oriented representation of a document's core data suggests that a small but comprehensive set of generic operations should be defined, one that could be used and reused by any of the exploration techniques. A case in point is the operation on subclasses of substructure-class that retrieves the value pairs or tuples of two or more variables. This operation is used by many of the exploration facilities described later, including filters, inquiries, the compare mechanism, the induction technique, as well as the precedent-based reasoning technique. During the process of incorporating exploration techniques into CrisView, the goal is to use, whenever possible, already existent operations or to define operations that are known to be needed in other parts of the system as well.

Since CrisView is a prototype and not a fully fledged data exploration system, "low-cost" extendibility is crucial. While experimenting with the prototype, many new ideas emerge for alternative ways of consolidating the information conveyed by the data. Similarly, various existing techniques—for example, statistical methods as well as knowledge-based techniques other than those supported in CrisView—represent potential candidates for exploring phenomenological data. Many of these techniques will require the same operations on the data as have been defined in the method interfaces to the object classes. Consequently, the system's functionality may be extended with little effort.

3.4.1 Exploration Techniques

Before a description of the windows of the user interface and the techniques associated with them is undertaken, the following list will present a brief overview of each of the techniques supported in CrisView and highlight its purpose for data exploration.

Browsing and inspecting Several browsing and inspecting operations are defined for inspecting the logical entities displayed in the windows of the user interface. The operations supported in the windows factorize and recombine the data in various ways, producing different views of the data. Operations that allow the user to browse quickly through logical entities such as variables, in order to retrieve their values or to find the units in which they occur, make use of acceleration structures.

Filtering and retrieval While the browsing operations support simple types of variable value filtering of the units in a document, CrisView offers more flexible filtering mechanisms. Templates consisting of variable value combinations can be defined (for example, Boolean combinations) in order to extract meaningful subsets of the data. Filtering mechanisms are a prerequisite for the successful performance of many types of analyses including inductive and precedent-based analyses. Furthermore, they provide the means of selecting and retrieving the specific subset of the data that a user may want to export.

Creating new logical entities Each datasets presents its own set of logical entities, starting with the units and decomposing them into logical entities on the substructure or variable level. Frequently, it is desirable to use additional descriptors, that is, combinations of existing logical entities in order to capture a certain characteristic of the phenomenon. These new entities can then be used by other explorative operations supported in CrisView. They are particularly important in experiments involving knowledge-based techniques where users frequently want a set of logical entities customized to their analysis needs.

Making inquiries Simple inquiry techniques focus on the properties of the phenomena, that is, the logical entities and values that characterize the units in the document's core data. Statistical methods are used to assess the correlation between selected properties and to determine their relative salience. These measurements can be used to formulate domain-specific hypotheses based on the relationships between properties. They are also important for setting up knowledge-based analyses experiments.

Comparing logical entities CrisView supports a mechanism for comparing pairs of units based on several similarity metrics. This mechanism can be used separately or as part of the precedent-based reasoning process.

Knowledge-based techniques CrisView supports two different types of knowledge-based techniques, or more specifically, learning techniques. The first is a domain-independent inductive analyses technique that has been developed for the analysis of complex structured datasets. It releases the data assumptions of earlier inductive techniques and can thus be applied to a much broader range of datasets in international relations and related domains. While inductive techniques provide a powerful tool for data exploration (for example, finding generalizations, capturing regularities, providing contingent projections), they require a certain number of examples from which they can learn. If the samples are too few, the results of inductive techniques are unsatisfactory. Therefore, CrisView incorporates a precedent-based reasoning technique. Rather than searching through large spaces of examples, precedent-based reasoning techniques search for previously seen units that are close to a certain base-unit. Chapter 4 discusses both techniques in detail.

3.4.2 Document-window

The document-window is the main window of the user interface. It is defined as an instance of the document-window class and is attached to an individual document. The window is created when a new document is created or when an existing document is activated (Figure 3.7).

The document-window, as with most of the windows displayed in the exploration component, contains several panels. The panels of a window are the different areas into which the window is divided (Macintosh, 1985, 50). Panels are used to show different parts of a document. Their functionality may differ depending on the type of the panel. In CrisView the panels represent either tables or editors.

The top-left panel of the document-window, called variable-panel, displays the names of the variables that have been used to describe a phenomenon. Two figures are provided, the first figure indicates how many different values have been counted for this variable (this number is either less than equal or equal to the cardinality of the variable's

Figure 3.7: Document-window

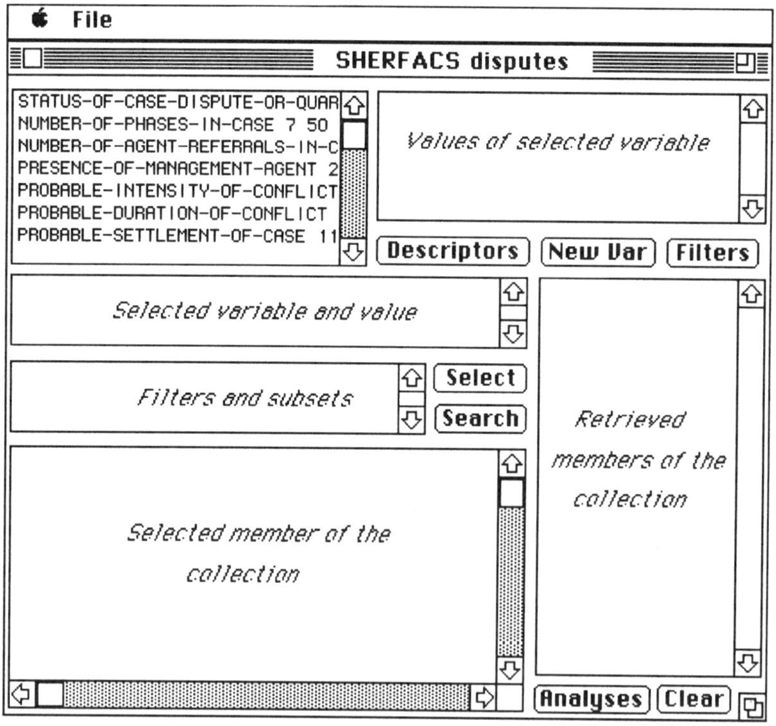

value domain), the second figure indicates how many times the variable has been used in the dataset. The other panels of the document-window are used for presenting the results of browsing and selecting operations.

Browsing and Inspecting The Data Displayed in The Document-Window

Besides the general browsing operations commonly supported in window-oriented user-interfaces, CrisView provides a set of application-specific operations. These operations have specific semantics, because they manipulate semantically predefined entities in the different panels of the main document-window (Figure 3.8). The following operations are supported:

Browsing through the values of a variable When a variable in the variable-panel is selected, its values are displayed in the value-panel. The value-panel shows the variable value together with the figure that

Figure 3.8: Browsing

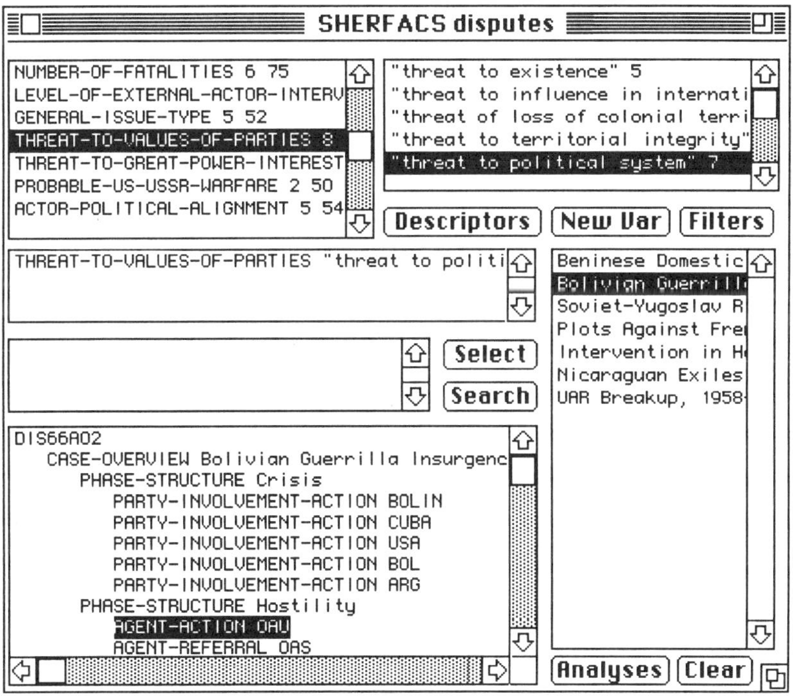

counts how many times this variable value combination occurs in the data. This enables the user to glance at the frequency of particular values in the data.

Browsing through units that contain a specific variable value If a value in the value-panel is selected, the units in which this variable value combination occurs are retrieved and displayed in the collection-panel. At the same time the variable-value combination is shown in the variable-value-panel. For instance, a user working with a document that represents SHERFACS data might wish to know the cases in which the United States was a primary party to a conflict. For this purpose he or she would select the variable "primary party" and then select "US" from among the variable's values.

Inspecting predefined partitions (select button) Predefined sets of units (subsets) can be selected and investigated. These subsets are either some filtered partition (the creation of filters and respective partitions are explained later) or they have been individually collected by the user. The units of the selected subset are displayed in the collection-panel.

Searching for a unit by name (search button) The user can find a particular unit in the document's core data by typing either its entire name or part of its name. If the name discriminates a unit from among the units in the collection, the unit is retrieved, and its name is displayed in the collection-panel. Otherwise, all the units whose names partially match the name supplied by the user are retrieved and displayed.

Inspecting the structure of a unit When the user selects an element in the collection-panel, the structure and content of the selected unit (that is, the hierarchy of logical entities below the unit level) is shown in a panel, called unit-panel. These entities are either instances of subclasses of substructure-class or variable-class, depending on the structuring of the documents' core data (see section 3.3.2).

Inspecting the logical entities in a unit The user can select any of the logical entities of a unit shown in the unit-panel and inspect it. An additional window is opened displaying the value(s) of the logical entity. This allows the user, for example, to inspect the variables and values of the feature vectors of a SHERFACS conflict case.

Intersection By repeating a variable-value selection, CrisView successively intersects the newly retrieved units with those retrieved earlier. This facility provides a filtering mechanism based on a conjunctive list of variables and values. The variable-value-panel shows the combination of variables and values that have been used for filtering. More sophisticated filters are described in the section about the filter-window.

Descriptor-Window

The variable-panel of the document-window displays only part of the entire set of variables that describe the units stored in the document. Two reasons account for the decision to restrict the number of variables shown in the panel: first, international relations datasets typically contain a large number of variables. Not all of them are of equal interest to the user. Rather, he or she will usually work with only a fraction of the variables, namely those related to their research question. The second reason is that small Macintosh computers may run into memory problems when importing datasets with too many variables. It is not the instantiating of the variables and their storing as objects in the document's core data, but rather the creation of acceleration structures that is memory intensive. In the SHERFACS dataset, for example, large cases have over 3,000 variable occurrences.

For these reasons the document-window's variable-panel initially displays about 50 variables. As this selection may not include what the user wants, it can be altered by invoking the descriptor-window (descriptor button). This window presents two tables: the first contains the variables that are actually displayed, the second contains the rest of the variables. To change the original setting, users select variables from the second table and add them to the first table, or they remove variables from the first table. Whenever a variable is transferred, the variable-panel in the document-window is automatically updated. Users can thus customize the selection of variables shown in the document-window. Acceleration structures are updated accordingly. When the document is saved, the present content of its variable-panel is saved too and can be reinstalled whenever the document becomes active again.

Analyses

While the filter-window and the new variable window are directly accessible from within the document-window, other windows and their analysis techniques are invoked from within the analyses-window. This window presents a menu from which the user can choose the desired exploration technique including inquiries, comparison, induction, rule-analyses, and precedent-based reasoning.

3.4.3 Filter-Window

The results of many analyses can be improved by operating on possibly coherent partitions of data rather than on largely heterogeneous datasets. Heterogeneity is a characteristic of many international relations, especially when they cover several periods of time and describe various aspects of the international system. Useful generalizations are more likely to be found in data that is partitioned based on some theoretical or practical criteria. At the same time, a partition of a document's units can also be viewed as a set of precedents for any unit that exhibits the same properties as the units of the partitions (for example, issue of a conflict, countries in a particular region). Indeed, searching for precedents in precedent-based reasoning systems (see Chapter 4) frequently employs filtering mechanisms for the selection and retrieval of certain units.

CrisView supports three types of filtering mechanisms. With the operations available to him or her, the user can define templates for retrieving specific subsets of units.

Boolean filtering In contrast to the mechanism presented in the document-window, which successively intersects subsets of units (conjunction of variable value pairs), filtering is based on an arbitrary Boolean combination of variable value pairs. Users can easily define such combinations (conjunctions, disjunctions, or negations) for selecting and retrieving the core data they are interested in. Working with the SHERFACS data, for example, the user can filter the data for conflicts that occurred in the Middle East, involved sub-national actors as primary parties to the conflict, but were not driven by ideological factors. A set of predefined filters for retrieving domain-specific data is also provided in the Feature Vector Editor developed by Mallery (1988b).

Interval filtering For variables whose values are numerical rather than nominal or ordinal, the user can specify the interval of permissible values for each variable. The filtering mechanism applies a predicate, testing whether the value of a variable of a particular unit is within the boundaries of the interval, and retrieves those units that satisfy the test.

Chronological filtering For datasets that contain chronological data, that is, descriptions of the phenomenon over time, CrisView enables the user to build temporal partitions of the data. Users specify a particular time period, and the filtering mechanism selects those units that occurred within this time period. Since the "occurrence" of a phenomenon does not necessarily denote a point in time but rather a period of several days, months, or even years, users may specify the temporal partitioning by defining a start and an end interval. A complex Time Indexation System to partition chronological data on the basis of temporal extent or co-occurrence was developed by Duffy (1991).

Figure 3.9 shows the filter-window that supports the necessary operations for defining Boolean formulae, numeric intervals, and time periods. The user selects the variables and values he or she wants to use for filtering. For numerical variables, the value interval for the variable is specified in a separate window, invoked by the "num. interval" button. Variable value pairs or variables and intervals can be added to panels, called or-panels. As a whole, the or-panels represent disjunctive elements of a Boolean formula, while the elements are conjunctive lists of the variables and values in an or-panel. In addition, time periods can be specified in a special chronology-window that is invoked by the "chronology" button. The "apply" button triggers the retrieval of the units that satisfy the desired criteria. These units are displayed in the partition-panel. Alternatively, a "complement" button can be pushed to retrieve those units that failed to meet the restrictions.

The specification of a filter and the resulting partitions can be stored in an instance of the class filter-class. If only the partition—that is, the retrieved units—are to be stored without specifying the criteria for their retrieval, an instance of subset-class is created. The slots of both classes include a name slot that contains a user-defined name for

Figure 3.9: Filter-window

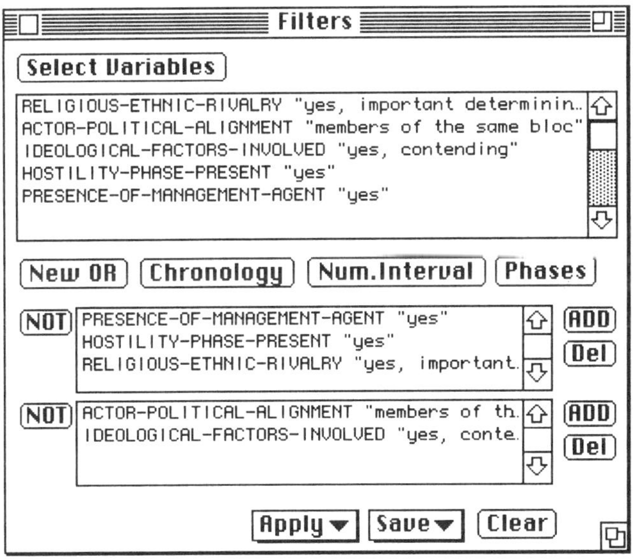

the respective filter or subset. An additional slot contains the indexes into the collection of units. Instances of filters have an additional slot, called template, which stores the combination of variables and values and, if present, the chronological time period. Instances of filter-class and subset-class are saved together with the document. They are available whenever the document becomes active again.

3.4.4 New-Variable-Window

The new-variable-window enables users to define new variables as combinations of existing variables and values. The creation of new variables is considered one of the filtering and retrieval operations, because, similar to filters whose templates can be used to retrieve units, a new variable defines a template for a part of each unit.

There are at least two aspects to the creation of new variables, both indicating the relevance of such a mechanism for effective data exploration. The first aspect is that the logical entities that describe the phenomenon in the dataset may fail to provide the information the user is interested in. A case in point is the SHERFACS dataset, in which the start and end data of each conflict is coded but not the duration of the conflict. Creating a new variable "duration" enables the user to access this information directly and to apply it in other types of analyses. Second, the introduction of new variables enables the user to include domain-specific knowledge in the exploration or analysis process. If the domain expert working with the system has a hypothesis, for example: *if A and B then C*, where A and B represent some logical entity and their value, and C represents some concept, this hypothesis can be tested on the data in the system. Exploring the data with new variables may also identify new analysis needs. CrisView supports three mechanism for building new variables:

Boolean combinations of existing variables Pairs of variable values are combined to define a new variable. Typically, a new variable takes on two values: 1, if the Boolean combination returns true, and 0, if it returns false.

Arithmetic formulae Simple numerical expressions are formed with existing numerical variables. CrisView supports only the most basic arithmetic operations. The value of the variable is calculated from the values of the variables in each unit.

Merging of variables Depending on the characteristics of the dataset, it might be desirable to merge two similar variables into one. For example, the SHERFACS dataset describes many properties of a conflict in terms of "side A" and "side B." Frequently it is useful to consider the side A and side B variable to be of the same type so as to form one variable, thus combining their values.

Figure 3.10 shows the window that is presented to the user for defining new variables. The top-left window panel depicts the general structure of the data model of the core data the user is working with. This data model is particularly helpful in cases of complex structured data, because it shows the user how the logical entities in a dataset are connected to each other. In the case of a tree-structured feature vector data model, the panel shows the feature vectors and their dependencies. Clicking on one of the feature vectors displays a table with the permissible variables for this type of feature vector.

The user selects the variables he or she wants to use to compose the new variable. These variables do not have to belong to the same feature vector type. The variables that have been selected are listed in the variable-selection-panel. Next, the user chooses the combination type he or she wants to use, either "Boolean," "numerical," or "merge." The

Figure 3.10: New-variable-window

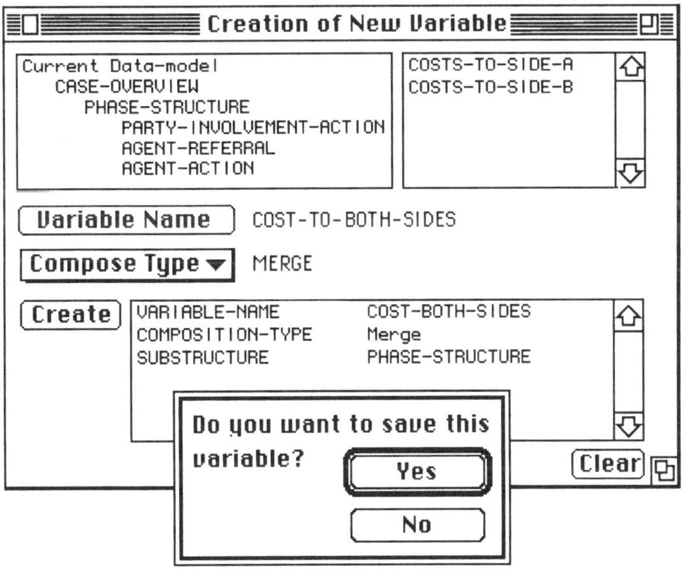

combination type is checked against the variables that have been selected. For example, if the chosen combination type is numerical, only variables with numerical values are admitted (the value type of a variable is stored in the variables class definition and is retrieved for this purpose). In case of a Boolean variable value combination, the user has to select a value for each variable and define the specific combination of variables and values. For this purpose, operations similar to the one defined in the filter-window are available.

Filters Versus New Variables

The process of defining new variables based on Boolean variable value combinations or templates appears to be very similar to Boolean filtering. The combination of variables and values might even be identical in the two cases. Indeed, as long as there are no multiple occurrences of variables in the core data, the difference is only one of purpose: filters are used to retrieve units, new variables are used to retrieve a property of units. For each unit, the new variable has a specific value. However, depending on the structuring of units in the document, the application of templates in the case of filters and new variables is different. If composed of variables that occur multiply in a single unit, a new variable may have multiple occurrences too. As a consequence, and in contrast to the application of filters, it is not sufficient simply to check whether a unit meets the restrictions imposed by the template. The values that the template returns for each occurrence of the new variable are required.

Example

Working with the SHERFACS dataset, the user defines a new variable (a template) whose value is the conjunction of two variable value pairs, namely "conflict side of party," "side-A," and "party-action-frequent-skirmishes," "yes." Both variables belong to the feature vector type party-involvement-action. The template returns either true or false for each of the party-involvement-action feature vectors that have been coded for each of the phases of a conflict (phase-structure feature vectors). In each phase there may be several parties on either side, some of which is engaged in frequent skirmishes. The user wants to compress this information in order to know whether, for a given conflict phase, there is a party on side A that engaged in frequent skirmishes. The new variable is thus located on the level of the phase-structure feature vector, and its value is the disjunction of the templates for each conflict phase. The number of new variables is equal to the number of phase-structure feature vectors in a conflict case.

Operations for Defining New Variables

The operation that applies the template of a new variable to the units in a document embraces several methods, including the method specialized to the dataset-specific subclass of the unit-class in order to find the logical entities defined in the template. If the data are structured as in SHERFACS, additional methods are needed to search through the logical entities on the substructure level. Once logical entities containing the variables in the template are identified, another method extracts the value of each variable involved. If the variables in the template occur only once in a single unit, only one new variable will be defined, and its value is the single value returned by applying the template to the unit.

A new variable is defined as an instance of new-variable-class. Similar to the filter-class, this class provides a slot for the name of the object and a slot to store the combination of variables and values composing the new variable. A third slot is used to specify the location of the new variable. The "location" of a variable is either a subclass of unit-class or one of the subclasses of substructure-class. New variables can be used in the same way as the original variables in the core data. They are also incorporated into the acceleration structures to ensure fast access to the logical entities in which the value of this variable occurs.

3.4.5 Inquiries

A set of formal techniques, referred to as *inquiries*, is provided for analyzing a phenomenon's properties (that is, its variables and values) as well as the relationship between these properties. Methods operating on the instances of dataset-specific classes extract the values of either single variables or sets of variables in each unit. Since many of the methods required for operating on the data already exist, the set of formal inquiry techniques can easily be extended to meet new analysis requirements. Relating to the work on computer-assisted, statistical data analyses and applications (for example, Gale, 1986), new inquiry techniques could include various statistical methods considered useful for data exploration. Statistical packages such as SAS and SPSS (Hull and Nie, 1981) could be used as a source.

Mainly in order to illustrate the use of inquiry techniques, CrisView currently supports some simple functions to yield estimates about the relevance of a particular variable or the relationship between two variables. There are functions to return the entropy and conditional entropy of a variable and the salience of a variable relative to different subsets.

Entropy

A formula from information theory can be used to measure the uncertainty about a variable's value, or in other words, the randomness of its values. This measurement, the entropy of a variable *V*, is calculated by the following formula:

$$E(V) = \sum_{v \in V} p(v) \log_2 p(v)$$

where for all *v*, *v* is a value of *V*, and p(*v*) denotes the frequency of *v* in the units of a document. The smaller the entropy, the less random or more redundant the variable's values across the units.

Conditional Entropy

Another formula from information theory enables the user to measure the conditional randomness of a property (the independent variable *V*) concerning the values of another property (the dependent variable *D*). The formula to calculate the conditional entropy reads:

$$E(V,W) = \sum_{v \in V} p(v) \sum_{w \in W} -p(v \mid w) \log_2 p(v \mid w)$$

where *v* and *w* are the values of variable *V* and *W*, respectively, and p($v \mid w$) denotes the relative frequency of the joint occurrence of values *v* and *w*. Similar to covariance analysis, conditional entropy measures the degree of randomness in pairs of independent and dependent variable values. The lower the conditional entropy, the greater the number of homogeneous value pairs, and thus the greater the independent variable's power for predicting the value of the dependent variable.

Salience of a Variable

Measures of salience have been used in understanding metaphors (for example, Iawayama et al., 1990; Weiner, 1985). Iawayama and his colleagues determine the salience of a variable and its values by two factors, the information content of the variable and the distribution of this information among similar concepts. In CrisView, "similar concepts" are subsets of units; for example, conflicts with a particular issue type or countries in a specific region. The formula for calculating the salience of variables has been adopted from Iawayama et al. (1990). The user partitions the units into a number of subsets C_k. The system then determines:

Amount of information For a given subset C_k of units, the values v_i of a variable V_i and their frequencies $p(v_i)$ are collected:

$$\{v_{i1}\, p(v_{i1});\ v_{i2}\, p(v_{i2});\ ..\ ;\ v_{im}\, p(v_{i,m})\}$$

$v_{i,max}$ denotes the value with the highest frequency among the values of V_i. The amount of information, AI (V_i), of variable V_i is calculated by the following formula:

$$AI(V_i) = 1 - E_r(V_i)$$

where $E_r(V_i)$ is the relative entropy of V_i calculated by:

$$E_r(V_i) = \begin{cases} 0 & \text{if } m = 1 \\ E(V_i)/\log_2 m & \text{otherwise} \end{cases}$$

where E(V_i) is the entropy of V_i.

Difference of variable Given a number of subsets $C_{k \text{ in } \{1, 2, \ldots, i-1, i+1, \ldots n\}}$ the difference D(V_i) of a variable V_i is calculated by the following formula:

$$D(V_i) = \frac{AI(V_i)}{AI(V_i) + \sum_{Vk \subset Ck} AI'(V_i, V_k)}$$

where $AI'(V_i, V_k) = \begin{cases} AI(V_k) & \text{if } v_{k,\max} = v_{i,\max} \\ 0 & \text{otherwise} \end{cases}$

Salience of variable Given the amount of information and the difference of the variable, the measure of salience S(V_i) of a variable V_i is then computed by the formula:

$$S(V_i) = AI(V_i) \times D(V_i)$$

Each of these functions is associated with a separate window, providing the necessary menus and controls for selecting the variables and invoking the methods. Furthermore, each inquiry can be restricted to a subset of the units in the document.

Counted as an inquiry technique, CrisView supports a compare mechanism that based on several similarity metrics allows the user to compare pairs of units.

3.4.6 Compare-Window

An essential requirement for data exploration is the capability of the system to compare individual occurrences of a phenomenon. The operations supported in the compare-window (Figure 3.11) compare pairs

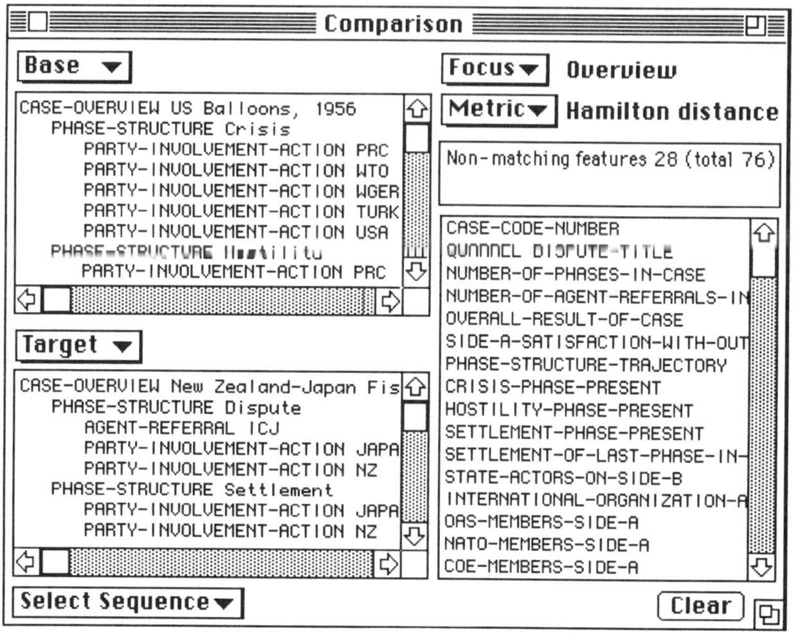

Figure 3.11: Compare-window

of units based on several similarity metrics. The user selects a *target-unit* and compares it to a *base-unit*. The terms target-unit and base-unit are adopted from precedent-based reasoning where the target denotes a new phenomenon (for example, a new situation, a new problem) that is compared to one previously known (the base), in order to transfer knowledge from the base to the target. If both target and base are units stored in the document's core data, the comparison serves to estimate the differences or similarities between the two rather than the transferring of knowledge. Each of the units is displayed in a separate panel in the compare-window in order to give users the possibility to inspect the units' content.

Since the individual units of a document can be viewed as a (possibly structured) sequence of logical entities and values, studies on sequence comparison and sequence analyses can be consulted for a variety of potentially useful algorithms and theoretical considerations. A good account of sequence comparison is provided, for instance, in Sankoff and Kruskal (1983). There are several ways in which users can come by an account of the similarity between base-unit and target-unit.

Hamilton distance The Hamilton distance is the number of positions in a sequence R (base-unit) where the elements are different from the elements in a sequence S (target-unit):

$$d(R,S)=\sum_{i\in N} f(r_i,s_i) \text{ where } f(r_i,s_i)=\begin{matrix} 0 \text{ if } r_i=s_i \\ 1 \text{ if } r_i\neq s_i \end{matrix}$$

The complement of the Hamilton distance (the number of positions in which corresponding elements are the same) is the number of identical features in both cases (in CASCON, this measurement is called *information statistic*). Apart form the Hamilton distance and its complement, the user can ask for the list of the matching variables and values in the base-unit and the target-unit. Similarly the list of nonmatching variables can be displayed.

Hamilton distance as well as other simple distance measurements such as Euclidean distance or City Block distance (Sankoff and Kruskal, 1983) assume that sequences are of equal length and are based on a comparison between corresponding elements. Different techniques have to be applied to compare sequences in which the correspondence between the elements is not known or simply sequences of unequal length. The former is not problematic in CrisView since all elements in a sequence are defined as instances of classes. Corresponding elements can be determined by referring to the class of these instances. The latter, however, is more serious. The documents' core data may contain units that have different numbers of logical entities and thus form value sequences of different lengths.

One way to establish the similarity between two sequences involves measuring the cost of transforming the base sequence into the target sequence. The theory of sequence comparison distinguishes three types of operations that change one sequence (the base or source sequence) into another sequence (the target sequence): substitution, deletion and insertion, compression and expansion. Substitution denotes a replacement of values in corresponding elements. Deletion and insertion either delete or insert new elements and values. The compression of two or more elements into one or the expansion of one element into two or more elements are a third type of operation. Based on this principle, Levenshtein (cited in Sankoff and Kruskal, 1983) introduced a concept of distance from a base sequence to a target sequence. Omitting some of the details of the original version, the Levenshtein distance can be described as follows:

> The difference between two sequences is measured based on a weighted sum of operations required to transform one into the other. The operations are substitution, deletion, and insertion, each of which has a certain "weight" attached to it. The sum of these weights determines the distance between the two sequences.

While Levenshtein distance has been used to measure the similarity of sequences of political events (Schrodt, 1984a; Mefford, 1984), it serves in CrisView to measure the similarity between two units. The difficulty of the approach lies in establishing the weights for the operations. Whether two occurrences of a phenomena are considered to be similar often depends on the perspective underlying the comparison. There are several possibilities for finding appropriate weights without relying on domain knowledge or some specific value system. Insertion and deletion operations may be weighted according to the salience of a unit's variable with respect to different subsets of units, its relative frequency, or its entropy as a measure of its randomness. The weight of the substitution operation may be determined by the absolute difference of the value codes of the variables in the base-unit and the target-unit, respectively. Or, the difference between the insertion and the deletion weight may be used, since substitution can be viewed as a deletion followed by an insertion. Alternatively, user-defined vectors of weights for each variable can be used. The object-oriented data representation of the core data in CrisView enables each variable to calculate its specific weight according to the weight matrix defined for substitution, deletion, and insertion.

Frequently it is desirable to restrict the comparison of units to only a part of their description, that is, to some of the unit's logical entities. Obviously, the options available for partial comparison depend on the unit that the user has selected as the target-unit. Consequently, these options dynamically change whenever the user selects a new target-unit and present the user with the logical entities that have been used to describe the unit.

3.4.7 Induction-Window

The induction-window (Figure 3.12) serves to set up and run induction experiments. Several choices have to be made by the user before an inductive analysis can be performed.

Setting Up an Experiment

First, the user has to pick which dependent variable is to be predicted and a set of independent variables from which to predict it. The next

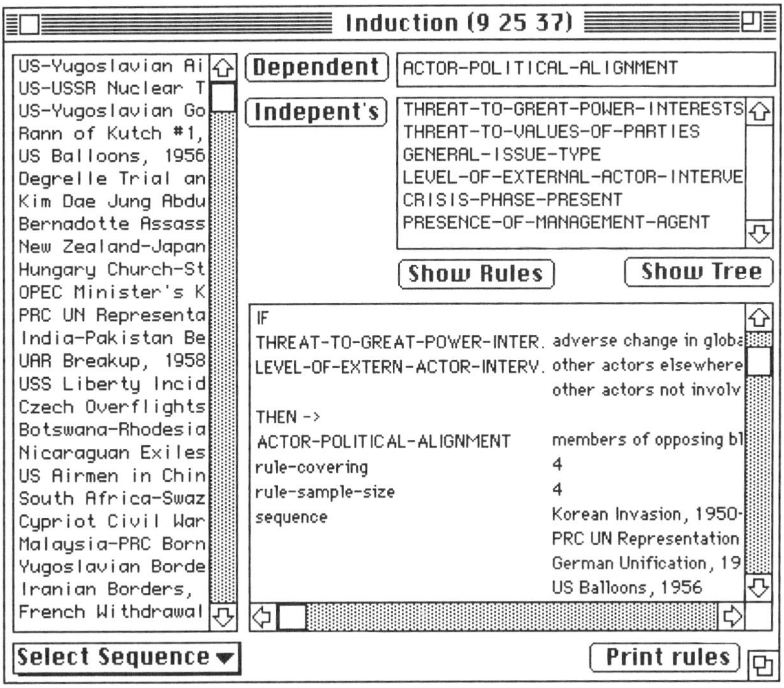

Figure 3.12: Induction-window

choice involves specifying the set of units from which generalizations are to be induced. This set is called a *training-set*, and its elements are the *training examples*. A pop-up menu, called subset, lists all the filtered partitions and the subsets (including the entire collection of units) that were defined earlier. By selecting an appropriate subset, the user can delimit the scope of the inductive analysis to the data he or she is interested in. Finally, a pop-up menu is presented to the user, allowing him or her to chose from three different variable pairing methods, each of which defines a different type of inductive analysis. The "show rules" button invokes the induction process.

Rule-Panel

The inductive algorithm creates a decision tree in which each path from the root to a leaf node corresponds to a set of constraints on the values of the independent variables in the examples. These constraints are represented by the node variables along the path and the branching value that lead from the node to the next node. The leaf node at the end of the path yields the value that is predicted for the dependent variable in the examples that meet the constraints. It has been argued that rules are easier to read than decision trees (for example, Quinlan, 1986a), therefore the different paths through the decision tree are transformed into a set of rules. The node variables and corresponding branching values along a path build the antecedents of the rule. The dependent variable and its value in the leaf node represent the consequent of the rule. The value of the dependent variable in the leaf node is the one that is most frequent among the training examples that reached the leaf node—ideally, all the examples share the same value.

Several operations are applied to the rules in order to compress the information yielded by the decision tree. The reduced set of rules is displayed in the rule-panel of the induction-window. These operations manipulate the rule set in the following way:

Thresholds There is a minimal coverage threshold that marks the minimum number of examples that have to be covered by the rule. The default is set to two, because rules that apply to only one example do not generalize the information in the data. However, this default value can be changed, if necessary. Rules below the threshold are discharged. A local precision threshold represents the minimal percentage of examples whose dependent variable value has to be correctly predicted by the rule (for example, a threshold of 0.6 says that 60 percent of the examples at the node have to be predicted correctly).

Disjunction of antecedent values The second reduction focuses on the antecedents of rules. When the consequents match, and the rules have the same number of antecedents (equal length of paths), and the antecedent variables are the same, and the variables have the same value except for one, rules are merged by combining the differing values.

Exhausted values of antecedents If, after merging, the values of an antecedent variable are exhaustive, that is, all values of the variable appear in the rule, the variable is dropped from the list of antecedents. The second and third reduction processes are repeated until the smallest set of rules is achieved.

Another rule reduction technique has been proposed by Quinlan (1986a). The method drops from the rules' antecedents those variables that are below some level of significance for determining the value of the dependent variable (Quinlan refers to Fisher's exact test in Finney,

Latscha, Bennett, and Hsu, 1963). Repeatedly, those rules whose set of antecedents and consequent are identical are merged. Since rules in CrisView are defined as instances of I^2D-rule-class, which is a subclass of rule-class, and contain all the information that is needed to calculate the significance of each antecedent with respect to the dependent value, Quinlan's reduction method can be implemented as a method specialized to the I^2D-rule-class.

To estimate the validity and relevance of rules, two numbers are attached to each rule: the global coverage or sample size of the rule, and the local precision. The former shows the number (and percentage) of training examples satisfying the conditions specified in the rule's antecedents. The latter shows the number (and percentage) of examples that satisfy the conditions of the rule and match the dependent value that was predicted by the rule. This figure can be used as an estimate for the likelihood of predicting a new example's dependent value. Since domain experts are frequently interested in knowing which examples were covered by a rule, a rule also lists the names of examples that satisfied its antecedent.

In addition to looking at the rules that have been induced by the inductive analysis, the user can inspect the decision tree from which they have been derived. The "show tree" button opens a tree-window in which the decision tree, that is, the hierarchy of its nodes, is shown (Figure 3.13).

Each node shown in the tree-window is mouse sensitive. When a node is selected, a separate node-window is opened containing two tables (Figure 3.14).The first table displays information about the node variable, including the range of possible variable values, the value types, and, if present, the name of the substructure to which the variable belongs. The second table shows the contents of the node.

Each tree node is defined as an instance of node class. The slots for this class are:

Node variable The name of the variable chosen at this node.

Superior node The node on the next higher level in the tree from which a path leads to the node. If the node is the root node, its superior is the tree itself—that is, an instance of tree-class. Otherwise it is an instance of node-class.

Branch value The value of the superior node variable that has been used for branching.

Node subset The training examples that have reached this node.

Dependent value The most frequent value of the dependent variable among the examples in the node subset.

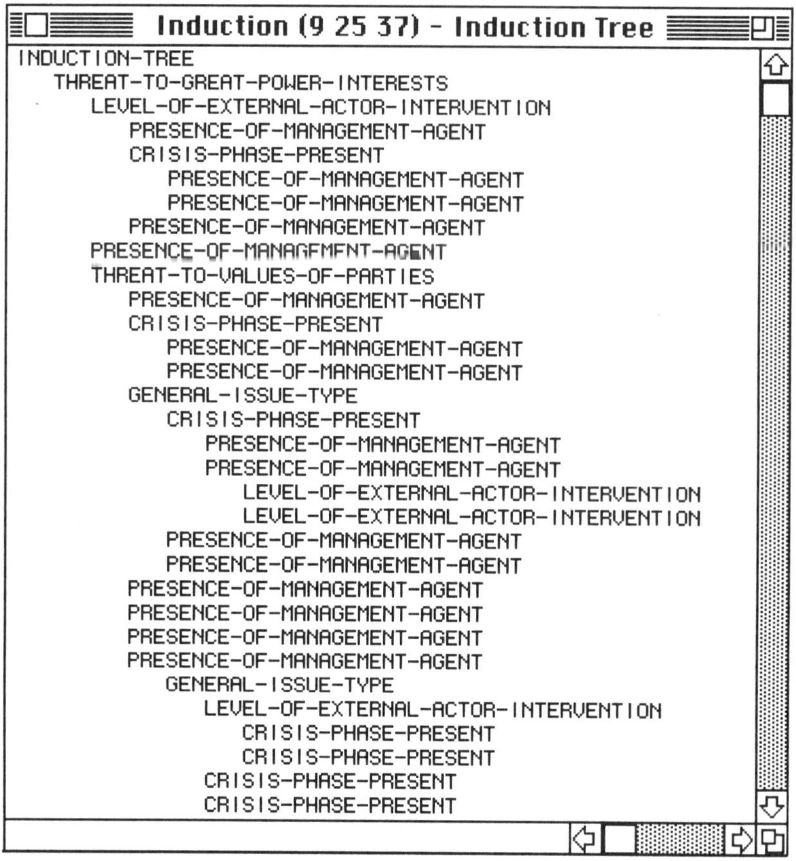

Figure 3.13: Tree-window

Inferiors The children of the node—that is, all nodes on the next lower level that can be reached from this node.

Remaining variables A list of independent variables that have not yet been used for branching along the path that leads to this node.

Node assessment Several results derived in the process of determining the variable selection and the creation of the node (explained in Chapter 4).

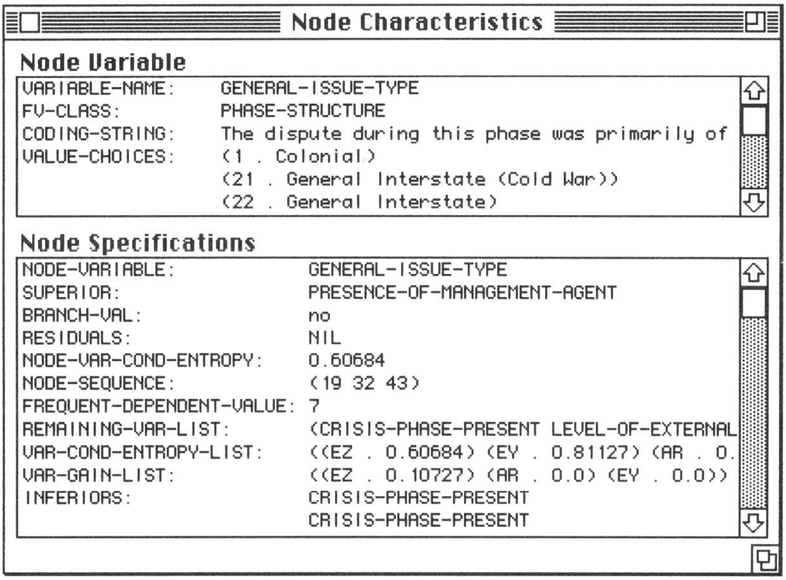

Figure 3.14: Content of a node

Collection of Induction Analysis

Most windows in CrisView are instantiated only once—when the window is used for the first time—and then dynamically change the content in their panels according to user interactions. In contrast, a new instance of induction-window-class is created each time the user wishes to carry out a new analysis. The window is pushed onto a list of induction-windows referenced in the document-window. At the same time, a new item with the name and creation time of the induction-window is added to the induction pop-up menu in the analysis-window. The menu item has a pointer to the induction-window. Consequently, the user can go back to a previous inductive analysis by selecting it from among the menu items of the pop-up menu.

3.4.8 Rule-Analysis-Window

The analyses-window contains a "rule-analysis" pop-up menu whose items correspond to the inductive analyses that the user carried out during a session with CrisView. When an item is chosen, a rule-analysis-window is presented to the user (Figure 3.15).

The rule-analysis-window is an instance of rule-analysis-window-class. It is instantiated when the user wishes to analyze a set of rules. Later, when the user chooses another rule-analysis pop-up item for analyzing a different set of rules, the same instance of the rule-analysis-window-class is shown but with a different content. The content of the window changes dynamically, displaying the rules that belong to a particular inductive analysis. The top-left panel of the window lists the names of these rules. When a rule is selected, its content is displayed in the adjoining rule-content-panel.

Rule Analyses

The rule-analysis-window supports the operations that enable the user to apply rules or parts thereof to various partitions of units:

Figure 3.15: Rule-analysis-window

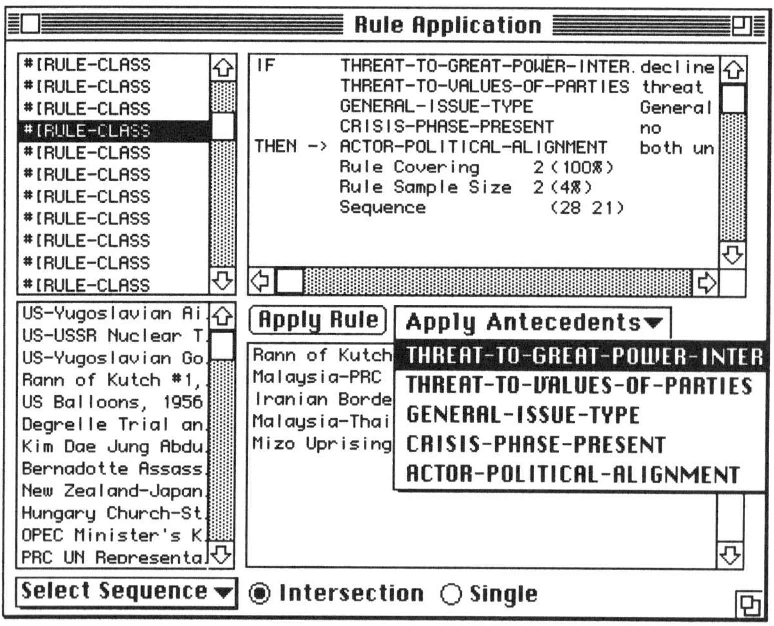

Unit selection The user can select the units to which he or she wants to apply a rule or parts thereof. A pop-up menu, identical to the one presented in the induction-window, presents the filtered partitions and subsets (including the entire collection) that have been defined earlier. The units of the selected subset, that is, their names, are displayed. Subsequent rule application is restricted to these units.

Applying a rule to a subset of units The rule shown in the rule-content-panel can be applied to the subset of units that was previously selected. The result, that is, the units that satisfy the rule's antecedents and consequent, are shown in the window's result-panel (bottom right). If the subset is identical to the training set, and the rule's local precision is 100 percent, then the units shown in this panel are the same as those listed with the rule. However, a local precision of less than 100 percent implies that the dependent variable value of some of the units does not match the predicted value. In this case, the units shown in the panel are a subset of those listed with the rule. The rule can also be applied to another subset to measure the validity of the rule for units that have not been included in the training set. Rule validity and the comparison of different sets of rules are discussed in detail in Chapter 4.

Applying single antecedent or consequent to a subset of units The user can individually apply each antecedent or the consequent of a rule to the units that were previously selected. The result-panel shows the units of the subset in which the variable value pair (an antecedent or the consequent) occurs. When applied to the entire collection, this operation is identical to the simple variable value retrieval supported in the document-window. When applied to the training set, or to any other subset, it enables the user to investigate closely the effect of each variable value pair on the retrieval of units from the core data of the document.

Intersecting single antecedents and consequent Instead of applying a single antecedent or the consequent of a rule to a subset, the user can investigate the effect of arbitrary combinations of antecedents and consequent. Again, if the subset is the entire collection, this operation is identical to the intersection mechanism supported in the document-window. When applied to the training set, it reproduces the induction process step by step along a single path of the decision tree. Applying rule segments to other subsets is of particular interest. It can be used to test the rule's capability to generalize if any one of the antecedents is missing and, similarly, to identify the effect of each antecedent with respect to the global coverage of a rule. Both results are relevant for estimating the validity of a rule. Furthermore, experimenting with rule segments across different subsets helps to detect additional regularity patterns in the data.

Generating New Rules

In addition to the analysis of rules that have been derived from a decision tree, the user can define his or her own set of rules and explore their effect in the way described earlier. The menu item labeled "new rule" in the rule-analysis pop-up menu opens the rule-analysis-window. Rather than displaying the set of rules produced by an inductive experiment, the rule-analysis-window called by the new-rule menu item is empty. Instead there are two additional buttons in the window, a "select" button and a "save" button. The former is used to select the variable and value pairs for the antecedents and the consequent of a new rule. The latter defines an instance of the class new-rule-class and stores the specified antecedents and consequent in the slots of the new instance. Both the new-rule-class and the class of the rules derived from decision trees, the I²D-rule-class, are subclasses of the same abstract object class rule-class. The reason for defining two subclasses rather than using the same class for both types of rules is that different methods are needed—for example, to display the instances of these classes in the windows of the exploration environment. In addition, new rules have a user-defined name, while the inductively derived rules do not.

The creation of new rules involves similar methods to those needed for the creation of filters. Rules and filters have a lot in common; indeed, a filter can be regarded as a kind of *synchronic* rule to recategorize units. In synchronic rules, synchronic relations hold between the elements in the antecedents and the consequent (Holland et al., 1989, 15). This type of rule is typical for datasets that provide a description of phenomena at a given point in time (for example, the World Facts dataset). However, filters differ from rules when they are *diachronic*. A diachronic rule represents temporal transitions between state descriptions. Chapter 4 presents an algorithm that is part of the I²D technique, producing diachronic rules for chronological datasets. In addition, filters and rules differ in their expressive power: filters allow for the inclusion of disjunctive variable value pairs and their negations, while rules consist of conjunctive variable value pairs only (the values of a variable may be disjunctively connected).

3.4.9 Precedent-Window

The precedent-window (Figure 3.16) serves as the user interface to the second knowledge-based technique incorporated in CrisView, namely

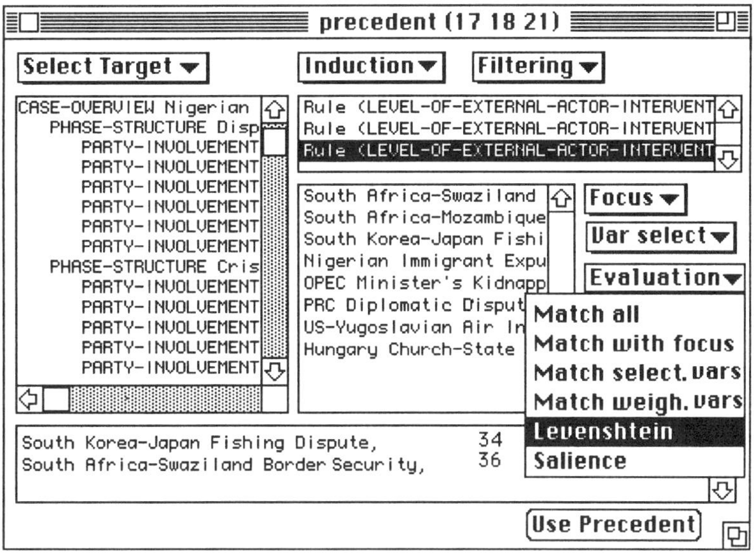

Figure 3.16: Precedent-window

precedent-based reasoning. It provides basic operations for retrieving and evaluating precedents for a target-unit (see section 4.3).

There are two ways for the user to specify a target-unit: selecting a unit from among the units of the document's core data or creating a new unit.

Selecting a target-unit The user is presented with the list of all the units in the document. The unit selected is treated as the target-unit, a "new" unit for which precedents will be retrieved from among the remaining units in the document. Similar to the display of a unit in the document-window, the precedent-window features a panel to display the target-unit. This panel shows the logical entities contained in the unit. The content of the target-unit can be investigated by clicking on these logical entities.

Creating a new target-unit The user can create a new target-unit and enter the variables and values that describe properties of this unit. It is important that the data model of the new target-unit should be the type of data model that characterizes the organization of the core data in the document (for example, tree-structured data model, flat data model). A special tree-editor-window is presented to the user where he or she can configure the structural elements of the target-unit. If the data model of the target-unit is flat, the tree will contain just one node. In the case of a more complex data model, the user inserts the necessary nodes at each level of the tree. These nodes represent the logical entities on the substructure level. Once the data model is built, the user specifies the variables and values in each of these logical entities. The entities that can be used in the process (for the logical entities on the substructure as well as on the variable level) depend on the document the user is working with. For each type of substructure specified in the data model, the user is presented with the list of variables that can be used to describe the new substructure. If a variable's value range is restricted, these restrictions are shown to the user. Within the limits imposed by the definitions of the corresponding classes, the user is free to draft his or her own version of a new unit. The new target-unit is defined as an instance of the dataset-specific subclass of unit-class. However, it is not permanently stored within the core data of the document.

Once a target-unit is defined, the user can experiment with several retrieval and evaluation mechanisms to find the best precedent for this target-unit among the units in the document. Many of the exploration mechanisms that have been defined elsewhere in the exploration component are supported by the precedent-window.

Selection of Potentially Relevant Precedents

Two techniques, the specification of filters and decision tree induction, are particularly useful for selecting potentially relevant precedents from a large collection of units.

The use of filters The precedent-window contains a "filter" pop-up menu that enables the user either to build a new filter or to select one of the previously defined filters. By using filters—or prototypes, as they are called, for example, in ReMind (1990)—the user can guide the selection of precedents to include only those units that satisfy a specific feature combination. The choice of such a feature combination depends on what the user believes to be relevant concerning the target-unit. The units that comply with the conditions specified in the newly created or selected filter are displayed in the retrieval-panel of the precedent-window. The filtering facility aids the user's memory, quickly identifying those units that, in some respect, are similar to the target-unit and are thus worth considering.

The use of induction While filters reflect the user's domain-specific belief that some characteristics of the phenomena are important and should therefore be used as qualifiers for the selection of precedents, induction is employed to divide the units into partitions that are homogeneous with respect to a specific outcome (some variable value). Neither the variables and values that determine this outcome nor their combination has to be known to the user. Theoretically, all the variables (except the outcome or dependent variable) can be used in the inductive analysis. Frequently, however, and in particular when working with variable-rich datasets, the user reduces the set of variables prior to the inductive analysis (see section 3.4.8). Similarly, if a target-unit has been created by the user, and only some of its features have been specified, the induction is automatically restricted to those variables that have been defined in the target-unit.

The induction pop-up menu gives the user the choice of either carrying out a new inductive analysis or using the results of some previous analysis. In the context of precedent-based reasoning, the interesting results of an inductive analysis are the units that have been generalized rather than the predictive structures that a rule or a path through the decision tree defines. The rules derived from a decision tree are displayed in the rule-panel of the precedent-window. The user can then select those rules whose consequent shows the value he or she is interested in. The units that have been generalized by these rules are listed in the window's retrieval-panel.

CrisView supports yet another way to retrieve precedents. It establishes a retrieval template based on a precedent that is provided by the user. The button "use precedent" opens a window in which the user can select from the document's core data the unit he or she believes to be a good precedent for the target-unit. Similar to the precedent-window, this window supports menus to specify a focus on a particular substructure of the data model and to restrict the variables that are used for comparison. A button labeled "make template" compares the supplied "precedent-unit" with the previously selected target-unit and constructs a template with the matching and nonmatching features of the target-unit and the precedent-unit. This template is stored and can be used in the current and in later precedent-based reasoning analyses.

Choosing The Best Precedent

Several options are available for fine-tuning the selection of the best precedent(s) either from among the candidates that have been preselected and displayed in the retrieval-panel or from among all the units. These options include several similarity functions, some of which have also been used for pairwise comparison (see section 3.4.6). The following menus support the user in fine-tuning the selection process:

Focus A focus pop-up menu serves to restrict the application of similarity functions to a particular substructure of the data models of the target-unit and base-units, respectively. The items of the menu are installed when the target-unit has been selected. They correspond to the logical entities in the target-unit's data model. If the target-unit, for example, is a SHERFACS conflict, the menu items list the case-overview feature vector, the specific phase-structure feature vectors that have been used to describe the conflict phases, and the substructure below each phase. Obviously, if the data model of the target-unit is flat, the focus menu contains no items.

Variable selection The variable selection pop-up menu enables the user either to select a specific set of variables or to associate a weight factor with some of the variables. If a focus has been defined, then only those variables that actually appear in the selected structure of the data model are presented for selection. To restrict the variables, the user simply selects the variables he or she wants to subject to the similarity functions. The second option, the specification of weights, presents the variables together with a set of predefined weighting options, ranging from 0 to 10. The default is 1, indicating that a variable is used for comparison but does not have an extra weight. If the value 0 is associated with a variable, then this variable is excluded from the comparison. Higher values make a variable more important since they affect the result of the similarity estimate.

Evaluation The evaluation pop-up menu lists the functions that assess the similarity between the source unit and potential precedents. Discussed in more detail in section 4.3, these similarity functions include nearest neighbor matching (or negative Hamilton distance), matching substructures of the data model, matching of restricted variables, matching of weighted variables (weighted nearest neighbor), as well as Levenshtein distance and salience measurement (sections 3.4.8 and 3.4.5, respectively). The matching extends to the units displayed in the retrieval-panel, either a subset of units or the entire collection. It is restricted to those parts of a unit (substructure or particular variables) that the user specified in the menus named focus and variable selection. If no restrictions are present, the matching applies to the entire unit. Upon selecting one of the menu items, the system compares the source unit with each of the candidate precedents.

The result of the evaluation procedure is a sequence of units. The sequence order indicates the relevance of each unit: the first unit in the sequence is the one that, for a given similarity function, is most similar to the target-unit. The sequence of units and their similarity measures are displayed in the result-table of the precedent-window. When clicking on a unit, the nonmatching features of this unit and the target-unit are shown in a table. This enables the user to investigate the effects of projecting the precedent onto the target-unit. In particular, if the target-unit is one of the units in the collection, and all its features are known, the correctness of the projection can be tested.

Collection of Precedent Analysis

The precedent-window is an instance of the precedent-window-class. Similar to the induction-windows, a new instance of this class is created each time the user carries out a new precedent analysis. The new precedent-window is pushed onto a list of precedent-windows stored in one of the document's slots. Each precedent-based analysis is accessible from a pop-up menu in the analyses-window whose items correspond to the previously performed analysis. The user can go back to a previous precedent-based analysis by choosing the respective item.

ENDNOTES

1. Generic functions are functions that contain, among other information, a set of methods—that is, a set of bodies of code— of which a subset is executed when the generic function is invoked. The subset chosen for execution and the manner in which the selected bodies of code are combined are determined by the classes or identities of the arguments to the generic functions and by the method combination type (Steele, 1990).

Chapter 4
KNOWLEDGE-BASED ANALYSES TECHNIQUES

A major challenge in dealing with large amounts of data is data reduction: to condense the information that is conveyed by the data as well as to recognize those pieces that are relevant to a specific research question. The use of knowledge-based techniques for approaching these tasks is not new in the computationally oriented sector of international relations. As mentioned in section 2.4, these techniques have become popular largely due to the limitations inherent in more traditional techniques such as statistical methods. In addition, their potential for symbolic modeling has allowed scientists to address new research questions.

Artificial intelligence offers a variety of techniques for data analysis. Some of these techniques rely on, or require, domain-specific knowledge. The performance of rule-based systems, for example, depends on the knowledge that has been acquired from domain experts and put into rules. Explanation-based learning systems are an example where learning from single examples is based on domain-specific knowledge supplied to the system prior to learning. The bottom-up, data-driven approach to data exploration that has been proposed in section 2.2., however, precludes the use of techniques that require domain knowledge. Rather, the knowledge-based techniques in a data exploration system should extract relevant information from the data in the absence of domain-specific knowledge or theories. The choice of such techniques is particularly important in domains such as international relations where there is little consensus about the theories explaining political phenomena, and where—unlike many other domains such as Newtonian physics—the nature of dependencies between various factors or even their existence are frequently unknown. The choice of knowledge-based techniques is also affected by the nature of the data. International relations data are often heterogeneous, incomplete, redundant, and even erroneous. Techniques that are sensitive to the noise in the data are less suited for the kind of data found in international relations. Section 4.4 addresses some of the problems surrounding the analysis of "natural," hand-crafted collections of real-world phenomena.

4.1 Selection of Knowledge-based Techniques

CrisView currently supports two knowledge-based techniques: an induction technique and a precedent-based reasoning technique. Both are believed to be essential for data exploration, and both are sufficiently robust with regard to the characteristic of the domain and the data. In addition, induction and precedent-based reasoning techniques complement one another: on the one hand, inductively derived results can be further refined by precedent-based reasoning (ReMind, 1990); the precedents identified in the reasoning process, on the other hand, can be used as training sets for inductive analysis (Skalak and Rissland, 1990). Furthermore, knowledge can be gained about the relevance of specific factors by explaining discrepancies between precedents and units that satisfy a particular induction rule.

CrisView's inductive capability is based on an extended version of a decision-tree induction technique that works with arbitrarily structured data. This flexibility is crucial in order for the technique to be applicable to different datasets. Similarly, the precedent-based reasoning technique in CrisView can be applied to different datasets. Both techniques benefit from the object-oriented representation of the phenomenological data.

4.2 Inductive Learning

According to Holland et al. (1989), induction encompasses all inferential processes that expand knowledge in the face of uncertainty. Understanding these processes has been a major concern for artificial intelligence. Most work on induction in the field has focused on the purely syntactic aspects of induction rather than on pragmatic aspects such as the goals and the context in which induction takes place. Evidently, the latter requires a system to incorporate a model of the problem domain. This requirement, however, is incompatible with the purpose of data exploration as proposed in this study. Rather than becoming locked in on a particular type of model, the aim is to support techniques that are data-driven in nature. Arguments against such "universal learning techniques," as these data-driven techniques are often referred to, can be found, for example, in Holland et al. (1989) and Buntine (1990).

The inductive technique incorporated in CrisView considers only the formal structuring of the data. A kind of *weak domain-specific knowledge* (Buntine, 1990) is introduced, however, by the user and his or her deliberate choice of the data to be included in the inductive process. This choice concerns the examples in the training set and the independent variables to predict or explain the outcome. Carefully choosing the training examples helps reduce the noise in the induced generalizations and increases the chance of detecting interesting patterns in the data. By selecting a particular set of independent variables, the user can apply his or her domain-specific knowledge of the relevance or irrelevance of certain variables.

The inductive learning technique introduced in this chapter belongs to the family of decision-tree induction techniques. The literature refers to this type of learning simultaneously as similarity-based learning, learning from examples, concept learning, that is, concept definition learning, or concept attainment. As will be discussed in the next section, induction techniques, although generally ascribed to the domain of machine learning, have also been developed and widely employed in the social sciences. Over the years, many variants of decision-tree induction techniques have evolved, deepening the general technique and addressing various problems that prevented earlier algorithms from yielding satisfactory results. However, what finds itself neglected in these more recent and improved approaches to decision-tree induction is the treatment of complex structured datasets. The algorithms that lie behind the techniques generally assume that the data are represented as fixed-length feature vectors, an assumption that complies with the data representation of many natural and most of the artificially constructed datasets. However, in a domain such as international relations and, possibly, in others, new datasets have been generated that, in order to provide more comprehensive accounts of the domain's phenomena, are much richer and frequently employ complex data models to represent individual occurrences of the phenomena.

The decision-tree induction technique incorporated in CrisView has been developed in an attempt to make already powerful techniques even more widely available, especially for inductive analysis of real-world data. It generalizes the data assumptions of other decision-tree induction techniques in order to find regularities in complex structured datasets. Furthermore it extends inductive modes beyond cross-sectional analysis to include time-dependent comparisons. Before describing the technique, it would be useful to briefly review the development and employment of decision-tree induction techniques in social science and machine learning.

4.2.1 Overview

The following paragraphs provide an overview of some of the pioneering work on decision-tree induction as well as some of the better known algorithms in both social science and machine learning. However, this account is far from exhaustive. Inducing decision trees and learning classification rules are part of ongoing research work in machine learning and application domains.

Social Science

Inductive discovery of classification schemes from examples and the use of trees in regression appeared in early social scientific approaches to categorical data (for example, Morgan and Sonquist, 1963; Hunt et al., 1966; Alker and Greenberg, 1971; Alker and Christensen, 1972). These techniques seek to induce decision trees, or rule sets, which explain most of the given domain examples that are described by a set of variables and values. The decision trees can then be used either as classifiers or as devices that help uncover the predictive structure of the data. While classification employs decision trees to propose categories for new examples based on their variables and values, prediction uses the decision trees to test certain combinations of variables and values to hypothesize other variables and values, or outcomes.

Decision-tree induction techniques, termed "Interaction Seeking Stepwise Procedures" (Alker, 1969) in polimetrics, neither search for nor assume a fixed relationship between variables. This is their main advantage over alternatives such as regression analysis, discrimination analysis, or cluster analysis. In discrimination analysis, a regression-like equation predicts the value of unknown cases of a dependent variable from known cases (Garson, 1987). Although cluster analysis reduces data to clusters of similar items, it does not provide an optimal scheme for the classification of new examples with respect to a dependent variable. In contrast, decision-tree induction explores the interaction effects between the variables and creates subgroups with different orderings of variables. By exploiting *all possible* degrees of freedom and for reasons already mentioned at the beginning of this chapter, namely the incomplete knowledge about the nature of the dependencies between various factors or even the existence of dependencies, this data-driven approach is particularly suitable in domains such as international relations.

Machine Learning

Learning concepts, or inducing classes, from examples has figured prominently in artificial intelligence and its subfield, machine learning, for over two decades. Winston learned concepts from examples represented in a relational graph (Winston, 1975). Other systems induced concepts from data expressed as feature vectors. These included Hunt's Concept Learning System (CLS), a decision tree that classified objects based on a minimal classification cost scheme (Hunt et al., 1966), and its descendants. Probably the best-known CLS descendant, Quinlan's (1979) ID3 entropy-based decision-tree induction algorithm has received widespread application in many domains, including international relations. Although often successful elsewhere, Schrodt argued that ID3 was not particularly useful for predicting international events (Schrodt, 1987a, 13). ACLS (Patterson and Niblett, 1983) is a generalization of ID3, permitting variables to range over unrestricted integer values. ASSISTANT (Kononenko et al., 1984) further generalizes ACLS by operating on continuous real values. It also included the use of hierarchically related class-values. ID5 (Utgoff, 1988), finally, is an incremental version of ID3. Motivated by the early efforts of social scientists to cope with actual problems and data and by programs such as Sonquist's (1971) Automatic Interaction Detection (AID), Breiman and others developed the CART system (Breiman et al., 1984).

The challenge for inductive learning techniques is to find the shortest decision tree or the smallest set of rules that correctly predicts the value of the dependent variable of most domain examples. Several methods of efficiently selecting the ordering of the variables in the decision tree have been developed. Hunt applied measurements of classification and misclassification costs at each stage of the tree building process (Hunt et al., 1966), Sonquist's AID relied on variance (Sonquist et al., 1971). ID3 measured the conditional entropy of pairs of variables (Quinlan 1979, 1983). Lopez de Mantaras measured the distance between partitions of variables (Lopez de Mantaras, 1991). Finally, Breiman and his colleagues chose the partition that most reduces the node impurity. The "impurity" of a node is largest if the partition contains all classes equally mixed together and smallest if the partition contains only one class.

Cumulative research has produced a number of improvements in decision-tree induction techniques:

Tree pruning Various pruning techniques for obtaining statistically significant trees of smaller size (Quinlan, 1986a; Breiman et al., 1984; Mingers, 1989b). Breiman, as well as Mingers, notes that effective pruning techniques are more relevant for improving the accuracy of the decision tree than the method that is chosen to establish the variable ordering.

Coping with noisy data Techniques were devised to operate on noise-affected data, such as nonsystematic errors in the values of the variables, or in class information. Test procedures that determine the dependence, or independence, between variables and classes are applied to exclude inadequate variables. Probability measures or default values have been used to prohibit decision trees from becoming unnecessarily complex (Quinlan, 1986b, 1986c; Niblett, 1987).

Biased samples Techniques were proposed to correct bias in decision trees that arose from training data with missing values (Breiman et al., 1984; Quinlan 1986b).

Biases in the apparent information content of variables Techniques for coping with the bias in the selection process of the variables (Kononenko 1984; Quinlan 1985; Lopez de Mantaras 1991). A bias occurs when the independent variables have unequal value ranges.

In addition, theoretical work in the field of computational learning theory concerned with identifying classes of concepts that can be learned from examples (Rivest, 1987; Haussler, 1990) has provided guidance for the designers of inductive algorithms.

CrisView's induction technique embodies many of the improvements that have made decision-tree induction techniques more robust and more reliable. However, shifting the focus from refining the algorithms to broadening their scope with respect to the data models they can handle causes a number of problems that have not yet been dealt with. They are discussed in the next section, together with the solution that has lead to the development of an extended version of a decision-tree induction technique. This technique, called Inductive Interaction Detection (I^2D), was first implemented on a Symbolics LISP machine (Unseld and Mallery, 1992).

4.2.2 Algorithm Generalizations

Conventional decision-tree induction techniques induce concepts and learn classification rules from examples with a flat feature vector data model. Each example of the problem domain is described by a single, fixed-length feature vector and represented as a sequence of values for which the indices of the sequence correspond to the variables to which the values belong. Different methods have been used to compare the values of variables (a dependent variable or class variable, and each of a set of independent variables) and to select at each stage of the tree building process the one independent variable that produces the best possible division of examples into homogeneous partitions.

Problems of Comparison

Several problems emerge when, instead of a flat feature vector model, the examples of the problem domain are presented in a tree-structured feature vector model. Figure 4.1 shows such a model. The model represents an individual conflict from the SHERFACS dataset (due to limited space only a part of the feature vector is shown).

The SHERFACS dataset provides an excellent opportunity to study the kind of problems that challenge traditional decision-tree induction techniques and other methods that assume a flat feature vector data model, because its structure exhibits several "anomalies." These include the unequal number of feature vectors along the branches of the tree, multiple occurrences of feature vectors of the same type, and the hierarchical, as well as temporal, dependence between feature vectors. In addition, the data models for each conflict case are different, that is, include a different number of feature vectors. A solution that complies with the complex structured SHERFACS data is likely to address the problems generally encountered when dealing with other complex structured datasets:

Inability to perform global comparisons Whenever examples of a dataset do not conform to the flat feature vector model, global comparisons between examples become problematic. Tree-structured feature vector models satisfy the conditions for global comparison only in exceptional cases.[1]

Multiple-occurring independent variables The absence of a flat feature vector model means that independent variables may appear more than once within a single example (for example, variable *D* in Figure 4.1). Instead of ordinary one-to-one comparisons, this situation requires one-to-many comparisons between the values of the variables.

Multiple-occurring dependent variables Similarly, the dependent variable may have multiple values within a single example, requiring many-to-one comparisons, or even many-to-many comparison when independent variables have multiple occurrences as well. At the same time, there are serious uncertainties about which value to predict.

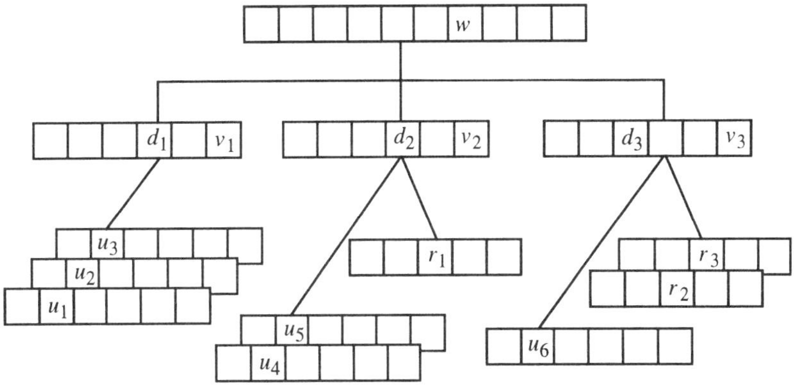

variables	values
D	$d_1\ d_2\ d_3$
R	$r_1\ r_2\ r_3$
U	$u_1\ u_2\ u_3\ u_4\ u_5\ u_6$
V	$v_1\ v_2\ v_3$
W	w

Figure 4.1: A tree-structured data model

All these problems arise from global information measures. To solve these problems a unifying solution is proposed: decomposition of domain examples into local observations where one-to-one comparisons again become possible and the recombining of local comparisons to arrive ultimately at global measurements.

Solution: Decomposition of Complex Data Models

Without loss of generality, it is assumed that the data models of the examples treated by the induction technique are tree-structured feature vector data models. Given the data import format of CrisView—an arbitrary structured list that can be represented as a tree—this is a reasonable assumption. The nodes of the tree are the variable-sized feature vectors that have been used to describe individual phenomena, that is, the domain examples.

The decomposition process works along the horizontal dimension of the data models, preserving only the hierarchical structure between the elements in an example. Each example is decomposed into a number of local observations. A local observation consists of the nodes along a single path from the root of the tree to one of its leaves. These paths can be of unequal length because the number of nodes may vary along different branches of a tree. Intuitively the result of this decomposition process can be conceived of as a series of (overlapping) pictures each showing the same object from different positions, possibly at different points in time. The structure of the local observations is much simpler than that of the original examples. Each variable in an observation can occur only once. As an illustration of this, the data model shown in Figure 4.1 yields nine local observations (the number equals the number of leaves in the tree).

Major Differences between I²D and Traditional Decision-Tree Induction Techniques

The Inductive Interaction Detection (I²D) technique differs from the traditional approach in two fundamental ways:

Local observation If the data models of the examples are tree-structured, I²D decomposes the examples into local observations and uses the values of these observations for constructing the decision tree. Since the structure of the observations is much simpler and does not contain multiple variable occurrences, it becomes possible to apply mechanisms for comparing the variable values that are similar to those found in traditional techniques. Of course, the examples whose data model is flat are not decomposed (there is only one node).

Pairwise comparison of variables In general, the input to decision-tree induction techniques consists of a rectangular matrix where each row contains the values of the selected dependent variable and independent variables in a single example. The input to I²D are the values of the variables for each of the local observations. However, rather than construct the lists of values for the different local observations, I²D works directly with the pairs of dependent and independent variable values. This allows for more flexibility as to the type of pairing that is performed. I²D distinguishes several types of *pairing methods.* Each of these methods is discussed later.

Complex structured datasets remained largely nonanalyzed because they violated the data assumptions of traditional induction techniques and other methods that require global one-to-one comparisons between variable values. The decomposition of the examples into local observations and the pairwise comparison of dependent and independent variables allow an inductive analysis of complex structured datasets.

The new approach to decision-tree induction has an impact on the kind of knowledge that can be inferred by the inductive process. While constructing the decision tree, I^2D dispenses with the unity of a domain example (for example, a dispute, a country) by decomposing its original description and by assembling different parts according to their relevance with respect to a particular phenomenological property (variable and value). The resulting structure contains the characteristics regularly associated with that property. This is important for international relations data because many variables in the datasets represent theoretical concepts rather than simple quantitative factors that can be easily measured. Furthermore, the new approach has a number of technical implications that will be discussed in the section on technical aspects.

Impact of the Generalized Algorithm

Most decision-tree induction techniques focus on classification, seeking to recover preexisting categories (classes or concepts) that discriminate the instances of the phenomenon. I^2D performs a more general task, namely regularity detection. Due to the decomposition of complex structured examples into local observations, I^2D can identify manifest relationships between the descriptive aspects of phenomena, regardless of whether these descriptive aspects discriminate the examples of the phenomena. Its impact is twofold:

The choice of the dependent variable In traditional decision-tree induction techniques the dependent variable is assumed to be a variable whose values unambiguously classify each example as an element of one of several distinct classes. Due to this quality, these variables are frequently referred to as "class variables" (of course, the term class here has nothing to do with a class in an object-oriented language). As mentioned before, this assumption does not hold for the variables in tree-structured datasets that occur multiply in a single example. For example, if a dataset contains descriptions of houses, in which each house has a property, door, with a different value for each of the doors in the house, then the variable "door" does not unambiguously classify the houses. A similar situation is encountered when attempting to classify, for example, complex structured conflicts based on variables that have multiple values for a single conflict. The way in which I^2D has been designed, however, makes it possible to use any variable in the dataset as the dependent variable.

Concept definitions from partial examples By abolishing the restriction on the type of variable for which predictive structures can be learned, it is possible to infer the definition of concepts that cover only parts of the phenomena. Again, the dataset that describes the properties of houses serves to illustrate this capability. In that case, the I²D technique can infer the definition of the concept "door" that covers doors inside a house, or the concept "door" that covers the doors that lead to the backyard, and so on. These definitions are learned from the local observations that contain the locally relevant independent variables and values for predicting the value of the dependent variable, door. Depending on the choice of the dependent variable, the traditional one-to-many relationship between concepts and examples is replaced in I²D by a many-to-many relationship: a concept may be found in different examples, and an example may embody different concepts. The free choice of dependent variables makes it possible to detect such concepts within the possibly multifaceted layers of phenomenological descriptions.

While the decomposition of examples extends the range of variables for which predictive structures can be identified, the pairwise comparison of dependent and independent variables provides new ways to explore the relations between the variables and values that describe the domain's phenomena.

Before discussing the different pairing methods incorporated in the I²D technique, it would perhaps be helpful to summarize the employment of information-theoretic entropy measurements in the variable selection process of decision-tree construction. These measurements have been used, for example, in ID3 (Quinlan, 1979), ASSISTANT (Kononenko et al., 1984), CN2 (Clark and Niblett, 1988), and others. Since the purpose of I²D is more general than classification, given that it involves the finding of predictive structures for arbitrary variables in complex structured feature vector data, the formulae for selecting the variables differ from those implemented in other systems. These differences are highlighted in the section on pairing methods (4.2.4).

4.2.3 Entropy-based Decision-tree Induction

Entropy metrics have been used in decision-tree induction techniques to select independent variables according to their information content during decision-tree construction. A decision tree can be viewed as "an information source that, given an object, generates a message that is the class of that object" (Quinlan 1983, 467). If p(c) is the proportion of examples with class c, the entropy E(C) provides a measure for the amount of uncertainty in the message about the correct classification of the example:[2]

$$E(C) = \sum_{c \in C} -p(c)\log_2 p(c) \qquad \text{for an arbitrary number of } c \text{ classes}$$

In other words, this formula determines the amount of information that a classification rule must supply. At each stage of the tree-building process, the goal is to select the independent variable V that most reduces the uncertainty about the classification of the example. The conditional entropy E(C, V) of V with respect to the classes in C, measures the amount of uncertainty in the subtrees that result from branching with the values of V:

$$E(C,V) = \sum_{v \in V} p(v) \sum_{c \in C} - \; p(c \mid v)\log_2 p(c \mid v)$$

p(v) denotes the proportion of examples whose variable V has value v; p(c | v) denotes p(v) with class c. Hence, the reduction of uncertainty or the gain in information obtained by branching on variable V is:

$$\text{Gain}(V) = E(C) - E(C,V)$$

The information gain is calculated for each independent variable, and the process is repeated at every level of the tree, until either all the examples can be classified or no independent variables remain for testing.

4.2.4 Pairing Methods

On the one hand, the existence of a tree-structured data model renders the task of induction more difficult. On the other hand, the structure of the data in a dataset encourages the definition of new types of inductive analysis. This section discusses several pairing methods—that is, ways of collecting the value pairs for dependent and independent variables in the examples of a training set. The pairing methods currently supported in CrisView include cross-sectional, time-lagged, and sequential pairing. While the first method can be applied to any dataset, the other two methods assume temporal relations between the data in the dataset. This section also explains the mechanism that underlies the induction of predictive structures once the pairs of variables have been collected.

Cross-sectional Pairing Method

The *cross-sectional pairing method* denotes a method that collects the variable values of an example across sections. In the case of tree-structured data models, the term *section* refers to the local observations—that is, the result of decomposing a data model along its horizontal dimension. The cross-sectional pairing method simply collects the values of dependent and independent variables in each section. Cross-sectional pairing is the method that performs the type of analysis found in ID3 (Quinlan, 1979), CART (Breiman et al., 1984), and similar techniques, generalized, however, to complex data models. If the data models are flat, the sections are the examples of the domain, and the values for the dependent and independent variables are collected for each of the examples in the training set.

Collecting value pairs from tree-structured data models, as well as the iterative process of selecting the variables for the nodes at each level of the tree, is best explained by working through an example. The data model that will be used is the one shown in Figure 4.1. Five variables, positioned in different parts of the tree, have been explicitly indicated: a dependent variable *D*, and the independent variables *R*, *U*, *V*, and *W*. With the exception of variable *W*, all variables have multiple values.

Decomposition The decomposition along the horizontal dimension of the data model yields nine local observations. Instead of collecting the list of values from each of these observations, I^{2}D focuses on the value pairs of variables.

Cross-sectional value pairing I^{2}D collects the value pairs for dependent and independent variables in each local observation. In the case of a flat data model, a single example would yield only one value pair for each independent variable. The data model shown in Figure 4.1 yields the following value pairs:

For variable *R*: (r_1, d_2), (r_2, d_3), (r_3, d_3),
For variable *U*: (u_1, d_1), (u_2, d_1), (u_3, d_1), (u_4, d_2), (u_5, d_2), (u_6, d_3),
For variable *V*: (v_1, d_1), (v_2, d_2), (v_3, d_3),
For variable *W*: (w, d_1), (w, d_2), (w, d_3).

Once all the examples in the training set are decomposed and their values assembled, the conditional entropy $E(D, VAR_i)$ is calculated for each of the independent variables with respect to the dependent variable. E(D, VAR_i) determines the amount of uncertainty in the subtrees that results from branching with the values of the independent variable, VAR_i.

$$E(D, VAR_i) = \sum_{\text{var}_i \in VAR_i} p(var_i) \sum_{d_j \in D} -p(d_j \mid var_i) \log_2 p(d_j \mid var_i)$$

where p(var_i) denotes the proportion of value pairs whose variable VAR_i has value var_i and p($d_j \mid var_i$) denotes p(var_i) with dependent value d_j. The variable to be selected is the one that reduces the overall amount of uncertainty in the decision tree—that is, the variable that maximizes:

$$\text{GAIN}(VAR_i) = E(D) - E(D, VAR_i) \quad \text{where } E(D) = \sum_{d_j \in D} -\ p(d_j) \log_2\ p(d_j)$$

In the traditional entropy-based approach, the number of examples and thus the number of value pairs for each independent variable is constant throughout the building of the decision tree. I^2D, on the other hand, operates on local observations and on value pairs that vary for each independent variable. Since the proportion of value pairs with dependent value d_j varies for each independent variable, no single value E(D) can be calculated. Therefore, a value $E_{VARi}(D)$ is computed for each of the differently sized sets of value pairs. The use of the symbol E_{VARi} (D), instead of E(D), indicates that the figure depends on the independent variable and the number of value pairs that can be created for that variable. The so-called ***relative gain*** for each of the variables R, U, V, and W can now be determined:

$$\text{Relative Gain}\,(VAR_i) = E_{\text{VAR}_i}(D) - E(D, VAR_i)$$

A final adjustment is made with respect to the method's bias toward variables with large value ranges. As has been noted by several researchers, independent variables with a large number of possible values tend to discriminate better among the values of the dependent variable than variables with fewer values. The former are favored in the entropy-based selection process. A variety of alternatives has been proposed to remedy this problem (for example, Kononenko et al., 1984; Quinlan, 1985; Lopes de Mantaras, 1991). Kononenko and his colleagues in their inductive inference system, ASSISTANT, circumvented the problem by allowing only binary branching at each node of the decision tree. Quinlan introduced the notion of gain ratio to counter the bias. Both approaches have their shortcomings: binary testing may lead to decision trees that are unintelligible to human experts and may require an increase in computation (Quinlan, 1985). On the other hand, the use of gain ratios is limited because a ratio may not be defined, or its value may be misleading for variables whose initial gain is not at least as high as the average gain of all the variables (Quinlan, 1985, Lopez de Mantaras, 1991).

Lopez de Mantaras developed a selection criterion for variables that is based on a distance measurement between partitions of variables. To solve the bias problem, he normalized the Gain(VAR_i) by the mutual information of the two partitions P_D (for the class variable) and P_{VARi} (for any independent variable). The mutual information of two partitions P_D and P_{VARi} can be reformulated as $E(D, VAR_i) + E(VAR_i)$. The Normalized Relative Gain for the independent variable VAR_i in $\{U, V, W\}$ thus becomes:

$$\text{Normalized Relative Gain}(VAR_i) = \frac{\text{Relative Gain}(VAR_i)}{E(D, VAR_i) + E(VAR_i)}$$

The variable with the highest normalized relative gain is chosen as the root node, and for each of its branches (the values of the root node variable) the process of assembling the values, calculating the normalized relative gain, and selecting the node variable for the nodes on the next lower level is performed, recursively.

The following two pairing methods operate on time-dependent data—that is, on datasets in which the data that describe a single unit have been collected over time. The time-lagged pairing method finds predictive values in adjacent time periods. The sequential pairing method steps from one time period to the next in order to establish interactions between variables across time. The construction of the decision tree follows closely the mechanism described earlier, the difference being the value pairs that are used in the process.

Time-lagged Pairing Method

The time-lagged pairing method accounts for the temporal dependencies between the data at some level in the data model of the domain examples. Based on the values of the independent variables in a time period, time-lagged analysis aims at predicting the value of the dependent variable in the next time period. The data model that served to illustrate the cross-sectional pairing method (Figure 4.1) is used to explain the steps carried out by the time-lagged pairing method. In SHERFACS, the phase-structure feature vectors describe the development of an individual conflict over time. Since the values of the variables in different phase-structure feature vectors, or in any feature vector below the phase structure, form a sequence of values over time, the temporal relationship between these values can be exploited.

As before, the variable D denotes the dependent variable with values that range over $\{d_1, d_2, d_3\}$. In a first step, the example is decomposed into local observations that are then grouped according to the time period to which they belong. The grouping depends on where time-dependency is present in a data model. In SHERFACS, time-dependency is found at the level of phase-structure feature vectors. The information about the temporal relationship between the feature vectors can be stored in the class definition of the corresponding object classes (here, the phase-structure-feature-vector-class). The data model in Figure 4.1 shows three time periods. The values in the different time periods $t_{i \text{ in } \{1\ 2\ 3\}}$ are:

t_1: d_1, u_1, u_2, u_3, v_1, and w
t_2: d_2, r_1, u_4, u_5, v_2, and w
t_3: d_3, r_2, r_3, u_6, v_3, and w

The value w appears in every time period because it is bound at a higher level than the time-dependent values and, hence, remains valid over all three periods. However, an argument can be made for excluding the variable W from time-lagged analysis: because the value of this variable is valid over all time periods, the temporal relation between this value and the dependent values is not known and thus cannot be relied upon. If the variable is nevertheless included in the analysis, the comparison between the values of this variable and the values of the dependent variable in the examples is cross-sectional in nature rather than time-lagged, and the interpretation of the result should take this into account.

The next step builds the value pairs of dependent and independent variables. Yet, in contrast to the assembly process employed by the cross-sectional pairing method, a time lag is introduced between the two values, taking the value of the independent variable at time t and the value of the dependent variable at time $t + 1$. This allows I^2D to use the information of a prior time period to predict the dependent value in a subsequent time period. The following value pairs of dependent and independent variables constitute the input to the tree building process the mechanism of which has been discussed earlier.

For variable *R*:	(r_1, d_3)
For variable *U*:	(u_1, d_2), (u_2, d_2), (u_3, d_2), (u_4, d_3), (u_5, d_3)
For variable *V*:	(v_1, d_2), (v_2, d_3)
For variable *W*:	(w, d_2), (w, d_3)

The time-lagged pairing method adds an additional dimension of analysis for datasets whose instances of the phenomenon are described chronologically. Applied to the SHERFACS data, time-lagged inductive analysis allows the study of escalatory and de-escalatory movements of a conflict, based on the characteristics of preceding time periods.

The Sequential Pairing Method

Similar to the time-lagged pairing method, the sequential pairing method supports inductive analysis of temporally structured data. However, instead of retaining only the temporal relationship between values in adjacent time periods, the sequential pairing method preserves the whole chronological order of the data.

The sequential pairing method explores the interaction effects between variables in different time periods, similar to time-series analysis. In contrast to time-series data, however, the description of political phenomena in the respective datasets rarely exhibits a strict time metric (Schrodt, 1984a). What matters more in international politics is the order in which political phenomena develop, and this is the focus of the sequential pairing method. Consequently, the relations between variables in the decision tree denote "before" relations and "after" relations. Turning to the example that served to illustrate the previous two methods, the sequential pairing method collects successively the values of the local observations in each time period. The value pairs for the three periods are:

	Period 1	*Period 2*	*Period 3*
For variable *R*:	-	(r_1, d_2), (r_2, d_2)	(r_2, d_3), (r_3, d_3)
For variable *U*:	(u_1, d_1), (u_2, d_1), (u_3, d_1)	(u_4, d_2), (u_5, d_2)	(u_6, d_3)
For variable *V*:	(v_1, d_1)	(v_2, d_2)	(v_3, d_3)
For variable *W*:	(w, d_1)	(w, d_2)	(w, d_3)

The first time period yields the value pairs that are used to determine the root node. Having selected the variable whose normalized relative gain is highest as the root variable, the subtrees below each of its branches can be built. The selection of the variables below the root level is based on the value pairs in the second time period. Again, the variable that yields the highest normalized gain is selected. The process continues until the values in all time periods have been examined (the example considered provides values for only one more time period).

Unlike the methods previously described, the sequential pairing method yields a decision tree that tests for different values of a variable more than once along the same path. Each path in the decision tree corresponds to a chronological path through the description of the examples as they were coded in the dataset. It is therefore possible that a variable already selected for the prediction of the dependent variable in one time period is selected again in one of the subsequent periods. Although the sequential pairing method is capable of expressing connections between the values of multivalued variables, it uses only one variable in each time period, thereby ignoring other, less significant but possibly relevant variables in the same period. In other words, the sequential pairing method does not treat the interaction effects between variables within a given time period.

Of course, there are other types of value pairing methods that can be added to extend the technique's functionality. There are other types of relationships between the variables that could be learned. Useful pairing methods for the datasets in CrisView could include, for example:

For SHERFACS The paring of values of side A and side B can be used to detect interaction patterns of conflicting parties. This type of "specialized" cross-sectional pairing is applicable to any dataset whose phenomena involve two parties or two sides—for example, defendant and suspect. An additional time-lagged pairing method could be defined, introducing a time lag of two or more periods. A new sequential type of pairing method could be employed where, in addition to a path through time periods, interactions within time periods would also be accounted for.

For World Facts The paring of values of neighboring countries (the independent values from one country, and the dependent value from a neighboring country) can be used to study the effects of common borders. Similarly, pairs of values from trade partners could be used. In both cases, the focus is on the relationship between pairs of units in the dataset and hence defines a "cross-two-sectional" type of analysis in contrast to a cross-sectional type of analysis.

4.2.5 Technical Aspects

Technical aspects that are specific to I^2D are a result of the "anomalies" imposed by arbitrary tree-structured feature vector data models of the examples in the training set. The most significant difference between tree-structured and flat-structured data models is the multiple occurrence of feature vectors in single examples and thus the multiple occurrence of variables. The decomposition of examples into local observations proved to be an adequate solution. The structural complexity of examples is reduced to a form that can be dealt with by the mechanism found in traditional decision-tree induction techniques. However, there are several differences between local observations and equally simple flat-structured examples. Local observations are the intermediary elements between, on the one hand, the value pairs collected by the paring methods and used for variable selection in the tree construction and, on the other hand, the examples that the user sees and that are recursively partitioned into more and more homogeneous groups along the tree. The following paragraphs discuss differences between I^{2}D and traditional decision-tree induction techniques and take a look at issues that demand a special treatment in I^{2}D due to these differences.

Traditional Decision Trees versus I^{2}D Decision Trees

In traditional decision trees, the step from one node to the next represents a one-to-one relation between the variable and value of a flat-structured example. At each node (starting with the root node), the examples of the training set are tested against the condition imposed by the node variable and each of its branch values. If a test succeeds, the examples are passed down along the corresponding branch. The path along which a particular example reaches a leaf node is thus unambiguously determined by the single values of the example. The leaf node provides the "answer"—that is, the value of the dependent variable that, in flat data structures, denotes the class whose definition is represented by the path from the root to the leaf node. If the examples have been indexed, those that have been generalized by a path can be found in the leaf node of the path.

The situation is different for decision trees that are built from complex structured examples. Since I^{2}D first decomposes the examples of the training set into local observations, a step from one node to the next represents a one-to-one relation between the variable and value of a local observation—not an example. As a result, the same example may appear more than once in different nodes at the same level of the tree. Whenever an example contains one of the variable value combinations, that is, a node variable and a branch value, it is passed down to a node that is selected at the next lower level (the possible restriction of values along the path of a tree is discussed in later paragraphs). For many analysis tasks, the retrieval of the examples that reached a leaf node is relevant. The international relations scholar may not only be interested in the predictive structure of the decision tree but also in the individual examples to which the predictive structure applies. For this purpose, the I²D technique not only yields the predictive structures but also the examples that satisfy the conditions along the path.

Residuals in the Modes of the Tree

Traditional decision-tree induction techniques assume that the number of variables is constant for all the examples in the training set. Although the literature proposes solutions to the problem of missing variable values, the problem of "missing" or, more precisely, absent variables is not treated. If decision trees are constructed from tree-structured examples in which the number of occurrences of certain variables varies from none to several, this problem has to be addressed. It is not solved by the decomposition of examples into local observations, since they cannot contain variables that are absent in the example. The problem manifests itself during tree construction when a variable is selected at a given node that does not appear in all the examples that have reached that node. The normalized relative gain may be very significant for that variable but only relative to the examples that contain the variable. All the other examples are either "lost" because they do not satisfy the node variable and any of its branching values, or they are misled by being passed down an arbitrary branch. In both cases, the result is less than satisfactory.

I²D provides two solutions for the treatment of *residuals*, the name given to those examples that arrive at a node where they cannot be further partitioned. The first solution involves the explicit identification of the residuals and their association with the node they have reached. When displaying the decision tree in the tree-window of the CrisView exploration environment, the nodes can be inspected to determine whether a node contains residuals, and, if so, what the residuals are. Alternatively, when the tree is transformed into a set of rules, the residuals of a rule are displayed (that is, the residuals of the nodes along the path that was transformed into a rule). The second solution is more sophisticated. It tests the residuals against new variables—that is, the variables that have not been used at that level of the tree. The variable that yields the highest normalized relative gain is chosen as the variable of a new node, and the residuals are passed down to that node in the usual way.

Restricting Variable Values During Tree Construction

The data model of an example mirrors the ontology with which data collectors and coders perceived the phenomenon. The logical entities on the different levels of the data model carry a specific semantics that applies to the logical entity and its substructure—that is, the logical entities on lower levels of the data model. The decomposition of domain examples into local observations runs the risk of loosing the semantics associated with the logical entities in the data model. By definition, the local observations preserve only the unidirectional hierarchical relationship between low-level and higher-level logical entities in the data model. Other relationships between the entities are ignored, although they may be relevant for certain analyses.

A case in point is the time-dependency between the phase-structure feature vectors in the SHERFACS data. Intuitively, each conflict phase represents a semantic entity whose elements, the facts and actions that have been coded, constitute it for this phase but not necessarily for other phases. Furthermore, given the significant difference between conflict phases, a human expert would probably expect to find different predictive structures for different conflict phases. This implies that the values used for inferring a predictive structure (that is, the values along a path in the decision tree) should be restricted to a particular conflict phase. More generally, it should be possible to restrict the values along a path in the tree to any substructure in the data model in order to meet consistency restrictions that might be relevant. This is a technical rather than a domain-specific problem, because the substructures one may want to use to impose constraints on the values during tree construction are the logical entities of the data model that are represented as instances of subclasses of the substructure-class, and that are, hence, individually accessible.

Tree-building with value constraints The selection of the root node of the tree is based on all the value pairs that are provided by the respective pairing methods. The values of the node variable determine the possible branches to lower-level nodes. As mentioned earlier, the same example may run through different branches if it has different values for the root node variable. For each branch, the selection of the node on the next lower level is based on the values of the examples that satisfy the variable value determined by the root node and the branch value. Instead of assembling all the possible value pairs from the local observations of these examples, consideration is afforded to only those observations that belong to the substructure that imposes a value constraint. The individual substructure relevant to each local observation is the substructure that contains the root node variable and the corresponding branch-value. The resulting value pairs represent only a subset of the value pairs that would have been collected had the values of all local observations been used. This restriction ensures that the values along the path of a tree are not arbitrarily collected from any part of the example but only from the substructure that has been selected.

The possibility of restricting the values that are used along a path is particularly important for time-lagged analysis. Without a restriction ensuring that the values of the independent variables along the path of a tree belong to the same time period, the result may be misleading. Independent variables from any time period—except the last in each example—would be used, each paired with the dependent value of the adjacent time period.

For cross-sectional analysis two alternatives are provided. The analyst may indeed be interested in knowing the predictive structures for the values of a dependent variable across all local observations regardless of the substructures to which they belong. In this case, the decision tree yields the patterns most frequently found in all the examples. Alternatively, the analyst may want to restrict the values to a particular substructure that may be a time period. In the case of sequential analysis, the pairing of values is already independently performed for the values in each time period. It is possible, however, that restrictions other than temporal restrictions are to be imposed (in SHERFACS, for example, restrictions on the parties, which thereby affect the collection of values from different party-involvement feature vectors). Such restrictions would have to be accounted for by all the pairing methods, including the sequential pairing method.

Testing Decision Trees

Breiman and his colleagues describe three different decision-tree estimates, which are useful for testing decision trees: the resubstitution estimate, the sample estimate, and the V-fold cross-validation estimate (Breiman et al., 1984). The first two estimates have frequently been used in induction experiments (for example, Quinlan, 1979; Mingers, 1989a; Schrodt, 1987a), albeit with examples that conformed to the flat feature vector data model. The estimates differ in that they use different sets of examples (test sets). While the resubstitution estimate uses the same examples that were employed for constructing the tree, the sample estimate uses a new test set. For the V-fold estimate, the domain examples are partitioned into *v* subsets. Different decision trees are constructed from the examples of *v-1* subsets and then tested against the one subset not used for tree construction.

Flat-structured examples can easily be run through a decision tree because the path along which a particular example reaches a leaf node is unambiguously determined by the single values of the example. However, if the variables have multiple values, as in examples with tree-structured data models, the branching at a given node becomes ambiguous. There are at least three ways in which the estimates mentioned earlier can be applied. First, a single branching value can be selected at each node among the possible variable values of an example. The I^{2}D experiments described in Unseld and Mallery (1992) used a branching value that was determined by relative entropy (the formula has been given in the section on inquiries). The value whose relative entropy is lowest has the highest probability and is also most redundant. However, this first approach is likely to yield distorted results because of the artificial selection of branching values. A second testing alternative uses local observations instead of the original examples. Problems with this approach arise when the local observations do not contain the variables that have been used in the nodes of the decision tree. More seriously, local observations cannot be used to test the results of time-lagged and sequential analyses. In the former case, the local observations do not contain the value of the dependent variable in the adjacent time periods. This value is needed to test the dependent value in the leaf node. In the latter case, the paths in the tree represent a path through different time periods. Yet the local observations represent a hierarchical segment of an example's data model, and thus the two are not compatible.

The third and probably most obvious way of testing tree-structured examples follows the rationale that underlies the construction of the decision tree. Instead of maintaining that examples have to follow one particular path of the decision tree, an example can simultaneously appear in several paths, depending on the values of its variables. As with the training examples used for tree construction, the test examples possibly reach more than one leaf node. The dependent value in that leaf node is compared with the dependent value of the example in order to yield an accuracy estimate. If variable restrictions apply along a path, the testing examples are restricted accordingly. If no variable restrictions have been used and the dependent variable of a test example has several values, the procedure checks whether the dependent value in the leaf node is among the example's dependent values. Instead of testing the decision tree, estimates can be obtained from the set of rules that have been generated. The local precision that is originally associated with the rules (see section 3.4.7) yields a resubstitution estimate—that is, a figure that indicates how many of the training examples have been correctly generalized by the rule. In order to perform a sample estimate, each test example is run through the set of rules to determine whether or not it is covered by at least one rule.

Quality and Usefulness of Results

When discussing and interpreting the results of inductive analyses, a second look at the algorithm that creates the decision trees and the rules sheds light on some of the less justifiable or less useful findings. As the algorithm searches among the independent variables for those that are most relevant in discriminating the examples along a path of the decision tree, some rare but highly discriminating variable values might produce a homogeneous partition of examples early in the process. However, the path itself (that is, the node variables and branching values) does not provide the analyst with much information. Candidates of such information-poor paths are typically created from examples in which a particular independent variable value is observed only together with a specific value of the dependent variable. As a result, the conditional entropy for all other variables is zero, and the induction technique creates a leaf node. In the path from the root to this leaf node, and later in the rule corresponding to this path, this independent variable and its value play an important role; they may even form the only antecedent of the rule. However, it is often the case that the variable in question is too general an indicator to allow for a projection of conflict development or outcome and hence fails to be of much use to the analyst.

Results are furthermore affected by the fact that international relations datasets are, in a statistical sense, heavily modal. Schrodt, who carried out inductive experiments on conflict data, noted that "because the modal category accounts for about 55 to 75 percent of the phenomena, the simple rule 'predict the mode' will have an accuracy of 55 percent to 75 percent" (Schrodt, 1987a, 7). In some cases, the modal category may even account for over 90 percent of the phenomena. An example is the SHERFACS variable "agent-referral-outcome," which only in rare cases departs from the mode "referral accepted." Obviously, few analysis techniques are likely to beat the "predict the mode" result in these circumstances. What is more serious is the fact that the presence of high modality often prevents the few remaining outliers from being recognized by inductive techniques, since they do not provide enough information for generalization. In this situation, an "analysis by example" technique, such as precedent-based reasoning, is more appropriate.

The shortcomings mentioned earlier, which relate to the technique as well as to the data, stress the importance of setting up meaningful analysis experiments. This requires a fair amount of familiarity with the dataset under investigation. Knowing the variables and what they represent, the range of their values, the distribution of individual values over the sample space, and the significance of variables with respect to a certain dependent variable is a prerequisite for the effective use of induction. CrisView supports users in acquiring such knowledge by means of browsing, inspecting, and filtering the data and hence assists them in working with datasets that have been generated by others.

4.2.6 Object-oriented Induction

While the general concept underlying the I^2D technique (the decomposition into local observations, the use of value pairs of the dependent and the independent variables, and the different pairing methods) can be implemented in a number of ways, an object-oriented implementation produces an effective and elegant solution.

As has been mentioned before, the data-structures used during decision-tree induction are defined as instances of object classes. These include the decision tree, the nodes, and the rules. Operations defined directly on these classes provide the means to delegate much of the functionality to the objects involved. Operations on rules (reduction of the rule set) have been described in section 3.4.8. Several of the technical aspects discussed in the last section can be conveniently dealt with by defining operations on node objects.

Constructing inferiors The decision on whether or not to expand a node into further sub-nodes (inferiors) is made by the node object at each level of the tree. The information required for this decision is available at each node. No further branching takes place if, for the value pairs of all remaining variables, either the conditional entropy is zero (without a perfect match between the values), or the normalized relative gain is zero. While the former indicates that in all the value pairs considered, the dependent values or the independent values are identical, the latter implies that no more information can be gained by further branching on the variable. A perfect match between the values of the value pairs indicates that the respective independent variable varies exactly with the dependent variable. The conditional entropy yields zero but one more level of nodes is needed to divide the examples into groups of equal dependent value. In all other cases, the next level of nodes is constructed.

The case of a perfect match between value pairs deserves some further comment. A perfect match can be accidental but it may also reflect the presence of a causal relationship between the independent variable and value (the cause) and the dependent variable and value (the effect). In theory, a causal relation postulates that the cause is always present when the effect is. A perfect match along a path in the decision might therefore suggest that some independent variable is causally related to the dependent variable. However, this conclusion is only justified under certain assumptions, including the assumption that the effect was not caused by factors *not* described in the dataset.

Retrieving information from nodes Each node is defined as an instance of node-class and contains the information about the status of the tree at that node level. The slots of the node-class have been described in section 3.4.7. In particular, a node contains the examples that have reached the node (node-subset). Therefore, the information about which examples satisfied the conditions along a path in the decision tree can be acquired from the leaf node of that path.

Processing of residuals The treatment of residuals as described earlier is a typical example of a local operation. It depends on the residuals themselves and on the variables that are available for further branching. Since this information is stored with the instances of a node, each node object can process its residuals by calling the paring method used in the current analysis and invoking the calculations for selecting the next best node variable. These new calculations are based on the values of the residuals and the variables that remain to be tested.

Constraining values along the paths of the tree The imposition of value constraints ensures that the values along a path belong to the same substructure—for example, to the same time period. During tree construction the examples along a path are reduced to include only those variables and values that belong to the substructure. This reduction process can be achieved in at least two ways:

> *Definition of partial examples* Partial-examples can be defined as instances of the object class partial-example-class. This class is defined as a subclass of the example's class (the dataset-specific subclass of the unit class) since it shares most of the behavior of the example's class. The definition of partial examples is particularly convenient because the same mechanism for variable selection and node construction can be used, as before, in the case of "entire" examples. Partial examples are decomposed into local observations in order for the paring methods to collect the value pairs. Since each partial example "knows" to which example it belongs, the original examples can always be retrieved, for example, at the leaf node.

Use of acceleration structures Another way of restricting the values along a path is to make use of acceleration structures. One of the acceleration structures in CrisView combines each variable and value with the substructures and the units (the examples) in which it appears. A partial acceleration structure containing the dependent and independent variables used in the induction can be extracted from the original acceleration structure and stored in the root-node of the tree. At lower levels in the tree, when the value restriction becomes relevant, the partial acceleration structure is further reduced to contain only those variable values that can be used along a path. Each node stores the new partial acceleration structure that is relevant at that level (retaining only those examples that have reached the node and imposing on each example restrictions as to the values that can be used). This solution is very efficient because it eliminates the need to build additional objects, using instead data structures that are already available. The first solution, however, conforms more closely to the object-oriented philosophy.

Most of the operations needed during the I^{2}D induction process are defined as generic functions whose methods have been specified to the various classes (if acceleration structures are used, operations on these structures are the exception to the rule, because acceleration structures are not modeled as objects). As a result, the technique can easily be extended to include, for example, new pairing methods, new tree pruning or rule reduction techniques, and so on, without affecting other parts of the process.

4.3 Precedent-based Reasoning

Learning from past experience, and reasoning from individual or collective historical episodes, is undoubtedly an important cognitive ability of human beings. Expressed in formal terms and cast in computer programs, it has been viewed as a promising alternative or a valuable addition to many qualitative or quantitative methods for problem solving, learning, and decision making. Precedent-based or case-based reasoning,[3] as it is generally called in artificial intelligence, has become a general research paradigm with two orientations. The first is grounded in psychological theories of human cognition and addresses issues such as memory organization, learning, and problem solving.[4] The second, a more technological orientation, is concerned with building artificial intelligence systems for problem solving and learning from experience. This chapter focuses on the technological aspects of precedent-based reasoning.

Precedent-based reasoning and analogical reasoning are based on the assumption that situations similar in some respects are also similar in other respects. Both types of reasoning refer to a knowledge transfer from some previously encountered situation (the base) to some new situation (the target). Mallery and Hurwitz distinguish among precedent-based reasoning and analogical reasoning by introducing the concept of inductive distance. This concept refers to the language user's domain-specific classification hierarchies or lattices and the levels (levels of inductive generalization) on which base and target are located (Mallery and Hurwitz, 1987, 17). Precedent-based and analogical reasoning are, in abbreviated form, defined as follows:

Precedent-based reasoning The base is an instance with the same relations among elements in the same categories as in the target but occurring at an earlier time.

Analogical reasoning Base and target are more distant than in precedent-based reasoning and usually in different domains, but most of the relationships between the elements are the same.

This distinction is often blurred in the literature, and the term *precedent* may denote the result of an analogical or of a precedent-based reasoning process (for example, Winston, 1982). As regards the definitions, most systems or system components in substantive areas such as international relations perform a precedent-based type of reasoning—that is, the focus is on relations among elements in the same categories. This is also the type of reasoning supported in CrisView. Since it is desirable to apply precedent-based reasoning to datasets that do not contain chronologically ordered data, such as the World Facts data, the condition "occurring at an earlier time" in the preceding definition is relaxed to include priority ordering as well as temporal ordering. In World Facts, the "precedents" would be those country profiles whose characteristics are most similar to those of the target (another country). In other words, precedents for a target are chosen from the units that have been stored in the system.

4.3.1 Overview

The study of reasoning by example or precedent-based reasoning can be traced back to Aristotle who, in his Prior Analytics, distinguished this type of reasoning from inductive and deductive reasoning (Mefford, 1988). Rather than infer the general from the particular as in induction, or the particular from the general as in deduction, reasoning by example moves from the particular example to another example.

The Abductive Nature of Precedent-based Reasoning

Like inductive learning, reasoning by example or precedent-based reasoning is not truth preserving—that is, the conclusions that are inferred may be invalid. The reason for this is that the form of inference used in precedent-based reasoning is abduction. The term ***abduction*** was used by C. S. Peirce (1950) to denote an inference to a hypothesis that provides a possible explanation of some puzzling phenomena (Thagard, 1988, 51). The general schema of abduction reads as follows:

> q is to be explained
>
> if p then q
>
> therefore, hypothetically p

where p and q denote propositions that are not further specified. Since the second premise is equivalent to "not p or q" and given that q is known to be true, the truth of p cannot be inferred with certainty. The possibility of other explanations for q brings about the question of whether abduction—that is, the inference to an explanatory hypothesis—can be a kind of justification or only a form of discovery. Thagard elaborates on this question by focusing on hypothesis formation and, later, on hypothesis evaluation and the inference to the best explanation. He introduces four types of abduction: simple abduction, which can be represented formally by the preceding schema and produces hypotheses about individual objects; existential abduction, which postulates the existence of previously unknown objects; rule-forming abduction, which produces rules that explain other rules; and analogical abduction, which uses past cases of hypothesis formation to generate hypotheses similar to those that already exist (Thagard, 1988, 54ff).

While the first three types of abduction depend on having relevant hypotheses or rules already formed, analogical abduction sheds light on how such hypotheses may be found. The inference mechanism of analogical abduction is the same as that which is present in precedent-based reasoning. Both analogical abduction and precedent-based reasoning involve a mapping from some previously encountered situation or problem to a new one. The mapping generates hypotheses or hypothetical facts about the new situation or problem that can then be explored further. The recourse to previous cases (theories, situations, or problems) in both analogical abduction and precedent-based reasoning guides the search for a relevant hypothesis in the absence of readily applicable rules.

Hypotheses or hypothetical facts that are inferred abductively can be expected to be doubtful or wrong. Therefore, much emphasis is placed on the evaluation of these hypotheses and various strategies for hypothesis evaluation can be found in the literature on abduction (Josephson et al., 1987; Punch et al., 1990). Holland and his colleagues list three criteria that an abductively inferred hypothesis should satisfy. First, the hypothesis must not be incompatible with other knowledge of the domain. Second, the hypothesis should explain as much data or observations as possible. Third, the evaluation of the hypothesis needs to be comparative, ensuring that the hypothesis is a better explanation than its alternatives (Holland et al., 1989, 137). The third criteria is the most critical, and the problem of inferencing to the best explanation has been the topic of many philosophical and theoretical studies (Harman, 1965; Thagard, 1988). Studies on the complexity of abduction have shown that the abductive problem—that is, finding the most plausible combination of hypotheses for explaining all the data—is generally intractable (Bylander et al., 1991). Thagard takes a more pragmatic view and argues that analogies, or precedents, are a legitimate criterion for inference to the best explanation because they play an important role in improving explanations. Some sets of phenomena can be better understood if the kind of explanation used is similar to those that are used already (Thagard, 1988, 94). The same pragmatic view lies at the heart of precedent-based reasoning.

Precedent-based reasoning or reasoning by example is probably the type of reasoning most frequently employed by human beings in tasks that range from problem solving and planning to decision making. It is particularly relevant in international relations, where learning from past experience (lessons of the past) allow reduction of the world's complexity.

Precedent-based Reasoning in International Relations

A number of international relations researchers have incorporated precedent-based reasoning in their computer models. Early work in this field is reviewed in Mallery and Hurwitz (1987, 7–16) and includes Bloomfield's CASCON system for crisis management (Bloomfield and Beattie, 1971); the studies by Alker, Greenberg, and Christensen on "precedent logics"— that is, rules for accumulating experience in an action predisposing way (Alker and Greenberg, 1971; Alker and Christensen, 1972); Tanaka's CHINA-WATCHER for modeling Chinese foreign policy masking (Tanaka, 1984); Mefford's investigation of Soviet responses to crises based on historical analogies (Mefford, 1984, 1987); Bonham and Shapiro's expert system for studying Middle Eastern politics (Bonham and Shapiro, 1976); Schrodt's analyses of events data using different techniques to find relevant precedents (Schrodt, 1984a, 1985, 1987a, 1987b). Other applications include Farrell's reconstruction of the assumptions on which political opinions are based (Farrell, 1987), the use of precedent-based reasoning in negotiation and mediation (Kolodner and Simpson, 1988), the analysis of military history (Dupuy, 1988), and battle planning (Goodman, 1989). While many of the systems or programs mentioned earlier use feature vector data as their input, more recent work on precedent-based reasoning focuses on processing textual information. In particular, Mallery and Hurwitz (1987) mention their work on analyzing sequential prisoner's dilemma (SPD) narratives (Hurwitz et al., 1986), using the RELATUS Natural Language system (Duffy and Mallery, 1986).

Precedent-based reasoning in international relations serves a number of goals:

Predicting outcome or further development Precedents can be used for making contingent projections about the likely outcome of a situation or the consequences of some actions. The projections are drawn from the descriptions of known phenomena (for example, past situations) that share some degree of similarity with the current phenomenon (the target). This is particularly useful if the data that are used describe international conflicts or crisis situations. The precedents are used to specify expansion of the target and the developments that can be expected (Mallery and Hurwitz, 1987, 17). This contrasts with the role of precedents in domains such as law, one of the most prominent substantive areas in which this type of reasoning has been applied (Rissland and Ashley, 1987; Skalak and Rissland, 1990), where precedents are used to discriminate the relevant relationships among the elements in the target.

Policy making Precedents can be used in a problem-solving sense—that is, to develop a course of action based on the actions that were successful in the past. They can also be used to justify a course of action and to shape the opinion of others by drawing their attention to a particular aspect of a situation. This leads into another type of research, which, rather than search for relevant precedents, investigates the choice of particular precedents. Since this choice depends on the premises that have been used in the abductive inference process, studying these premises sheds light on the belief systems of political actors as well as on the hypotheses about political phenomena held by scholars in the field (Unseld, 1990).

Developing innovative typologies The precedents that have been retrieved for a particular phenomenon can be used to define new typologies or categories into which the phenomena collected in a dataset can be grouped. The new typology embraces all those phenomena that have some characteristic or observed pattern in common.

Precedent-based Reasoning in Artificial Intelligence

Reasoning by example, and transferring previously acquired and successfully applied knowledge to new situations or problems, has motivated many research projects in artificial intelligence and machine learning. Precedent-based or case-based reasoning systems and programs have been developed to address tasks such as planning (Hammond, 1987, 1989a), diagnosis (Bareiss et al., 1987), legal reasoning (Rissland and Ashley, 1987), and design (Goel and Chandrasekaran, 1989). Work on precedent-based and analogical reasoning has been surveyed, for example, in Kolodner (1991); Slade (1991); Mallery and Hurwitz (1987); and Mefford (1988). A collection of current papers can be found in Kolodner (1988) and in Hammond (1989b).

Mefford (1988) has argued that precedent-based reasoning systems conform to the essentials of the information-processing model introduced by Newell and Simon (1972), which conceives of problem solving as a process of assembling in short-term memory information that has been retrieved from long-term memory. Following this line of argument, precedent-based reasoning refines the information-processing model by adding specific accounts of the way in which information in memory (the *knowledge-base* of a system) is structured and how relevant information is selected and retrieved. Most systems today, however, focus on the selection and retrieval of information rather than on the structuring of the information in the system's knowledge-base. In case-based reasoning parlance, the knowledge-base of a system is usually called *case-base*. "Cases" are the input to the reasoning process—that is, descriptions of instances of a phenomenon that have been previously encountered (for example, international conflicts (Bloomfield and Beattie, 1971), précis (Winston, 1982), recipes (Hammond, 1987), fault recovery protocols (Barletta and Mark, 1988), or federal income tax cases (Skalak and Rissland, 1990). Because the cases that are stored in a system's case-base belong usually to the same category, the search for precedents is limited to the cases of this category. What is eliminated thereby is the more difficult task of analogical matching of cases from different categories.

The basic processes employed in precedent-based reasoning systems include the selection of a target, recognition and retrieval of candidate precedents for the target from the system's case-base, evaluation of candidates and selection of a particular candidate, elaboration of the selected precedent to specify the extension or the reduction imposed on the target, and, finally, testing or justifying the result. The operations performed in each individual step, particularly step three and four, depend on the purpose of searching for precedents. Kolodner distinguishes two styles of reasoning from precedents: problem solving and interpretive (Kolodner, 1991, 55). In the former, the precedent is used to provide a solution to a new problem (the target). The solution of the precedent is adapted to fit the situation specified in the target. The new solution, combining features of the old and the new situation are tested against the current problem. If successful, the new solution is stored as a new case in the system's case-base. In the process, the performance of the system improves thanks to a more comprehensive set of cases from which precedent can be drawn. In the latter, the interpretive style, the precedent is projected onto the target. This process includes inferring action or situation predisposition, predicting further development, identifying the essential relationships among the elements in the target, classification, and justification. The result (the projected outcome) may be tested against the outcome of already known situations, and the retrieval mechanism can be adapted, based on the success or failure of past retrieval operations.

One of the major challenges of precedent-based reasoning is to search the system's case-base for cases that are potentially relevant and applicable to a given target. In the literature, this problem is frequently called the indexing problem (for example, Kolodner, 1991), denoting the process of marking those characteristics (partial descriptions) of a case in the case-base that qualify it as a precedent for some target. How does the system know what the relevant characteristics of a case are? To take a very simple example, a car of the same model may be a good precedent for estimating the price of some target car, whereas the car in the next parking lot that matches the color of the target car is not. Apart from manually constructing a set of domain-specific rules that contain the necessary conditions for selecting and retrieving cases, researchers have sought to improve the capability of their systems by including other learning mechanisms that guide or support the retrieving of cases—for example, exemplar-based learning (Bareiss et al., 1987), explanation-based learning (Barletta and Mark, 1988; Redmond, 1989), or inductive learning (Skalak and Rissland, 1990; ReMind, 1990).

Precedent-based Reasoning in CrisView

One common characteristic of the techniques supported in CrisView is that they do not require domain-specific knowledge to be built into the system. Rather, the user provides domain-specific knowledge when working with the system—for example by creating new variables, building filters, selecting the variables to be included in the inductive process, and so on. Apart from weak domain knowledge, the exploration techniques are data-driven, inferring their results from the data themselves (from the structuring of the data), possibly using other exploration techniques in the process. As a consequence, and consistent with the argument made for inductive learning (section 4.1), the precedent-based reasoning capability of CrisView dispenses with auxiliary techniques that rely on substantive amounts of domain-specific knowledge such as, for instance, explanation-based learning. However, precedent-based reasoning in CrisView makes use of and actually integrates many of the exploration techniques that have been defined in other parts of the system: inquiry methods (for example, measuring the salience of some phenomenological property), filters, comparison, and induction. Section 4.3.2 discusses the use of these techniques in combination with precedent-based reasoning.

The decision to develop a data-driven rather than a theory- or model-driven exploration system (see section 2.2), clearly has an impact on the employment of knowledge-based techniques such as precedent based reasoning. When people reason by example, they make use of past, individual and collective, experience according to perceived circumstances (including the purpose that motivates the reasoning). While their ability to use precedents and analogs for solving new problems or interpreting new situations is impressive, they are often less gifted in remembering relevant precedents or analogs (Genter, 1989). The hard part for precedent-based reasoning systems and programs, on the other hand, is not retrieving the precedents, but rather adapting them to new situations or problems. "Sufficient" domain-specific knowledge needs to be provided in order for the systems to cope with this problem. Since this knowledge is largely absent in a data-driven system, such as CrisView, the complementary strengths of human and system in a precedent-based reasoning process suggest a division of labor: the first two steps, retrieving candidate precedents and selecting the best candidate, are performed by the system. The remaining steps, adapting or interpreting, and, finally, justifying the results, are the user's responsibility, even if he or she is partially supported by the system (that is, the system projects the characteristic of the precedent onto the target and provides some testing procedures). This division of labor complies well with CrisView's notion of data exploration as an interactive process between the user and the system. Kept explicitly in the loop, the user interprets and bases his or her decisions on the results provided by the system.

4.3.2 Retrieving Precedents

The case-base of a precedent-based reasoning system corresponds to CrisView's collection of units in a document. CrisView's precedent-based reasoning capability incorporates several techniques to retrieve and select precedents for a target from among these units. Consistent with the terminology used in section 3.4.6 (CrisView's compare mechanism for pairs of units), the target is called *target-unit*. Three mechanisms, retrieval based on filters, retrieval based on user-specified precedents, and retrieval based on induction, serve to preselect a number of candidate precedents for a specific target-unit. In addition, a number of similarity metrics can be applied to these preselected candidates or to the entire collection of units in order to determine the best precedent.

Selection of Candidate Precedents

Retrieval based on filters The user may want to restrict the set of potential precedents to those units that meet some theoretical or phenomenological criterion (for example, conflicts after 1963, superpower involvement, economic issues). The filtering mechanism that has been described earlier can be invoked to specify the conditions under which the units in the document are to be partitioned. The precedents that are retrieved are merely those that satisfy the template defined by the filter. The more restrictive the template—that is, the more conditions that have to be satisfied by a unit—the smaller the set of retrieved precedents. Depending on the expectations of the user, the number of retrieved precedents may already be sufficiently small to be evaluated individually. Otherwise, similarity metrics can be applied to find the unit that most closely matches the target-unit.

Learning precedent templates Instead of using a filter and a feature combination that has been explicitly specified, the second precedent retrieval mechanism in CrisView derives relevant feature combinations from a precedent that has been provided by the user. Knowing a good precedent for the target-unit, the user might want to find out what other precedents exist (among the units stored in the system) and how similar they are to the target-unit. Based on the relationship between the precedent and the target-unit, the system constructs a template consisting of matching and/or nonmatching features. This template can then be applied to find other precedents for the same target-unit or precedents for a new target-unit. Retrieval based on a single precedent is the first step toward what might be called precedent-based induction—that is, the use of precedents as the training set for inductive experiments (section 4.3.3).

Retrieval based on induction This type of retrieval and selection is applicable if the user defines a specific outcome he or she is interested in—that is, a dependent variable and its value. The decision-tree induction technique of CrisView (I^2D) is invoked to partition the units into groups with equal dependent values. Inductive indexing in the context of precedent-based reasoning and further refinement of the results are described in section 4.3.3.

These techniques represent a kind of cluster-analysis procedure (Fisher and Langley, 1986), dividing the units into partitions or "clusters" that could possibly overlap. The clusters overlap if the units are represented by tree-structured data models in which variables appear more than once. These units may satisfy the conditions (variable value combinations) of more than one cluster. A fourth type of retrieval mechanism could be added—namely, a mechanism that makes use of the rules created by the user. Since the necessary operations for creating rules have already been defined (section 3.4.8), their access from within the precedent-window could be easily achieved. Like filters, the use of rules offers a way of including domain-specific knowledge that guides the selection of precedents. In the course of performing a series of experiments, these user-specified rules can be modified to account for success or failure in retrieval operations. Such "precedent-rules" have been constructed by Alker and Greenberg (1971) to retrieve conflict cases that match the antecedents specified in the rules (norms of the UN charter). The consequents of the rules represented action proposal or the status/outcome proposal derived from the UN charter.

Selecting the Best Candidate Precedent

Once a number of potential precedents from among the units in a document have been retrieved, the next step involves the evaluation of these candidates with respect to the target-unit. Precedent-based reasoning systems apply a number of different similarity metrics, which, based on the characteristics of the units (or cases), retrieve the "best" precedent(s). A simple version of a similarity metric, applied in many systems in international relations, employs feature matching (that is, matching the values of corresponding variables) between the units stored in the system and the target-unit. This type of matching is also called nearest neighbor matching (for example, ReMind, 1990). CrisView includes a number of other similarity metrics and evaluation techniques.

Nearest neighbor matching For each unit in a set of potential candidates, or in the entire collection of units, nearest neighbor matching performs a matching of the features in the potential precedent and the target-unit. This type of matching has already been described in section 3.4.6. The result is the complement of the Hamilton distance—that is, a score that denotes the number of matching features. The candidates are then ordered according to their score, and the highest scoring units are returned to the user.

Restrained feature matching As mentioned in section 3.4.6, it is frequently desirable to restrict the matching of features to a particular substructure of the units' data models, or to reduce the variables that are used for matching, or to manipulate the matching score by making some variables more important than others (that is, to associate a weight with variables or variables and values). The first option is relevant if the data models of the units are structured in a complex manner—for example, tree-structured. The second and third options are useful because international relations datasets are typically rich in variables. Reducing the number of variables to be matched or giving particular variables more "weight" than others makes the results more useful. Furthermore, reducing the number of variables that have to be matched may considerably speed up the performance of the matching operations. All these options are available to the user who wishes to determine the precedent that is "closest" to the target-unit in terms of matching features. Unlike the options in the compare-window, however, the matching operations are not just applied to one specific unit but to all units in the document or to a selected subset thereof.

Levenshtein distances Another similarity metric that has already been introduced is the Levenshtein distance (section 3.4.8). Applied to all the candidates in a subset or all the units of the document, this measurement associates to each unit the cost of transforming it into the target-unit. The units with the lowest score, the most cost-effective ones, are returned to the user.

Salience priority ordering This evaluation method can be used when a set of candidate precedents has already been selected. For the variables that have been used to describe these precedents (usually a subset of variables), the salience is calculated with respect to the remaining units. The variables are ordered according to their salience. Starting with the most salient variable, a feature matching is performed between each candidate and the target-unit. Those candidates whose variable value matches the value in the target-unit are selected, and the matching process is repeated with the next salient variable until the best candidate is found.

Recency factor If the instances of some phenomena in a dataset are chronologically ordered (for example, international conflicts), potential precedents can be selected and ordered according to their recency with respect to the target-unit. This procedure was suggested in Alker and Christensen (1972) and in Alker and Greenberg (1971). Intuitively, one could argue that recent memories provide stronger incentives for similar behavior than memories that go far back in time. However, counter examples call this argument into question. Furthermore, the recency factor is not applicable to nonchronological datasets.

4.3.3 Precedent-based Reasoning and Induction

There are a number of arguments for the joint use of induction and precedent-based reasoning in a data exploration system. Induction and precedent-based reasoning complement each other by augmenting each other's analytical power. On the one hand, induction offers a valuable precedent-selection criterion: the path in a decision tree or the rule into which it can be transformed identifies a concept or a feature combination that is characteristic for a specific group of units in the document's core data. The units that support the concept may not be very similar judging from their surface features but they form a homogeneous, although not necessarily discrete, group whose elements share exactly the feature combination relevant for determining a certain outcome. What is frequently considered one of the major disadvantages of inductive decision-tree techniques is the need for a sizable number of examples in order to infer generalizations. It is this requirement that, in the context of precedent-based reasoning, makes induction a useful tool in reducing the search space of potentially relevant precedents.

The decision tree divides the set of units into smaller partitions that can then be further analyzed.

On the other hand, the precedents that have been established for some target-unit form a highly useful training set of examples for inductive experiments: inductive techniques are based on the assumption that the data to be analyzed share common patterns that can be recognized. Large heterogeneous datasets may jeopardize this assumption, because even if common patterns exist, they might not be universal but could be local to specific parts of the dataset. An informed selection of training examples introduces a focus that can then be exploited by inductive generalization. The generalizations yielded by the decision-tree induction are less likely to carry noise since they are based on representative examples.

Inductive Selection of Precedents

The strength of decision-tree induction is its parsimonious selection of feature combinations in order to partition the units into homogeneous groups with respect to some outcome. The process is parsimonious because the variables selected along a path of a decision tree are those needed to induce the dependent value, mostly a subset of the variables included in the analysis. Since these feature combinations have been constructed using the information content of variables over the examples in the training set, the resulting partitions, viewed as a set of precedents satisfying the generalization, are not biased toward some theoretically or ideologically formed political orientation and, thus, are not affected by the tendency of human decision makers to ignore precedents that point to undesirable outcomes. Inductively derived partitions may thus carry an advantage over manually selected precedents and also over filtered partitions for which feature combinations have been explicitly specified by the user. Furthermore, the inductively derived feature combinations satisfy the criteria specified by the case-based reasoning community for precedent selection (Kolodner, 1991). These criteria are predictiveness, abstraction, concreteness, and usefulness.

Predictiveness The feature combinations along the paths of a decision tree are inherently predictive for a given outcome. Each feature has been selected on the basis of reducing the variance among examples with respect to some outcome (the value of a dependent variable). The accuracy of the decision tree (see section 4.2.5) provides an estimate for the degree of certainty with which the outcome can be projected.

Abstraction A feature combination, which corresponds to a path in the decision tree, retrieves only those units that exactly match the specified features (variables and values). This implies that a unit that shares the same outcome, but does not match all the features that have been specified, cannot be retrieved by this feature combination. However, since the decision tree splits on variables and each of its values, all feature combinations that project the same outcome are available. Taken together, this set of feature combinations allows for several values of the same variable and is thus applicable to a broader set of units. As an illustration of this, a specific feature combination induced from the SHERFACS data, characterizing a conflict between unaligned states, might contain the feature "threat to values of parties" (variable) and "threat to political system" (value). While the feature combination does not account for conflicts between unaligned states where the parties are threatened in other ways, for example, by a "threat to territorial integrity," the abstraction from the specific case is achieved by considering the entire set of feature combinations for this type of conflict.

Concreteness Since the feature combinations have been inductively derived from the concrete examples of the training set, they contain exactly those features that actually appear in the examples. No additional inference is needed to recognize the feature in other units.

Usefulness The inductively derived feature combinations are useful in the sense that they establish homogeneous partitions of units with respect to a certain outcome value. However, the statistical nature of the inductive selection process may favor some irrelevant variables, in which case the partition that is produced is rather accidental and its elements poor precedents. A closer inspection of the variables selected by the inductive technique helps detect such flaws.

The sets of inductively retrieved precedents can be seen as defining new categories or new typologies that classify, though possibly ambiguously, the units. These new categories or typologies are characterized by the feature combination and the projected outcome value. The user might not have been aware of these categories and their predictive power with respect to a specific outcome and might thus have failed to retrieve the appropriate precedents.

Precedents as Training Sets for Inductive Analysis

As mentioned earlier, precedent-based reasoning and induction both benefit if they are used together. Precedents can provide clusters of training examples that are representative for a specific type of phenomena (for example, in SHERFACS, the international conflicts that involved the great powers; in World Facts, the countries that are members of some international organization). The simplest method of obtaining precedents and some cohesive set of training examples is to apply filters (one of the retrieval methods used in precedent-based reasoning). Other methods include the use of similarity functions, some of which have been described earlier. The generalizations, or rules that are learned, help to gain insight into the characteristics of those phenomena that have been focused on. Skalak and Rissland (1990), who work on case-based legal reasoning systems, observed that the use of precedents in inductive experiments is particularly interesting in domains where one can assume different viewpoints and thus derive rules that favor one or the other side. They experiment with different training sets for inductive experiments including—for example, cases that are most favorable to one party or "conflicting" cases that can be used by either side. Clearly, international relations is a domain where different viewpoints abound.

Using precedents as training examples in inductive experiments provides a means of including domain-specific knowledge (implicit in the selection of precedents) to the otherwise purely syntactically based induction process. The selection of variables known to be relevant is an additional source of the knowledge transfer from the user to the induction technique. While generalizations learned from precedents are likely to carry less noise and represent more meaningful patterns in the data, they can themselves be fed back to precedent-based reasoning as general templates, or feature combination, for the retrieval of other precedents. This is an obvious extension of learning templates from single precedents (see earlier).

4.4 Problems of Analyzing Real-world Datasets

One of the greatest problems of formal data analysis in a domain such as international relations, namely the access to differently structured data, has been successfully addressed by CrisView's capability to import and manage differently structured data. In addition, Chapters 3 and 4 illustrate how a number of useful techniques and methods can be made available to analyze politically relevant data and to help synthesize the information conveyed in large datasets. However, the exploration of real-world, hand-crafted datasets, found in many social science domains, raises some additional technical as well as phenomenological problems. While CrisView can deal with some of the technical problems, most of the phenomenological problems are beyond it.

4.4.1 Divergence from the Coding Scheme

In contrast to datasets such as World Facts, datasets that have not been commercialized are often insufficiently cleaned and may thus contain many coding errors. Coding errors refer to discrepancies between the data and the specification in the dataset's codebook. CrisView performs a systematic check on all the logical entities that are imported into the system. This is possible because the object classes that are instantiated during the import process provide the information necessary to detect divergences (for example, structural violations) from the underlying coding scheme and coding errors such as value domain violations. Although flaws in the performance of the exploration techniques can be prevented by ensuring that the values comply with the specification in the coding scheme, the detected errors have to be corrected manually. For example, if a variable value that is imported fails to fall within the variable's specified value domain, the system—and sometimes even the developer or user—cannot guess what the correct value should be. For each dataset, coding errors need only be corrected once: at the time the data is imported. Unfortunately, the process is time consuming because the errors have to be traced back to the original data file.

4.4.2 The Heterogeneity of Datasets

The search for common patterns and regularities in a dataset may be challenged by the heterogeneity of the data that is being analyzed. In SHERFACS, for example, more than 700 instances of a phenomenon are categorized as international disputes. However, by sampling over various conflict types and conflicts between different parties, and, most of all, by collecting the instances of the phenomenon over several politically different, and in international parlance, "distinguished" historical periods, common patterns and regularities across all disputes may be difficult to find. Many international relations researchers have dismissed the assumption that conflict behavior remains regular across time, emphasizing instead that the international system and thus the short-range as well as the long-range indicators have the capacity for change (for example, Azar, 1972; McClelland, 1983). In other words, patterns of conflict development, although once accurate, can become invalidated by system transformation. Strong correlations between various facets of a conflict may weaken or disappear due to the nature of the phenomena, which evolves continually. Prediction of the future that is grounded in recurrence within a changing system is uncertain and may be dangerously misleading if it is serving as a guideline for further action.

A possible solution to this problem is to partition the dataset into several smaller but more homogeneous datasets. This was done, for example, in an analysis of the SHERFACS data reported in Sherman et al. (1992). The goal was to identify interesting regularities in different periods of international history as codified by the SHERFACS dataset. Based on hypotheses in the literature about changes in the behavior of the actors involved, several time periods were defined, and the SHERFACS international disputes were divided accordingly. Apart from historical partitions, partitions based on geographic regions, involved parties, or issue types of a conflict could be defined. A means of confirming or questioning the coherence of such partitions with regard to the behavior of international disputes provides the rules derived from an induction experiment. The fewer the rules, the more homogeneous a given set of disputes appears to be. A large number of rules, on the other hand, indicates a rather heterogeneous set with little regularity present. Unfortunately the partitioning of a dataset can produce an undesirable side effect, namely partitions that are too small for analysis techniques such as induction. With few samples but many variables, the induced models (that is, the decision tree) may be "overfitted," meaning that they capture all the details of the training data but perform very poorly on new samples.

4.4.3 Methodological Issues

Even more serious are the problems that touch on methodological issues of data collection and coding. A short and far from exhaustive summary of some of the major phenomenological problems surrounding the generation of coded structured datasets concludes this chapter. For a good account on issues such as source bias, subjective coding, and intercoder reliability, see Howell et al. (1986).

Misclassification Presumably, misclassification haunts nearly any kind of coding endeavor. Concerning the collection and coding of data, misclassification occurs when some phenomenon or a part thereof has been observed and reported, but those who collected and coded the data failed to code it correctly—that is, when the coded data do not correspond to what was observed or reported. Intercoder reliability tests are often used to remedy this problem. What is more difficult is the detection of misclassifications across different datasets, since the coding schemes that have been used may be incommensurable. Then the question is which of the datasets should be used as the "base" dataset, and, furthermore, which should be used for accurate analysis results. CrisView can help to experiment with different coding schemes and assist in evaluating their usefulness for specific types of analysis, but it cannot, and is not intended to, address the problem of misclassification.

Disinformation Disinformation refers to the recording of something that does not have a real-world correspondence, such as events that did not happen, or facts that do not prove to be correct (assuming for once that there is consensus about what the correct recording should be). Disinformation has an impact on all exploration techniques, because they are designed to make the results appear as though they were based on "realities."

Missing information The coverage bias in source material, amplified by the process of human (and/or automatic) editing of these sources, is at the heart of what Schrodt (1988) calls the "censoring" problem, understood in a statistical rather than a political sense. An existing dataset can only catch some percentage of the real phenomena and whether the information provided is considered sufficient and reliable depends on the purpose of the analysis. Particularly in domains where intelligent, purposeful agents such as humans and organizations engage in rational planning and counter-planning, relevant decisions may be based on information that is not coded in the dataset. As a result, the conclusions drawn from the data by employing techniques such as those supported in CrisView may not provide the key to understanding or projecting the processes or situations that have been investigated. Therefore, the results of these techniques must be interpreted with care.

Misclassification, disinformation, and missing information are all different instances of an erroneous mapping process from the real world to text strings and to the coded data in a dataset. Misclassification typically occurs in the second stage of mapping, from a text to a set of categories. Disinformation and missing information, on the other hand, are generally a product of the first mapping stage, from real world to text strings, where the mapping process is often affected by or based on subjective judgments on external "reality." In addition, many of the concepts that are used to describe social phenomena do not have easily observed empirical referents, which introduces therefore an inferential leap from some trace that is observed back to the phenomenon of interest (that often remains unobserved). These inferential leaps, which are subjective in nature contribute to uncertainties and ambiguities, and if propagated into the dataset, affect the analysis of the data.

ENDNOTES

1. Whenever the structuring of the data (for example, the number of elements at every level of the hierarchy) is uniform for every unitary example of a dataset, it is possible to flatten the structure into a single fixed-length feature vector format.
2. Decision-tree techniques have generally assumed that the variable to be predicted is a class variable. Each example of the domain is marked as an instance of a single class.
3. Although frequently associated with the Yale school of research (for example, Riesbeck and Schank, 1989; Kolodner, 1988), the term *case-based reasoning* is used for the entire field of "reasoning by example" research in artificial intelligence.
4. A review of research work on the cognitive aspects of case-based reasoning can be found in Slade (1991).

Chapter 5
SUMMARY AND CONCLUSION TO PART I

The initial motivation that led to this study was the desire to use and develop knowledge-based techniques that would help explain the possible causes for, and predict the likelihood of, conflictual interactions in the international arena. Knowledge-based applications that have been developed along these lines, seeking to contribute to crisis and war prevention or resolution, are reviewed, for example, in Trappl (1986, 1992), Trappl and Miksch (1991), and Trappl and Unseld (1993). However, the lack of systems general enough to access and represent different, often structurally incompatible, data collections, as well as the absence of convenient, flexible interfaces to the data for the retrieval of relevant information, changed the research agenda. Instead of providing an ad hoc solution by subjecting some specific set of data to a particular analysis technique, a more general approach has been favored. The objective became one of employing and investigating the use of object-oriented programming techniques and modern engineering practices in developing a system that supports systematic exploration of large bodies of phenomenological data. While this effort is continued in Part II of this study, the operational CrisView prototype contributes to the international relations community considerably more than would an additional analysis technique.

5.1 Summary of Features

CrisView's data management capabilities (importing and representing data from different datasets), and its exploration techniques, provide a general platform for working with phenomenological data. As mentioned in section 2.3.3, a data exploration system can be used by international relations scholars to test and refine domain hypotheses, to browse through and search for historical cases, and to extend analysis across datasets in order to compare findings from two or more related datasets and to detect interesting constellations that may warrant further analysis. This last task suggests that a data exploration system such as CrisView provides not only the means to analyze the data in a dataset with the help of different techniques. It can also be used as a basis for examining the extent and interaction of variables and for investigating the impact of different coding categories on analysis results. Various practices for coding phenomenological data have evolved in the international relations community, shaped by different assumptions as to the constituents of political processes and events (Sherman, 1987b; Leng, 1988; Davies and McDaniel, 1991). Studies suggest that analysis results depend to a large extent on the data that has been used in the process and may vary considerably across datasets (Howell, 1983; Vincent, 1983). Subjecting the data to various forms of explorative analyses helps to determine the usefulness of existing coding categories in solving specific domain-relevant problems, and to suggest, if necessary new or modified coding schema.

While a prototype for data exploration can be designed and implemented in a number of ways, the goal, both here and in Part II, has been to focus on object-oriented programming techniques in addressing the domain-specific problems of data exploration. The data-structures in CrisView are defined as objects and are thus easily identifiable, consistent, and traceable at every stage of the development process. A significant derivative value for data exploration comes from the fact that every piece of data imported into CrisView becomes an instance of some object class and can therefore be treated in a flexible and individual manner by operations defined on the classes of these instances. The use of documents as an integrated part of CrisView's object-oriented data management is another key characteristic of the prototype, facilitating not only the modular development and modification of the classes needed for new data, but also allowing users to work conveniently with the application and the data from different datasets. The following is a short summary of the most prominent aspects of the CrisView prototype.

Object-oriented Data Management and Exploration

Comprehensive data access The representation of all logical entities of a dataset as instances of object classes provides the type of comprehensive data access that is crucial in a data exploration system: it enables the exploration techniques to manipulate every piece of phenomenological data. Operations are defined on entire views, their parts, or individual objects so as to support exactly those data exploration mechanisms and techniques that are of interest to the user. These operations can be specified at the appropriate level of abstraction, thereby minimizing code duplication.

Processing of data from different datasets By building a hierarchy of abstract and dataset-specific object classes that define the structure and behavior of the data imported and managed by the system, CrisView offers an elegant, parsimonious, and flexible solution to the treatment of data from different datasets, regardless of their underlying data models. This solution draws upon polymorphism and the inheritance mechanism of object-oriented programming languages.

Functional extendibility The current set of exploration techniques supported in CrisView can be extended to include other techniques that appear to be suitable or desirable for data exploration. Many of these new techniques will require the kind of data access operations that have already been defined and can thus profit from reusing them.

Documents in an Object-oriented Environment

Working with documents Several advantages emerge from combining the concept of documents with object-oriented programming techniques: the simplicity and ease with which users can work with the datasets of their choice without having to care about the data management of the system; the ability to modify the structure and behavior of the document-class; the possibility to create new documents and to enlarge incrementally the data in existing documents while exploring the data; and the ability to save documents that contain coherent data partitions for use on other machines.

5.2 Leading Over to Part II

Throughout Part I it was emphasized that CrisView is not specific to a particular dataset. This statement has to be further qualified. While CrisView's object-oriented architecture makes it possible to represent and manipulate data from differently structured datasets, many definitions in CrisView have been specialized to the SHERFACS and the World Facts datasets. This is partly the consequence of a deliberate design choice: in CrisView, the object classes that correspond to the logical entities of a new dataset must be defined *before* new data can be imported and explored. These classes account for the information in the dataset's coding scheme and cannot be defined in a general way.

The benefits of this design choice are ease of use (loading one rather than multiple data files), consistency (checking the imported data for coding errors), and flexibility (dynamically changing the data configuration rather than working in a persistent, fixed environment).

However, the main effort in preparing new data input for the CrisView prototype lies not in creating a set of new object classes but in writing the code for the operations that account for and express the specific behavior of the logical entities in a dataset. It is the task of writing this code that has to be reduced or further facilitated if the prototype is to become more attractive and useful. Clearly, the user can take advantage of CrisView's object-oriented architecture by making use of existing classes and operations, thereby cutting down on the effort required to write additional specifications. In the course of handling more and more data, the reusability of existing code is likely to increase. Yet more can be done not just to help a user enlarge the prototype's data handling capability but also assist him or her in adding new functionality or even in designing new versions of the prototype or components thereof.

The first step in this direction is to look for functionality that is considered generic to data exploration systems and to provide this functionality automatically. The better the support of general functionality the less new coding is required. Second, assistance can be given to users who have specific research requirements and, hence, want to modify the existing system or add new features. Their task can be facilitated by placing at their disposal a set of building blocks consisting of predefined structures and behavior that can readily be used to implement the desired specializations. Third, if users are expected to take an active part in the process of enlarging or modifying the prototype, they need information about the structure and behavior of the system. This information can be made available by supporting browsing tools that enable the user to inspect the elements of the prototype, their interactions, and dependencies.

In order to provide the kind of assistance mentioned in the preceding paragraph, the CrisView prototype has to be extended. These extensions are at the center of the second part of this study. As will be shown, a specific requirement of these extensions is the availability of meta-information—that is, information about the structure and behavior of the prototype's implementation objects. Such meta-information is provided by the CLOS metaobject protocols—that is, interfaces to the CLOS language (Kiczales et al., 1991). Part II examines the potential of metaobject protocols in the realization of the prototype's extensions.

Part II
A Protocol for Data Exploration Systems

Part II seeks to improve and extend the technical and methodological support given to the exploration of phenomenological data from different sources. This is the second step in the development of data exploration systems, following the design and construction of an operational prototype. Apart from substantive continuance, Part II continues to pursue the methodological objectives that have motivated this research: it further investigates object-oriented techniques, particularly the use of metaobject protocols and their possibilities and limitations in realizing extensions to the prototype. More specifically, the goal is to propose new classes and methods that, on the one hand, facilitate working with CrisView and, on the other hand, allow the experienced user to specify the prototype according to his or her analysis requirements. There are two factors that render this goal possible. First, CrisView's object-oriented architecture ensures the flexibility that is needed to supplement and modify the prototype in a modular and convenient way. Second, the metaobject protocols documented in advanced object-oriented programming languages such as CLOS (Common LISP Object System) add a new dimension to the control and manipulation of the behavior of the language's basic elements, its classes, generic functions, and methods.

Developing and extending object-oriented systems is clearly an activity with many degrees of freedom, especially if the potential of metaobject protocols is used in the process. The same problem can be solved in a number of ways, and there is usually no clear guideline as to which solution is preferable. As a result, and like the first part, the problem-solving process is itself at the focus of attention. From a methodological point of view, one challenging question is how to employ and effectively use object-oriented techniques and advanced techniques such as metaobject programming in the face of new demands on the functionality of a system that is dedicated to exploring domain-specific data.

Part II assumes familiarity with object-oriented techniques and is intended for those interested in the technical details of expanding an object-oriented system. These details concern the identification and subsequent definition of new structural and functional elements as well as their interface to the existing system. Object-oriented software engineers may be particularly interested in Part II given that it focuses on the use of metaobject programming techniques.

Chapter 6
MOTIVATION

The prototype developed in Part I is operational and can be readily used by someone of limited experience to explore either the data in previously created documents or new data imported from datasets for which the required classes have already been defined. However, to operate on an entirely new dataset, the user has to provide the system with the definition of the classes that correspond to the logical entities of the dataset that is to be imported. These classes must be defined *prior* to the import and manipulation of new data. New classes inherit structure and behavior from abstract classes or subclasses thereof, but a part of their definition is dataset specific. Dataset specific information about the logical entities of a dataset (for example, their names, the data type of their values, or the coding choices) can be found in the coding scheme that was used to collect and code the data and has to be included in the definition of the corresponding object classes. In addition, a number of methods are needed to account for behavior that is specific to the logical entities of the dataset and, thus, not embodied in the inherited, more general methods of the super classes. Although the object-oriented architecture of CrisView allows for a modular definition of a class's method interface, defining the appropriate methods is not always simple, particularly when a dataset exhibits special properties, such as multiple relationships among variables, variable values that are annotated with additional information, or variables whose values have different data types.

Apart from the obvious need to work with new datasets, the user may also wish to experiment with new types of analysis techniques as well as specialize or refine certain operations on the data. In order to perform these tasks, some familiarity with the prototype is clearly necessary. More precisely, the user has to know the classes and method interfaces that have already been defined, what new classes have to be added and what their interaction with other classes will have to be, and what new methods need to be defined in order to obtain or ensure the desired behavior (a fair amount of experience with object-oriented programming techniques is an additional prerequisite for engaging in these tasks).

6.1 Providing Assistance to Users

A critical factor in maintaining the present and ensuring the future usefulness of a system is the extent to which it can respond to new user requirements. In the case of CrisView, these requirements concern the processing of new data, embedding new functionality, and the specialization or modification of certain parts of the system. As indicated earlier, there is always a certain amount of dataset specificity that cannot be dealt with generally; furthermore, there are functional requirements that cannot be foreseen when developing a system. However, what can be done is to facilitate the process of realizing new requirements.

Supporting general functionality Some of the operations defined in CrisView are specific to the datasets that have been imported, but they are known to be relevant for processing any new data. A case in point are the queries concerning the linkage of two or more logical entities. Part-whole relationships are present even in flat-structured data models, and the logical entities involved have to be accessible from either side. Providing classes and operations that automatically supply this kind of generic functionality helps reduce the effort involved in preparing new data input. Furthermore, there are repeated requests (from internal classes and operations) for statistical information about the data—for example, the number of instances of a particular class or the frequency of their values. This type of statistical information is independent of the actual data being processed, and hence the necessary operations to compute this information can be defined prior to any data input.

Supporting specialized building blocks Users of the prototype may have special functional requirements—for example, a new analysis algorithm—or they may want to work with a dataset whose particular properties require that new methods be included in the method interface of the corresponding classes. To assist them in writing the necessary specifications, a set of specialized building blocks can be provided. As with, for example, the elements of a graphical user interface library, users can benefit from predefined structures and behavior by instantiating these building blocks and adjusting them to their specific needs.

Clearly, it is difficult to foresee all the possible extensions a user may wish to make, and, hence, the development of a comprehensive set of building blocks is a process that will evolve over time and improve as more experience is gained. However, there are a number of structural and functional requirements that can be anticipated, and for which appropriate support can be provided.

Supporting class browsers In order to take an active part in enlarging or modifying the prototype, a user needs to be able to query the prototype about its classes, generic functions, and methods. Such queries can be supported by so-called class browsers—that is, methods that operate not on the instance level, like the data browsers that have been defined in CrisView, but rather on the class level. Class browsers are useful devices for inspecting a class's superclasses, subclasses, and method interface as well as for checking what classes or combinations thereof are affected by generic functions. It is this kind of meta-information—that is, information about the structure and behavior of the prototype's object classes—that enables users to make changes or additions to the prototype. Class browsers are also helpful for those users who merely wish to have some insight into the program and the interaction of the prototype's components.

The remaining chapters of Part II discuss the extensions to the prototype that make possible such additional support. The realization of these extensions—most prominently the implementation of class browsers—requires access to meta-information that is provided in CLOS by the metaobject protocols. These protocols allow the standard behavior of the language to be modified and specialized to satisfy new requirements. The additional flexibility gained by being able to make such modifications provides a new and often elegant angle to the solution of a particular problem.

6.2 OUTLINE OF PART II

Part of the intention to extend the CrisView prototype arises from the fact that CrisView's applicability to new data is impeded through the effort required to write new specifications. Another critical factor is the prototype's limited set of analysis techniques, which may not be sufficient for what the user wishes to do. Chapter 6 discussed three types of extensions that aim to facilitate working with CrisView and to help users adjust the system to their needs.

Chapter 7 presents the concept of metaobject protocols in object-oriented languages and illustrates the way in which similar to, and based on, the CLOS metaobject protocol, a special protocol for data exploration systems can be defined. The new protocol consists of three additional components whose classes support general functionality, specialized functionality, and introspective access to the elements of the prototype, respectively. Because these classes represent some of the key ingredients in an application framework, their definition can be viewed as a first step toward developing a dedicated application framework for data exploration systems.

Chapter 8 focuses on the joint use of object-oriented programming techniques and metaobject protocols in proposing and defining classes for the new components mentioned earlier. Much emphasis is placed on the development of "base" classes to support the kind of functionality that is generally required in any data exploration system. The CrisView prototype and, in particular, its import mechanism are both examined. Modifications and extensions are made to those classes that fail to be general enough to be used in other systems. The use of metaobjects is shown to be effective for making these modifications. The second component contains specialized classes capable of representing and operating on logical entities that exhibit special characteristics. The introspective classes of the third component are discussed in the context of different user groups. The final section addresses the generalization of the user interface that would allow a data exploration system to accept different types of data.

Chapter 9 concludes Part II. From a user's perspective the CrisView prototype is evaluated and its role in the field of international relations is highlighted. This chapter also evaluates the usefulness of metaobject protocols in addressing the problems encountered in extending the prototype and points out some of the drawbacks involved.

Chapter 7
PROTOCOLS

In object-oriented parlance, a protocol comprises the set of generic functions of an application and thus encompasses the complete behavior of the objects in the application (Keene, 1989, 30). The notion of protocol emphasizes the functional aspects of an application—that is, an object-oriented program is viewed in terms of generic operations on objects. A different perspective focuses on the objects that are manipulated by generic functions and methods and, hence, views a program in terms of objects. An object is depicted as a unity spanning structure and behavior. Consequently, the definition of an object class includes both the definition of its structure and its method interface. Both perspectives are valid and will be used in the following chapters.

Each application is built upon a particular object-oriented language whose programmer interface supports one of several possible object-oriented paradigms. These paradigms differ in the way they handle, for example, the organization of classes, the creation and initialization of instances (not all object-oriented languages distinguish between classes and instances), and the dispatch of the generic functions. In view of these different paradigms, CLOS (Common LISP Object System) has evolved in an attempt to define a standard object-oriented language extension to Common LISP, incorporating what are considered the most useful aspects of various object-oriented paradigms. The programmer interface of CLOS supports one particular model of object-oriented programming, but in order to enable users to customize their own applications and to experiment with other object-oriented paradigms, CLOS itself has been designed as an extensible protocol. This protocol is called the metaobject protocol.

7.1 Metaobject Protocols

Instances of an object class can readily be manipulated by defining the appropriate operations as methods specialized to this class. The class's structure and method interface determine the instances' characteristics, what they can do, and what can be done to them. What if a class, a generic function, or a method needs to be manipulated? What if one wishes, for example, to be able to store information about the value in the slot of a class, or to have a class count how many times it has been instantiated, or to modify the way in which instances are created, or perhaps to change the order in which multiple methods are executed? The answer to these questions is to conceive object classes, generic functions, and methods as being themselves instances of classes, namely instances of metaobject classes.

The notion of an object as being an instance of some object class leads at a metalevel to the notion of a metaobject (a class, generic function, or method) as an instance of some metaobject class. At this metalevel, the object-oriented language itself is viewed as an object-oriented program whose objects, the metaobjects, represent the fragments of that program. The link between an object and a metaobject is the same as between a user-defined protocol and a so-called metaobject protocol (Kiczales et al., 1991). Like the protocol of a user-defined application, which encompasses the behavior of the objects in the application, the metaobject protocol encompasses the behavior of the objects in the underlying program, in this case, the metaobjects of the object-oriented language.

Metaobject protocols add a new perspective to the design of object-oriented applications in a given language because they can be used to modify the otherwise fixed semantics of the programming language. Kiczales and his colleagues describe the characteristics of metaobject protocols as follows:

> Metaobject protocols are interfaces to the [programming] language that give users the ability to incrementally modify the language's behavior and implementation, as well as the ability to write programs within the language. (Kiczales et al., 1991, 1)

Rather than being confined to a single language design that reflects one particular model of object-oriented programming, the metaobject protocol approach enables the user to explore other language designs within the space of all possible designs and implementations. Specialized metaobject classes can be viewed as representing fragments of a user-defined, extended language built from instances of the standard metaobject classes of the implementation language and including constructs that extend the implementation language itself.

7.2 Drawing Analogies to Data Exploration Systems

An object-oriented application such as CrisView constitutes a particular extension of the object-oriented implementation language and, hence, can itself be viewed as a language. From this point of view, some analogies can be drawn between an object-oriented language such as CLOS and the CrisView data-exploration prototype.

Problem analogy Among the reasons that led to the development of a metaobject protocol for CLOS were, first, the incompatibility of different object-oriented languages (extensions to LISP) each committed to large bodies of existing code, and, second, the need for special extensions of particular projects (Kiczales et al., 1991). On a different level, a data exploration system faces similar difficulties: large bodies of domain-specific data have been collected in datasets whose data models are largely incompatible. In addition, users who want to explore their data have different, present and future, analysis needs. A data exploration system cannot support all the functionality that is required, nor can it foresee what kind of additional operations may be needed to cope with new data and satisfy new analysis requirements.

Solution analogy Those who developed CLOS designed the language as an extendible protocol, thereby encouraging the user to engage actively in the design process. Because the metaobject protocol provides control over the basic elements of the language, users can modify and extend the language's default behavior, documented in the metaobject protocol, thereby adjusting it to their own requirements. As no single solution can possibly be universally appropriate, extendibility, and in particular user-defined extendibility, is desirable both on the programming language level and on the application level. Users of CrisView need to be able to extend the prototype and, in particular, to add new specifications in view of new data or new analysis requirements. As with the metaobject protocol for object-oriented languages, the goal is to facilitate their tasks by providing an extended data-exploration protocol for the CrisView prototype.

The metaobject protocol approach does not just provide the idea and motivation for a similar approach at the application level; the CLOS metaobject protocol itself is used to develop an extended protocol for CrisView.

7.3 A Protocol for Data Exploration Systems

As mentioned earlier, the set of generic functions of an object-oriented application constitute the protocol of the application. Thus, the CrisView protocol comprises the set of generic functions that were defined during the development of the prototype in Part I. Extending the prototype means extending its protocol. Each extension to the prototype can be viewed as a new protocol component that—given the functional perspective implied in the notion of protocol—extends one particular functional aspect of the prototype. Together these components define a protocol for data exploration systems.

7.3.1 Three Additional Protocol Components

Section 6.1 discussed three extensions to CrisView for the purpose of making the prototype a more useful and versatile tool for data exploration. These extensions include the provision of functionality that is considered generic to the task of data exploration, the support of building blocks to facilitate the implementation of new functionality and allow the user to customize the prototype to specific needs, and the definition of class browsers that help inspect the elements of the prototype.

The access to metaobjects and metaobject classes is an obvious prerequisite for building class browsers, since it is this access that allows the prototype "to reflect about" its classes and method interfaces. However, the other two extensions to the prototype challenge the implementation language even more, because they demand the structure and behavior of classes to adapt and respond to new requirements. The classes, or more precisely the sets of generic functions, that will be defined for each of the two extensions will be referred to here as *intercessory protocols*. This is the term used by Kiczales and his colleagues for protocols that include specialized metaobjects (Kiczales et al., 1991, 71). The prospective intercessory protocols discussed in this study will contain both specialized metaobjects and standard CLOS metaobjects. The set of generic functions defined for the third extension will represent an *introspective protocol* (Kiczales et al., 1991, 71) in reference to operations on but not specialization of metaobjects.

Two Types of Intercessory Protocols

Considering the first extension to the prototype, the goal is to identify and define classes and operations that cover as much as possible of the functionality that is generally required for the processing of phenomenological data. To a large extend, this functionality can be found in the CrisView prototype, since the prototype has been designed to represent and analyze data from different dataset. However, part of CrisView's functionality is expressed by methods that are specialized to dataset specific classes and, hence, these methods are not generally applicable. Other classes and operations are generic but limited in the functionality they support. As has been mentioned before, dataset specific classes and methods cannot be avoided altogether, because they store information that cannot be generalized. Rather, the goal is to elaborate further on the classes that have been defined and to advance their method interfaces. It involves thus redefining some of CrisView's classes and operations in such a way that they support generally required functionality more effectively, and extending, if possible, the set of abstract classes and their method interfaces. Both tasks help reduce the amount of specifications the user needs to write in order to enlarge the prototype's database or to ensure the exploration of new data.

The second extension includes a set of specialized building blocks that can be employed by experienced users when implementing new functionality or designing specialized versions of the prototype. From the viewpoint of extendibility, it is this extension that comes closest to the ideas put forward by the metaobject protocol approach in object-oriented languages. Concerning flexibility, however, the objective is significantly different. A metaobject protocol documents and provides access to the basic elements of the programming language in order to allow users to take an active part in the design process of a language that fits the requirements of the programs they intend to write. Apart from compliance with the syntax of the language, the user faces no restrictions; on the contrary, he or she is faced with an almost overwhelming range of possibilities in implementing a given problem. The extension to the prototype, however, offers a set of building blocks whose predefined structure and behavior can be used and combined selectively. Ideally, these building blocks would provide all the structure and functionality that are required by the user.

An Introspective Protocol

In general, the user of an object-oriented application has no access to the application's protocol but sees only the effects of the application's behavior when issuing the commands in the user interface. This situation can be changed by defining a set of operations that allows the user to inspect the structure and behavior of the prototype. Added to CrisView's user interface, these operations extend the browsing facility, which so far involved only the data, to the elements of the prototype. Such operations are considered generally useful as an analysis tool for querying an application about its classes, generic functions, and methods. Their main function in CrisView is to give users access to the information they need in order to write the necessary specifications for enlarging the prototype's database or adding new functionality.

7.3.2 Steps Toward a Dedicated Application Framework

The preceding paragraphs described the three components of an extended CrisView protocol. The goal of defining such a protocol is to provide the user with an interface to a set of basic, yet semantically meaningful, generic operations to develop further the CrisView prototype and possibly design other data exploration systems. While the notion of a protocol imposes a functional perspective (generic functions defined on objects rather than objects and their method interface), the goal can be formulated from an "object-oriented" perspective. From this perspective, the goal is to provide the user with a set of classes encompassing the functionality that is required to extend the prototype and build new versions of data explorations systems.

Pursuing this goal can be seen as a first step toward developing an application framework for data exploration systems, because the classes that are included in the components of the protocol represent some of the key ingredients in an application framework. The first component yields a set of *base classes*—that is, definitions of classes and method interfaces, which seek to encompass the functionality required by all future framework-based applications. The second provides a set of *specialized classes*—that is, definitions of classes and method interfaces, which support specialized functionality to build new data exploration systems or add new parts to the CrisView prototype. The third component, finally, comprises a set of *introspective classes*—that is, definitions of classes and method interfaces—to inspect the elements of the CrisView prototype as well as of future framework-based applications.

The CrisView prototype plays an important role with regard to developing an application framework for data exploration systems. Firstly, the generic parts of CrisView, together with additional base classes, cover an essential part of the structure and behavior of a data exploration system and, hence, can be used to define the kernel of an application framework. Second, experience gained from working with the CrisView prototype, as well as considerations of the requirements for exploring new data, help to define a set of specialized classes. These specialized classes become part of the framework's class library, enabling the user to compose new applications in an effective and convenient way. In addition, the CrisView prototype has an impact on the choice of the major design principles. Here, the prototype helps to identify those parts that have proved vital or desirable for data exploration. The major design principles to be adopted by all future framework-based applications include the use of documents as the main entity managed by a data exploration system, the definition of classes prior to the import of new data, and the fully object-oriented representation of domain-specific data.

While the notion of an application framework refers to a general concept for developing software that provides flexible means of modifying existing applications or designing new ones, extending the CrisView protocol is a step toward realizing this concept for a dedicated type of application, namely data exploration systems. The components of an extended protocol, once they are developed, yield an *operational specification* of some of the key ingredients of an application framework for data exploration systems. Chapter 8 proposes a number of definitions for the classes that make up the components. Clearly, the definition of base classes, specialized classes, and introspective classes account for only a fraction of what could, possibly, be included in a fully fledged application framework.

7.3.3 Development of Components

Knowing the kind of functionality that the components of a data exploration system intend to support, their definition, more precisely the definition of the classes they comprise, involves two sets of decisions. First, it has to be decided what operations are needed and what objects they manipulate. This touches upon the question as to whether and to what extent existing operations and classes in CrisView can be extended and what new classes and operations have to be defined. Second, decisions have to be taken as to how object-oriented programming techniques, including metaobject programming techniques, are going to be employed to define the necessary classes and operations.

Prospective Classes in Each Component

Experience gained during the course of developing the CrisView prototype identified some of the critical elements in using the prototype and suggested a number of possible improvements. These suggestions provide the basis for developing the components of an extended protocol for data exploration systems.

Base classes The classes to be included in the first component of the extended protocol should support functionality that is either generally required or considered useful in data exploration systems, including the CrisView prototype. A closer look at the prototype developed in Part I helps indicate which classes in CrisView qualify as base classes, which classes need to be modified in order to account for general data-exploration requirements, and what additional functionality needs to be supported. Concerning this type of question, the operations interfacing the prototype and the external world are of particular interest. These operations and the classes they affect, as well as the parts of CrisView that directly depend on them, are most relevant and most critical in view of supporting general functionality. Similarly, the requirements of exploration techniques may indicate where more powerful, yet still generally applicable, operations can and should be provided.

Specialized classes The classes to be added to the second component should represent specialized building blocks that can be used to define specific extensions to the prototype. Information about useful building blocks can be derived from considerations of structural idiosyncrasies of data or from the likely analysis requirements of users who work with domain-specific datasets. As regards users' new analysis requirements, the objective is to provide classes that enable the user to enlarge the prototype's exploration capability in a convenient and modular way.

Introspective classes The classes of the third component should support generic browsing operations that can be applied to the prototype as well as to various extensions thereof. The classes for this component can be derived from considering what kind of information a user needs with regard to the structure and behavior of the CrisView prototype.

Methodological Concerns

The primary task is to decide where metaobjects come into play. For some of the classes to be defined, the standard CLOS forms (defclass, defgeneric, and defmethods) can be used. For others, it is necessary to have access to metaobjects as well as the possibility to change the behavior of the standard classes, generic functions, and methods. Obviously, class browsers cannot be constructed without access to what Kiczales and his colleagues call "backstage fixtures" (Kiczales et al., 1991), namely the standard metaobject classes, because it is their structure and behavior that the browsers have to show. For the other two components the choice is less obvious. The default behavior of CLOS may already provide much of the flexibility required to build the required classes. However, the use of metaobjects may offer an alternative and even more elegant way to obtain the desired functionality.

Another important issue involves the decision as to how a particular specification should be formulated. This issue was already raised during the development of the CrisView prototype and becomes even more important with the ability to modify the CLOS metaobject classes. Should a particular specification be expressed as a restriction on a generic function or on its methods? The specification of a standard generic function governs system and user-defined methods alike, whereas the specification of a standard method does not restrict user-defined methods on the generic function (Kiczales et al., 1991, 111). There are no clear-cut answers to these questions; rather, the choice of one or the other way of formulating a particular specification depends on what is considered to be more useful or convenient.

Chapter 8
EXTENDING THE CRISVIEW PROTOCOL

This chapter elaborates on the kinds of classes that are included in the components of a protocol for data exploration systems. Much emphasis is being placed on the development of the first component, referred to as *base component* in view of the classes it seeks to embrace. Assuming that CrisView supports the functionality needed to explore specific datasets, the objective is to identify and modify, if necessary, those classes and operations in CrisView that are considered indispensable or highly desirable in any data exploration system. The development of this component is interesting for three reasons. First, unlike the theoretically unlimited number of classes qualifying for the second component, the number of potential base classes is limited. Second, in contrast to the third component, which comprises many classes that can be used for any object-oriented application, the base component is dedicated to data exploration. Third, defining the classes of this component may indicate alternative solutions to problems addressed in Part I.

8.1 Developing Base Classes

The main functionality of CrisView as well as of other data exploration systems encompasses data access (data import and management) and data analysis. Ideally, this functionality is supported by a set of classes powerful enough to cover as many of the structural and functional requirements of data exploration as possible, while at the same time general enough to account for the characteristics of various datasets and data models. The CrisView prototype provides a good starting point for defining base classes. First, in the course of developing the prototype, experience has been gained concerning the kinds of classes and operations essential for exploring phenomenological data from different datasets. This experience is crucial in proposing possible base classes. Second, the prototype is an operational system representing a solution to the problem of data exploration. This solution embraces the classes and operations that were needed to address the problems of data access and data analysis. They can now be reviewed to propose generalizations or modifications of those definitions that are specialized to some dataset or those that are limited in their functionality. Third, because the prototype is an example of a data exploration system, it can be used for testing the base classes that are developed. Included in the prototype, these base classes should neither interfere with nor impede the behavior of those parts of the prototype that are specialized to some dataset. In addition, all the functionality that is not dataset-specific should be covered by the base classes.

The following paragraphs examine the mechanism of data access and data analysis in CrisView. The focus is on the classes and operations that import and manage new data. They are the prime candidates for the definition of base classes because they control the structuring and content of the elements that are later analyzed by the exploration techniques. Furthermore, enlarging the prototype's database and updating its data management capabilities are possibly two of the major concerns of users who wish to explore phenomenological data. Both tasks evolve around the definitions of classes and operations involved in accessing new data.

8.1.1 Mechanism of Data Access and Data Analysis

Evidently, the document-class plays an important role in the process of accessing and analyzing data: the document is the main entity managed by the prototype. It controls the object classes that correspond to the logical entities in the dataset. It further controls the supplementary data—for example, the windows of the user interface to which the various exploration techniques are associated—and the acceleration structures defined on top of the core data. The structure of the document-class is shown as follows:

```
(defclass document-class ()
  ((file-pathname :initform *file-pathname*)
   (modified-p :initform nil)
   (unit-collection :initform nil :accessor unit-collection)
   (variable-unit-structure :initform nil)
   (variable-substructure-unit-structure :initform nil)
   (document-window :initarg :document-window)
   (descriptor-dialog :initform nil)
   (filter-dialog :initform nil)
   (new-variable-dialog :initform nil)
```

```
    (analyses-dialog :initform nil)
    (filter-list :initform nil)
    (subset-list :initform nil)
    (new-variable-list :initform nil)
    (i2d-induction-dialog-list :initform nil)
    (precedent-dialog-list :initform nil))
  (documentation "structure of class document-class"))
```

When new data are imported, several slots (or instance variables) of the currently active instance of the document-class are updated (they are initially bound to nil).

Unit-collection The value of the slot unit-collection is an instance of the class collection-class. This class contains the units that have been imported from a dataset (that is, instances of dataset-specific subclasses of unit-class) and the indexes of these units, each pointing to the position of a unit in the collection. The data are stored regardless of their content or structure, and hence the process of establishing such a collection is generic—that is, identical for all datasets that are processed. The operation that creates the collection of the units is part of the import operation (discussed later).

Acceleration structures The values of the slots named variable-unit-structure and variable-substructure-unit-structure contain two specific acceleration structures that are built (or updated) when new data are imported into the prototype. Acceleration structures are an indispensable feature of CrisView because they provide the access from lower-level to higher-level logical entities (Part I, section 3.3.1). The current representation of the core data in a document does not support this kind of "bottom-up" access. It provides only "top-down" access, from the instance to the instances stored in its content slot (for example, from a unit to its substructures). Typically, the definition of an acceleration structure depends on the data model of the dataset and the kind of access to the data that is required. This seems to imply that acceleration structures are customized to particular datasets. Indeed, the methods that construct the acceleration structures in CrisView are part of the definitions that have to be supplied when new data are imported. However, because these structures are vital in CrisView and similar data exploration systems, the construction of acceleration structures—at least those whose content can be derived from the imported dataset—should be part of the functionality provided by the base component.

Document-window The document-window that is associated with the document is stored in one of the slots of the document. This window is affected by the import of new data to the extent that it displays the variables used in a dataset. The window's variable-panel shows the variable names, the number of different variable values, and the number of variable occurrences. However, this information is not stored in the document-window but supplied by an acceleration structure. Both acceleration structures in CrisView contain sublists of variables, values, and indexes that point to the units stored in the document. These sublists yield exactly the information that is displayed in the variable-panel. They also provide the links exploited by the operations defined on the panels. In other words, the document-window is not tied to the particularities of a dataset but depends, rather, on the acceleration structure for the information it requires. The document-window assumes, however, that this acceleration structure contains a structured list of variables and units. The examination of the document-window in CrisView highlights again the role of acceleration structures and confirms the importance of delegating their construction to the base component. It also shows that the window is specialized to structured coded data. This implies that the definition of the document-window-class would have to be changed if the restriction on the data were to be relaxed (see section 8.4).

Other windows The document-class provides additional slots to store the instances of windows that can be directly invoked from within the document-window (Part I, section 3.4.2). These windows support different techniques for analyzing phenomenological data and display different parts of the data. Like the document-window, the data are not stored in the windows but supplied either by an acceleration structure or acquired directly by assessing the value of the document's unit-collection slot. This means that the windows are not customized to one particular dataset. Some of them are, however, adjusted to an acceleration structure, and most of them support operations that assume the data to be structured, at least in terms of units and variables. To account for other types of data (for example, unstructured data), a new set of windows and operations would have to be defined, raising the question as to the kind of operations suitable for exploring other types of data.

User-defined views There are five slots that contain data-structures defined by the user during data exploration: namely, subset-list, filter-list, new-variable-list, I^2D-induction-dialog-list, and precedent-dialog-list. The values of these slots are initially bound to nil and are updated when the user explicitly adds new elements to these lists. The value of the slot subset-list is updated for the first time when new data is imported into the document. A "subset" embracing all the units stored in the document is added to the initially empty list. Like the unit-collection, the creation of the subset is independent of the structure and content of the data.

The examination of the document as the main entity affected by the process of importing and representing new data indicated two areas where definitions of the prototype's classes and operations should be modified. The first area pertains to the definition of the import operation and the classes involved. The import process as it is currently defined in CrisView and the modification that allows it to extend its capabilities are discussed in the next section. The second area concerns the definition of new windows in the exploration component. This area will be touched upon only briefly by outlining a generalized approach that, depending on the type of data imported into the document, invokes one of several document-windows. Each window is specialized to the type of data being processed and supports the operations considered germane for the analysis of these data. For structured coded data, the CrisView document-window together with the various other windows of CrisView's exploration component already support the required user interactions.

8.1.2 Generalizing the Import Behavior

The import operation interfaces the application and the external world, converting the "raw" data into their internal representation. Two reasons suggest that the import behavior of data exploration systems should be rendered more powerful: first, the import operation is responsible for establishing the content of the core data and, thus, may store much of the information (structural and statistical information) about the data at an initial stage. Second, while the import operation initializes the dataset-specific classes, it can incrementally build acceleration structures that represent links (for example, bottom-up) between the instances of these classes.

CrisView's Import Process

When a new document is created in CrisView, it contains no data, and the document-window associated with the document is empty. Data is entered into the document by issuing an import command that in turn triggers the import process. The following code shows part of the import method specialized to the document-class (additional behavior such as constructing the initial subset of units, calling the methods for building the acceleration structures, and filling the variable-panel in the document-window are omitted).

```
(defmethod import ((ob document-class))
  (catch :cancel
    (with-open-file (infile (choose-file-dialog))
      (with-cursor *watch-cursor*
        (let ((arg-list (read infile)))
          (unless (slot-value ob 'unit-collection)
            (setf (slot-value ob 'unit-collection)
                  (make-instance 'simple-collection-class))
            (dolist (unit arg-list)
              (let ((unit-instance
                     (make-instance (car unit) :content nil)))
                (import unit-instance (cadr unit))
                (add-to-collection ob unit-instance)))))))))
```

The file from which data are imported is in import/export format (see Part I, section 3.2.2) and, hence, is a structured list whose sublists represent the individual phenomena in the dataset. A sublist contains the logical entity on the unit level, followed by the entities on lower levels. For each unit, the import method specialized to the document-class creates an instance of the corresponding class (subclasses of the abstract class unit-class). The method then calls the import method specialized to the unit-class to fill the unit's content slot with the logical entities on the next lower level. Finally, it adds the new unit to the collection. The import method specialized to the unit-class reads:

```
(defmethod import ((ob unit-class) arg-list)
  (let ((allowed-content (slot-value ob 'allowed-content)))
    (dolist (element arg-list)
      (when element
        (if (member (car element) allowed-content)
          (let ((content (make-instance (car element) :content nil)))
            (import content (cadr element))
            (pushnew content (slot-value ob 'content)))
          (error "invalid content for unit-class: ~s element: ~s"
                 (class-name (class-of ob)) element))))))
```

The method uses the value of the "allowed-content" slot to check whether the imported data match the classes defined in the system. If no class exists for a given logical entity, the method signals an error. A similar import method has been defined for the substructure-class. The import of variables frequently requires methods specialized to the dataset-specific subclasses of variable-class in order to perform dataset-specific validity checks on the imported values. Restrictions on a variable's value type or value domain are specified in the definition of the dataset-specific subclass and can be checked by methods specialized to the corresponding classes. Variables whose values are not restricted can be imported by a general import method defined for the abstract class variable-class.

The import methods successively build up the core data of the document. The instances of subclasses of the unit-class are added to the collection in the document's slot. Each instance stores the instances on the next lower level up to the variable level where the content slot of the instances contains the variable's value. This process works for an arbitrary number of levels (that is, several layers of substructures) carrying over the structuring of the dataset into the internal representation of the data in the document. However, CrisView's import process is limited in the amount of information it conveys about the imported data. Furthermore, it rests on certain assumptions that affect other parts of the prototype:

Container information The instance that appears in the content slot of another instance carries no information about its so-called *container*. In order to find the container of an instance, a top-down search would have to be performed, searching all the units in the document's core data and, in each unit, the logical entities on each level until the requested instance is found.

Different types of logical entities in a content slot The current assumption in CrisView is that all the instances in a content slot are of the same type. This means that the content slot of a unit is assumed to contain instances of subclasses of either variable-class or substructure-class, and the content slot of a substructure is assumed to contain either instances of subclasses of variable-class or instances of other subclasses of substructure-class. Clearly, variables just store their values. While the data of World Facts comply with this assumption, some of the feature vectors of SHERFACS (subclasses of substructure-class) would be more accurately represented if their corresponding classes contained a set of variables *and* other feature vectors, given the relationship among the feature vectors (Part I, Figure 3.6).

Additional structure among logical entities The import process further assumes that the structure of the file containing the phenomenological data reflects in detail the structure of the logical entities in the dataset. Additional structural relationships among logical entities that are not depicted in the imported data cannot be accounted for.

These limitations are different in nature and require different approaches. In order to provide container information, two adjustments have to be made. First, the structure of the unit-class, substructure-class, and variable-class have to be modified to include an additional slot, called "container" slot. Second, the import operation has to be adjusted to add to every instance that is created the information about its container. These adjustments are described in the next section.

As for the content slot and the possibility to store different types of logical entity in it, the import methods defined in CrisView are general enough to store instances of all the classes listed in the allowed-content slot. This corresponds to the most general notion of a content slot. Any object may be stored in the content slot as long as its class is among the classes in the allowed-content slot. It is the user's responsibility and choice to determine the classes whose instances can be stored in the content slot. What are affected, however, are the operations that seize the value of the content slot. In CrisView, the instances in the slot belong all to the same class and can thus be processed in a uniform way. Once these instances belong to different classes, the operations have to be specialized. In many cases, this can be achieved by adding another method to the generic function that implements the operation. For example, if an operation has been defined with the purpose of returning the values of the variables in a content slot, and the slot contains instances of subclasses of variable-class and substructure-class, two methods have to be present. One operates on the variables as before, the other recursively applies the first operation to the value of the content slot of each substructure.

A more serious problem is that of missing information concerning the relationships between the logical entities of a dataset. In CrisView, additional methods have been defined to query an object for this additional information (for example, in SHERFACS, the relationship between the feature vectors). For a new dataset, similar methods would have to be added explicitly to the method interface of the dataset-specific classes.

Adding Container Information

As mentioned earlier, the present import process does not store the container of an instance—that is, the instance in whose content slot an instance appears. This information, however, is needed by browsing and retrieval operations, including the operations that create filters and new variables. To store an instance's container while the data are imported into the prototype, the structure of the corresponding classes needs to be extended. Modifications are made at the level of abstract classes, because all dataset-specific classes need a container slot. The following code shows the structure of the new unit-class.

```
(defclass unit-class ()
  ((content :initarg :content)
   (container :initarg :document
              :allocation :class
              :accessor container))
  (:documentation "abstract class unit-class"))
```

The container slot of the unit-class has been specified as a class slot (that is, a slot whose value is shared by all instances of the class), because the value of the container of each unit is the document to which they belong. In addition, an accessor function or *reader method* has been defined to access the value of the slot by calling a method named "container." The structure of the substructure-class and variable-class are similar, except that the container slot is no longer a class slot. Substructures belong to different units, and hence the value of their container is not shared by them all. The structure of the substructure-class reads:

```
(defclass substructure-class ()
  ((content :initarg :content
            :accessor content)
   (container :initarg :container
              :accessor container))
  (:documentation "abstract class substructure-class"))
```

Once the container slot has been added to the structure of all abstract classes, the import methods need to be modified to supply the required slot value. The modification is minor because the links between an instance and its container are known at the time the import methods transform the phenomenological data into their internal representation.

```
(defmethod import ((ob document-class))
  (catch :cancel
    (with-open-file (infile (choose-file-dialog))
      (with-cursor *watch-cursor*
        (let ((arg-list (read infile)))
          (unless (slot-value ob 'unit-collection)
            (setf (slot-value ob 'unit-collection)
                  (make-instance 'simple-collection-class))
            (dolist (unit arg-list)
              (let ((unit-instance (make-instance (car unit)
                                                  :content nil
                                                  :container ob)))
                (import unit-instance (cadr unit))
                (add-to-collection ob unit-instance))))))))))
```

The container information serves several functions. First, it provides access to the logical entities from both directions, not just top down. Second, it helps to determine the location of a logical entity in the core data of a document. The path from an instance to the instances in one or more containers also gives access to the document to which an instance belongs. This is important in case several documents are open at the same time. Third, containers facilitate the establishment of simple acceleration structures that are general enough to be used for any dataset. An alternative to the container would be to store with each instance the path that leads from the document to this instance. The path to the unit level is identical to the value of a unit's container. Each level adds another segment to the path. The path information unambiguously identifies each instance within the core data of a document and, like the container information, makes it possible to move between the levels of a data model.

For instances of the subclasses of the substructure-class, there is another value that may be stored in the container slot. Rather than storing the units in which they appear, the index into the collection of units can be stored. This complies with the way units are accessed—that is, by means of their index. Only a small change is required to implement this modification. When the import method of the substructure-class creates the instances that belong to the content of the unit, the method provides the index of the unit rather than the unit itself as the value to the container argument:

```
:container (get-index collection ob)
```

This modified version of the method makes use of the fact that units have been stored in a collection from which they can be retrieved by their index. A similar collection could be built for substructures in order to store the indexes rather than the substructures in the containers of variables. The difference between storing an instance or storing its index becomes visible when the value of a container is stored with the class of some instance, a procedure discussed in the section on acceleration structures. If instances are stored in a class—that is, in a metaobject—they cannot be "garbage collected" until the pointer to these instances in the class is removed. If only their indexes are stored, the instances themselves can be garbage collected while their indexes are still contained in a slot of the class. In the former case, the user who is opening and closing a series of documents while working with CrisView faces a growing number of instances collected in the corresponding classes. Only some of them actually belong to the active document at that time. Explicit care has to be taken to remove the instances from their storage when a document is closed. In the latter case, the instances that are created when a document is activated or new data are imported are automatically garbage collected once the document is closed. However, the user still needs to take care of the information stored in the class even if it is only a list of indexes. This list will be obsolete as soon as the user closes a document, because the indexes refer to data structures that no longer exist. Evidently, the indexes occupy less storage than the instances, but failure to deal with them explicitly is likely to cause errors when new data are explored. This issue will be taken up again in later parts of this chapter, in particular section 8.2.2, where classes are required to have control over their instances.

The following comment concerns the relationship between logical entities not depicted in the structuring of the dataset. The SHERFACS dataset, for example, does not convey the relationship between the various feature vectors. Based on the import/export format of the file that contains the data, the feature vectors that describe a conflict are all represented as instances of subclasses of substructure-class regardless of the relationship between them. Consequently, if a feature vector is queried for its container, an instance of the subclass unit-class is returned (the individual conflict in which the feature vector occurs), rather than the feature vector on the next higher level in the data model. Here, the definition of a new "container" method has to account for these special cases, without affecting the general container behavior of the core data in other documents. For this purpose an ***around method*** specialized to the dataset-specific subclasses of the substructure-class can be added to the methods of the generic function "container." Around methods have a higher precedence than all applicable primary, before, and after methods. They specify the code that is to be run instead of other applicable methods, though it is possible to cause some of the other methods to run as well.

The following code shows the around method of the feature vector type phase-structure. Clearly, this method is dataset specific.

```
(defmethod container :around ((ob phase-structure))
  (let ((case (slot-value ob 'container)))
    (case-overview case)))
```

The method seizes the value of the container slot in order to obtain the instance of the subclass of unit-class—that is, the conflict case. The expression (slot-value ob container) accesses this value without calling the reader method. A method called "case-overview" yields the case-overview feature vector, which is the feature vector that "contains" all the phase-structure feature vectors in a data model. Whenever the method "container" is called and an around method is present, the code of the latter is executed. Otherwise, the reader method defined in the abstract class is called, returning the value originally stored in the container of the instances.

Similar methods need to be defined for the feature vector classes party-involvement-action, agent-referral, and agent-action. No additional method is required for the case-overview feature vector because the value of its container is an instance of a subclass of unit-class, and this value is returned by the general reader method of the substructure-class. The following is the around method specialized to the party-involvement-action feature-vector class. The "container" of these feature vectors is the phase-structure feature vector (see Part I, Figure 3.6).

```
(defmethod container :around ((ob party-involvement-action))
  (let* ((case (slot-value ob 'container))
         (phase-structure-fvs (phases case)))
    (find (phase-number ob) phase-structure-fvs :key #'phase-number)))
```

The link between a phase-structure and the party-involvement-actions defined for this phase is established by matching the value of the variable "phase-number." This variable appears in the phase-structure feature vector as well as in the party-involvement-action feature vectors (it also appears in the feature vectors agent-referral and agent-action).

The modifications, mentioned earlier, of the import process and the classes involved, extend and automatically support functionality that is generally required in data exploration systems. Behavior for data whose structure is only partly deducible from the dataset can be easily accounted for by combining general behavior and methods specialized to the dataset-specific classes.

Providing Statistical Information

The import process can be extended further by making optimal use of the fact that the import methods work sequentially through all the logical entities of a dataset. This means that statistical information about the logical entities can be accumulated and stored during the import process. Statistical information about the core data in a document, including the number of instances that have been created for a given class and the frequency of their values, is requested by various exploration techniques. The induction technique, for example, uses this information to calculate the entropy and conditional entropy of variables and variable pairs, respectively. Similarly, comparison and precedent-based reasoning rely on this information to establish the similarity between the units in a document's core data. Currently, the CrisView prototype comprises several methods that compute the requested figures. Some of them can be replaced by storing statistical information with the classes of instances where it can be accessed in a uniform way.

Functionality derived from accumulating and storing statistical information when new data are imported into the system requires the introduction of new metaobject classes. Because the metaobject classes are responsible for instance implementation, it is possible to associate some additional functionality with this process. Instances of object classes are created when the import methods work through the logical entities imported from a data file. As has been shown, the import methods create for each logical entity an instance of the corresponding class. Then they call the import method of this class, providing as an argument the logical entities on the next lower level. The value of an instance's content slot is set after the instance has been created. The creation of instances is controlled by the standard generic function make-instance and the method defined for CLOS standard-class metaobjects. The low-level slot access function (setf slot-value) is responsible for setting or changing the value of a slot. Both functions—more precisely, their methods—have to be changed in order to collect information about the logical entities of a dataset at the time the data are imported.

In general, there are three steps involved in changing the standard behavior of object classes. First, a new specialized metaobject class is created as a subclass of standard-class, which is a default CLOS metaobject class. Instances of this class, that is, the user-defined classes, inherit structure and behavior from this new metaobject class. Second, generic functions and methods are specialized to this metaobject class to determine its behavior. Third, instances of the specialized metaobject classes are created, serving as classes for the application-specific instances. The following paragraphs discuss the modifications that are necessary if the new requirements are to be met. The first modification extends the behavior of the make-instance method to count and store the number of instances of a given class while the instances are created. The second modification concerns collecting the values of variable instances and computing their relative frequency while slot access operations are performed.

Specialized metaobject classes In order to store additional information about the logical entities, two new metaobject classes are created, information-class and variable-information-class. Metaobject classes can be "subclassed" as any other class. The first specialized metaobject class (information-class) serves as the class for all dataset-specific classes. It contains a slot, called number-and-location, to store the number of instances that have been created for a given class, and, more specifically, the number of instances in each container. The second specialized metaobject class is the variable-information-class. It is defined as a subclass of information-class and serves as the specialized metaobject class for subclasses of variable-class. This class has a slot called value-list to store the list of values and their frequency for each variable.

```
(defclass information-class (standard-class)
  ((number-and-location :initform (cons 0 nil)
                        :accessor number-and-location))
  (:documentation "metaobject class for dataset-specific classes"))

(defclass variable-information-class (information-class)
  ((value-list :initform nil
               :accessor value-list))
  (:documentation "metaobject class for subclasses of variable-class"))
```

Number of instances of a class When a new instance is created the standard method make-instance allocates an instance and calls initialize-instance to initialize it. Often, standard generic functions are extended by adding before or after methods to the generic function, thereby ensuring that the original functionality is still supported. Here, the behavior of initialize-instance is extended to count the number of instances created for each dataset-specific class and to store this figure with the corresponding metaobject. In addition, the new method assesses the number of instances in each container.

```
(defmethod initialize-instance :after
                     ((instance information-class) andrest)
  (unless (eql (class-name (class-of instance)) 'information-class)
    (let* ((container (container instance))
           (meta-slot (number-and-location (class-of instance)))
           (container-loc (car (member container (cdr meta-slot)
                                       :test #'equal :key car))))
      (incf (car meta-slot))
      (if container-loc
        (incf (cadr container-loc))
        (push (list container 1) (cdr meta-slot))))
    instance))
```

This method is called for the instances of dataset-specific classes and instances of the metaobject class alike. To prevent the latter from being affected by the new behavior, the method excludes them explicitly. Another possibility is to specialize the method to the dataset-specific classes themselves. Alternatively, it is possible to use the make-instance method instead of the initialize-instance method. However, this solution requires that a new primary make-instance method be written specialized to the information-class rather than adding an "after" method because the latter does not have access to the instance that is created. Only the class of the instance is known to the "after" method and hence this method cannot access the container of the instance.

Accumulating values of variable instances The CLOS function (setf slot-value) is a low-level slot-access operation responsible for setting or changing the value of a slot. This function calls the standard generic function (setf slot-value-using-class), which determines the required behavior of the slot. The latter is not yet supported in the current Macintosh Common LISP version (MCL 2.0). The specialized method shown later is based on the description of the standard method (Kiczales et al., 1991, 97). The standard method is modified in such a way that it accumulates the variable's values and updates their relative frequency during the incremental process of filling the content slot of a variable. The results are stored in the corresponding slot of the metaobject. As mentioned earlier, this information cannot be gathered by modifying the make-instance method, because the values of the variables are added to the variables' content slot only *after* the variable has been created. The modified method is specialized to the metaobject class variable-information-class. Since it clearly affects all the slots of classes whose metaobject class is the variable-information-class, the adjustment needs to be explicitly limited to the content slot. The qualifier :after specifies that this method is called after the primary method—that is, the standard method—has run.

```
(defmethod (setf slot-value-using-class) :after
           (new-value (class variable-information-class)
                      instance slot-name)
  (when (eql slot-name 'content)
    (let* ((meta-slot (value-list class))
           (number-of-values (car (number-and-location class)))
           (tail (member new-value meta-slot
                         :test #'equal :key #'car)))
      (if tail (incf (cadar tail) (/ 1 number-of-values))
          (pushnew (list new-value (/ 1 number-of-values)) meta-slot))
      meta-slot)))
```

Instances of the new metaobject classes To ensure the modified behavior for the classes involved, each class has to be defined as an instance of the corresponding metaobject class. The specialized metaobject class of the subclasses of unit-class and substructure-class is the information-class. For subclasses of the abstract class variable-class, it is the variable-information-class. Evidently, the metaobject class of a given class cannot be inherited by subclasses, and the metaobject option has therefore to be explicitly specified for each dataset-specific class. If no specialized metaobject class is defined, then the class is by default an instance of the metaobject class standard-class. The following code shows the class definition of the World Facts subclass of unit-class; container, content, and allowed-content slot are inherited from the unit-class.

```
(defclass country-class (unit-class)
  ((name :initform nil))
  (:metaclass information-class)
  (:documentation "class for World Facts countries"))
```

Once the data of a dataset has been imported into the document, the information about the logical entities collected during the import process is accessible in a uniform way. The country-class can be queried for the number of countries that have been created (they are all in the same container—that is, the document). This is done either by calling the accessor method number-and-location or, directly, by using the slot-value access operation:

```
(number-and-location (find-class 'country-class))
(slot-value (find-class 'country-class) 'number-and-location))
```

With this new information readily available once the data are imported into the application, some of the functionality of CrisView can now be expressed in a simple and general way. To find the most frequent value of a variable, for example, the slot "value-list" of instances of variable-information-class can be accessed, and the value whose relative frequency is highest can be selected. The information collected during the import process also prevents the same figures from having to be computed every time they are needed somewhere in the program.

Two comments on the modifications to the standard behavior of classes, discussed earlier, conclude this section. The first comment concerns the specification of user-defined classes as instances of specialized metaobject classes. As already mentioned, if a class is to be an instance of a specialized metaobject class, this has to be specified when the class is defined. Classes (metaobject classes and metaobjects) are created by using the *defclass macro*. When evaluated, this macro checks whether a specialized metaobject class replaces the default metaobject class standard-class. Since international relations data are usually variable rich, it follows that not only a large number of classes have to be defined (one for each variable) before the dataset can be imported into CrisView, but that, in addition, each class needs to be supplied with the appropriate metaclass information in order to ensure the modified behavior described earlier. To save users from having to specify the appropriate metaobject class for each of their data-specific classes, special defclass macros can be provided (called defclass-unit-class, defclass-substructure-class, and defclass-variable-class). The new macros automatically ensure that the classes they define are instances of the specialized metaobject classes that were introduced previously. This is achieved by changing the options supplied to the original defclass macro to include the appropriate metaobject class option. The preceding definition of the country-class for the World Facts dataset, for example, can be replaced by the following definition, producing the same class object:

```
(defclass-unit-class country-class (unit-class)
  ((name :initform nil))
  (:documentation "class for World Facts countries"))
```

The second comment relates to the modified method (setf slot-value-using-class). This method was used to extend the standard slot behavior in order to store information about the value of the content slot of an instance with the instance's class object. It is possible to delegate this functionality to the make-instance method by changing the import method specialized to the substructure-class so that the value to be stored in the content slot of a variable is available at the time the variable is created. Variables do not contain other logical entities in their content slot and hence their values can be directly added to their content slot. Although this solution does not depend on slot access operations not yet documented in the CLOS metaobject protocol, it implies that the values of variables are added to the content of an instance *before* they can be checked for coding errors. This is a serious disadvantage, because hand-crafted datasets frequently contain coding errors that, if undetected, may distort the results of exploration analyses.

Base Classes for Data Import

Modifications to and extension of the classes involved in the import process resulted in a small set of base classes that can be used as the classes of the first component of the extended protocol. Assuming that the data that are imported into a data exploration system are structured coded data, these classes include the document class and the three extended abstract classes, unit-class, substructure-class, and variable-class. Specialized metaobject classes have been added (that is, information-class and variable-information-class) to store and readily access the information that is requested by many operations in a data exploration system. The import behavior of all these classes has been changed by appropriate changes to the classes' method interfaces. The set of base classes in an extended protocol for data exploration systems typically includes abstract object classes but is not limited to these classes. The document-class is an example. Apart from the windows that are associated with the document-class, and in particular the document-window, the document-class can also be used for data other than structured coded data. Acceleration structures play an important role in various parts of CrisView. Possible modifications to the way in which these structures are defined and constructed are discussed in the next section.

8.1.3 Constructing Acceleration Structures

The purpose of introducing acceleration structures is to ensure fast access among the data structures of an application. As the name suggests, acceleration structures represent links between data structures that would have to be established each time they are needed. The data structures in the acceleration structure may be any data structure in the system, including application-specific data structures such as menus and windows. The acceleration structures discussed in this section focus, however, on the core data of a document. Their common characteristic lies in the fact that they connect logical entities that are on different levels of the data's underlying data model. Acceleration structures can be built, for example, to connect the substructure level to the unit level (if substructures are present) or the variable level to the substructure or unit level. The paths stored in an acceleration structure start from a *search key* and connect it to a *target*. Typically, the search keys are not instances of classes—although this may be desirable for certain tasks—rather, they represent some group or partition. For example, instances of variables can be partitioned into those of the same class or those of the same class and with the same value. The target are those instances in which the search key appears, for example, the units in which a particular variable value combination appears.

Acceleration structures for a document's core data may be quite sophisticated and specialized to a particular dataset. In the current version of CrisView, acceleration structures have been explicitly tailored to the data requirements imposed by the imported datasets. An interesting question concerns the way in which simple acceleration structures can be built up automatically, given the newly added container information for each of the logical entities in a data model. Because acceleration structures are vital for efficient data exploration, it seems appropriate to include their construction as part of the general functionality that is supported by the base classes of an extended protocol.

Acceleration Structures in CrisView

CrisView's current import process involves two methods for constructing acceleration structures. Both methods map through the core data of a document, thereby establishing the paths from each variable value pair to the unit in which they appear. While the first acceleration structure links the variables to the units, the second links the variables to the substructure in which they are contained and these in turn to the units. In both cases, variable value combinations represent the search key. The second acceleration structure is specialized to the SHERFACS dataset, containing a path from a variable value pair to the phase-structure feature vectors in which the pair appears, and from there to the conflict cases. This specific access structure reflects the semantics associated with the phases of a conflict. It is neither generic to datasets nor can it be derived solely from the structure provided by the imported data.

In view of specific requirements concerning the access to logical entities, two groups of acceleration structures can be distinguished. The first group embraces those structures that are automatically built when the data is imported into the application. They are available to users and exploration techniques alike without having to be defined explicitly. Presumably, the acceleration structures of this group are limited in that they can only rely on information that is available when the data are imported into the system. The second group contains more sophisticated types of acceleration structures, which are customized to a particular dataset. Building these structures can be facilitated by defining methods that accept different search keys and targets. The next paragraphs propose definitions for acceleration structures of both groups.

General Acceleration Structures

What can be derived from the CrisView prototype is the need for an acceleration structure that connects variable value pairs with the containers in which they appear. In a flat-structured dataset, the containers of a variable value pair are instances of the dataset-specific subclass of unit-class, while in a complex-structured dataset, they are instances of subclasses of the substructure-class, and, on the unit level, instances of the subclass of unit-class. In the case of a complex-structured dataset, two acceleration structures are needed, one connecting the variables to the units and the other connecting them to their direct container. The search keys in both cases are variable value pairs. Acceleration structures that contain the paths from variables and values to the units in which they appear can be established for any dataset containing structured coded data, regardless of the complexity of the underlying data models.

Before discussing how these general acceleration structures can be built, an abstract class called acceleration-structure-class is added as a base class to the extended protocol. All instances of acceleration structures are defined as instances of subclasses of this class. By representing acceleration structures as objects rather than structured lists, their classes can be inspected by appropriate class browsers (section 8.3).

```
(defclass acceleration-structure-class ()
  ((name :initform nil)
   (document :initarg :document
             :allocation :class)
   (key-target-list :initform nil
                    :accessor key-target-list))
  (:documentation "class of acceleration structures"))
```

The first acceleration structure needed in a data exploration system is a structure that provides fast access from variables to units. The acceleration structure should work for both flat and tree-structured data models alike. The form of this acceleration structure is as follows:

```
acceleration structure: = {search-key}
search-key: = (variable-name #values {value-list} )
value-list: = (value #occurrences unit-list )
unit-list:= (unit1 unit2 unit3 . . . unit n)
```

Defining the necessary base classes for the establishment of such a structure at the time new data are imported into the system involves the following steps. First, a subclass of acceleration-structure-class, called variable-unit-a-s-class, is defined. This subclass is instantiated by the import method of the document-class and the instance is stored in the document (the slot variable-unit-structure of the document-class depicted earlier can be used for this purpose). Second, an additional slot named variable-unit-path is added to the metaobject class variable-information-class. The value of this slot is accessible by an accessor function whose name is identical to the slot name. Third, the method (setf slot-value-using-class) is further extended to provide the required information about variable values and their container on the unit level. Fourth, a new import method qualified as an after method and specialized to the document-class is added to control the construction of the acceleration structure. The following paragraphs elaborate on the third and fourth steps.

Extending the method (setf slot-value-using-class) New code is added to this method in order to store for each variable the paths from its values to the unit in the corresponding metaobject. In addition, the method stores the number of variable value occurrences in each container—that is, in each unit. The function contained-in-unit is used to yield the instance of the subclass of unit-class in which the variable appears.

```
(let* ((meta-slot2 (variable-unit-path class))
       (var-unit-container (contained-in-unit instance))
       (value-loc (car (member new-value meta-slot2
                                :test #'equal :key #'car))))
  (cond (value-loc
         (incf (cadr value-loc))
         (unless (member var-unit-container (cddr value-loc))
           (pushnew var-unit-container (cddr value-loc))))
        (t (push (list new-value 1 (list var-unit-container))
                 meta-slot))))
```

In order to fill the value of the slot key-target-list in the new acceleration structure, the variables that are instantiated during the import process need to be queried for the value of their slot variable-unit-path. There are two methods that "know" what classes of variables are instantiated: the method specialized to the substructure-class that creates the variables (by a call to make-instance) and the import method of the variable-class, more precisely of the subclasses of variable-class.

Both are candidates for querying these classes about the value of the slot in which the paths for the acceleration structure are stored. However, the final path for each variable is only available after all the variables have been imported into the system—that is, after all substructures and units have been imported. It would be possible to write, for example, an import method qualified as an after method and specialized to variable-class that adds the path stored in each variable's class to the acceleration structure. Yet this seems impractical because the method would be called for every variable that is created, each time adding a new version of the path to the acceleration structure until finally the entire path had been established.

A better solution is to write an import method qualified as an after method and specialized to the document-class, which, at the end of the import process, establishes the acceleration structure. Yet, this method needs access to all the variable class-names that have been instantiated in the system. Of course, the document can be queried as to the dataset-specific classes by searching through the units in the collection, their substructures, and, finally, the variables. Alternatively, the class-names of dataset-specific classes can be stored with the document when instances of these classes are created. This can be done either by the import method specialized to the dataset-specific classes or by an extended version of the make-instance method specialized to the metaobject class of each of these classes. New slots are added to the document-class (labeled unit-class-names, substructure-class-names, and variable-class-names) in order to store this information with the document.

Defining an after import method for the document-class For each of the dataset-specific subclasses of variable-class (instances of the metaobject class variable-information-class), the method accesses the value of the slot key-target-list—that is, a list of variable values where each value is associated with the container on the unit level. The name of the class, the length of the path, and the path itself are added to the acceleration structure:

```
(defmethod import :after (ob document-class)
  (let ((var-class-names (slot-value ob 'variable-class-names)))
    (dolist (name var-class-name)
      (let ((path (variable-unit-path name)))
        (push (list name (length path) path)
              (key-target-list
               (slot-value ob 'variable-unit-structure)))))))
```

As mentioned earlier, a second acceleration structure can be provided for complex-structured datasets to connect variables to their direct container. The process of establishing this structure involves the same steps as outlined earlier: a new subclass of acceleration-structure-class is defined, named variable-substructure-a-s-class. It is instantiated by the import method specialized to the document-class, but only if the dataset to be imported contains logical entities on the substructure level. This information is clearly available once the data are imported into the application. However, the additional code that serves to establish the paths from variables to substructures in the method (setf slot-value-using-class) is only executed if an instance of the variable-substructure-a-s-class has actually been created, and this method runs before the entire import process has terminated. As a result, the new acceleration structure needs to be instantiated before the import process is started. A possible solution is to examine the structure of the imported file. If the logical units on the second level correspond to subclasses of substructure-class, the dataset contains tree-structured data models, otherwise its data models are flat. Since the method (setf slot-value-using-class) has access to the document, it can query the document for this information. Similarly, the after import method specialized to the document-class runs only if the acceleration structure has been created.

A final adjustment is made to the subclasses of acceleration-structure-class. In CLOS, the link between classes and their instances is retained only in one direction, namely from instances to their classes. Instances can be queried for their class, but a class does not have access to, and, hence, cannot be queried for, its instances. As mentioned earlier, the reason involves the mechanism of garbage collection. For subclasses of acceleration structures, however, it may be desirable to give the class control over its instances—that is, the individual acceleration structures created for a given document. Storing the instances of a class involves defining a specialized metaobject class and modifying the behavior of the initialize-instance method:

```
(defclass store-instance-class (standard-class)
  ((instances :initform nil
              :accessor instances))
  (:documentation "metaobject class for storing instances of classes"))

(defmethod initialize-instance :after
           ((instance store-instance-class) &key)
  (pushnew instance (instances (class-of instance))))
```

As instances of store-instance-class, the subclasses of the acceleration-structure-class inherit the behavior specialized by the after method that is added to the generic function initialize-instance. The structure of the class variable-unit-a-s-class is as follows:

```
(defclass variable-unit-a-s-class (acceleration-structure-class)
  ()
  (:metaclass store-instance-class)
  (:documentation "class of acceleration structures"))
```

Since the new initialize-instance method will affect all acceleration structures created in CrisView, querying a subclass of the acceleration-structure-class for its instances will return all instances of acceleration structures, not only those that belong to a specific document. This can be avoided either by removing a document's acceleration structures from the corresponding slot of the metaobject when the document is closed or by selecting among all the acceleration structures those that belong to a given document.

Specialized Acceleration Structures

For exploring tree-structured datasets such as SHERFACS, more sophisticated acceleration structures than those already discussed may be needed. However, the structures considered useful or desirable may depend on dataset-specific semantic information and, hence, on explicit instruction as to what information is to be used. Domain-specific considerations such as frequency of tasks have an impact on what the criteria for establishing these structures will be. The following paragraphs discuss possible search keys for specific acceleration structures and propose solutions for gathering the required information.

A first type of acceleration structures focuses on search keys on the substructure level, storing the paths to those instances on the unit level whose container matches a given search criterion. The second type of specialized acceleration structure addresses search keys for building paths from the variable to the unit level with an additional restriction on the instances of the substructure level. The idea is to build on the general acceleration structure available to all tree-structured datasets. This acceleration structure yields partitions of instances on the substructure level, each containing a given variable value pair. The elements of these partitions are subjected to a user-defined criterion, specifying how they are further divided into subpartitions.

Specialized acceleration structures connecting substructures to units It is assumed that the search keys for this type of acceleration structure are composed of the class name of the instances on the substructure level and the criterion provided by the user, specifying the characteristic by which instances are grouped into partitions. Typically, the criterion specifies one of the variables in the content slot of the substructures. For this variable (more precisely, its class), a metaobject class is defined as a subclass of the general metaobject class variable-information-class. This new metaobject class is called substructure-key-class. A new method is added to the generic function (setf slot-value-using-class). This method is specialized to the substructure-key-class, performing a similar function as the other specialized methods of this generic function. Yet rather than establish the path for the variable it is processing, the method builds the path for the variable's container. When the method is invoked, all the information to construct the paths from substructures to units is known: the variable's value (that is, the criterion according to which the substructures are partitioned), the substructure that contains this variable value, and the unit in whose content slot this substructure appears. The method accumulates the substructures that share the same variable value while at the same time keeping track of the units in which these substructures appear.

Because the method is specialized to the metaobject class substructure-key-class, it is called for those variables whose class is an instance of the metaobject class. This means that the specialized behavior can be limited to the variable that the user selected as the criterion for accumulating the substructures. To group them differently, only the definition of the class of the variable that corresponds to the new criterion has to be changed (it must be defined as an instance of substructure-key-class). The final construction of the acceleration method is carried out by the after import method specialized to the document-class. Additional code is added to this method to collect the paths for all the substructures and to add them to the new acceleration structure. This behavior can be conditioned on the existence of the corresponding acceleration structure. The form of the acceleration structures that can be built by incorporating a user-specified criterion is as follows (the partition-specification is one of the values of the variable that is used to partition the substructures):

```
acceleration structure: = {search-key}
search-key: = (substructure-name #partitions {partitions} )
partitions: = (partition-specification #occurrences unit-list )
unit-list:= (unit1 unit2 unit3 . . . unit n)
```

Clearly, the process just described requires that a new subclass of acceleration-structure-class should be defined, that this subclass should be instantiated, and that the new instance should be stored in the document so that it can be used by those operations that need this kind of access to the data. These tasks can be delegated to a modified initialize-instance method. The modified method is specialized to the substructure-key-class and qualified as an after method. When it is called with a variable whose class is an instance of substructure-key-class, it checks whether the acceleration structure already exists and creates, if necessary, a new subclass of acceleration-structure-class as well as an instance of this class. The advantage of delegating these tasks to a specialized method is that the required behavior can be specified where it is most appropriate. Rather than overloading the primary import method of the document-class, the acceleration structure is created by a method that runs when a variable is present whose class is an instance of substructure-key-class—in other words, when the user intends to build the corresponding acceleration structure.

Specialized acceleration structures connecting variables to units The procedure of building these structures differs from the procedures described previously in that it builds upon information that has already been collected for the general acceleration structure in documents containing tree-structured core data. The accumulated substructures for each variable value pair can be further partitioned according to the criterion supplied by the user. To implement this behavior, three steps are performed. First, a new metaobject class variable-substructure-key-class is created as a subclass of the general variable-information-class. The class of the variable that corresponds to the search criterion is defined as an instance of this metaobject class. Second, a new method make-instance is defined, specialized to the variable-substructure-key-class. The method stores the class name of the variable it initializes in the newly created acceleration-structure. Third, a method named built-a-s is defined and specialized to the document-class. Once the import process has terminated, this method is called from within the document's import method. It checks whether new acceleration structures have been built by searching the value of the document's slot specialized-acceleration-structures. Using the general acceleration structure that was defined earlier and the variable (the search criterion) whose values determine the partitioning of the substructures, this method maps through each of the lists of substructures that contain a given variable value pair and replaces each substructure by the value of the search criterion and the unit in which the substructure appears. The value of the search criterion by which a substructure is replaced is the value of the corresponding variable in this particular substructure.

The acceleration structures that can be built have the following form:

```
acceleration structure: = {search-key}
search-key: = (variable-name #values {value-criterion-list} )
value-criterion-list: = (value #occurrences {criterion-unit-list} )
criterion-unit-list:= (criterion (unit1 unit2 unit3 . . . unit n))
```

Like the first type of specialized acceleration structures, the procedure described earlier combines flexibility with generality. The user determines the partitioning of the logical entities on the substructure level simply by making one of the dataset-specific subclasses of variable-class an instance of the specialized metaobject class variable-structure-key-class. Due to the specialized behavior of instances of this metaobject class, the desired acceleration structure is defined, and its content is established without the user having to worry about where to collect the appropriate information. The process, which is the same for all the acceleration structures of this type, is carried out only if an instance of the metaobject class has been defined.

Base Classes for Acceleration Structures

Given the classes and operations specified earlier, two acceleration structures are automatically established when new data are imported. The classes and methods used for constructing these structures can be included in the base component of the extended protocol. They include the abstract class acceleration-structure-class, the subclasses of the two acceleration structures, and the method specialized to the metaobject class variable-information-class. An additional import method has been added to the method interface of the document-class in order to collect the information stored with the metaobjects of the variables and to establish the acceleration structures.

Although dealt with in this section, some of the classes and methods used for building the two types of specialized acceleration structures are not included in the first component of the extended protocol. In order to establish these acceleration structures, the user has to choose the variables that determine the partitioning of the substructures and define their classes as instances of the appropriate metaobject classes. He or she makes this choice when defining the classes that correspond to the logical entities of a new dataset. These definitions, together with the individual acceleration structures they create, are dataset-specific and belong to neither component of the extended protocol. The metaobject classes themselves, however, are part of the first component. Their method interface includes the specialized initialize-instance methods. Similarly, the built-a-s method whose code is executed when specialized acceleration structures have been created is part of the document's method interface and included in the first component of the extended protocol.

8.2 Developing Specialized Classes

The CrisView prototype currently operates on data from two different datasets. One of these is the SHERFACS dataset that uses tree-structured data models to represent its units. Since tree-structured data models subsume most of the other types of data models found in international relations datasets, including the flat data models of World Facts, many of the problems surrounding the management and exploration of data have already been encountered in CrisView. Some of these problems were solved by defining classes that were specialized to the SHERFACS or World Facts data. However, part of the functionality that these classes support is required for representing and exploring other datasets as well. Rather than define from scratch a complete, customized set of classes each time new data are imported or similar data-exploration problems arise, it seems preferable to build a set of building blocks that support special but nevertheless recurrent functionality. These building blocks are included in the second component of an extended protocol. The user can choose from among them to provide for the special requirements of a new dataset or a new analysis technique.

The following sections address only a small subset of the classes and operations that can be included in the second component. Focusing on some of the characteristics found in international relations data, and particularly in the datasets manipulated in Part I, section 8.2.1 proposes classes that facilitate the handling of new data. Intended for data that exhibit particular characteristics, the classes seek to provide appropriate structure and behavior that can be inherited by user-defined classes. They therefore bear some of the burden when the user writes the specifications for representing and managing the logical entities of a dataset.

A second set of classes, discussed in section 8.2.2, focuses on data exploration across different datasets. Part I mentioned some of the benefits of working with different datasets, including the possibility to search for corresponding patterns in datasets that cover different topics, to compare findings from two or more related datasets, and to investigate the impact of different coding categories on analysis results. In CrisView, users can work either simultaneously with two or more documents (each corresponding to one dataset or a subset thereof) or with a single document containing data from different datasets. However, the current prototype does not provide classes that are specifically dedicated to data exploration across datasets. Section 8.2.2 suggests a set of classes that allow the user to represent semantic connections between the logical entities of different datasets and, hence, render feasible subsequent operations such as data comparison across datasets.

8.2.1 Specialized Classes for Representing Data

Some of the characteristics of the SHERFACS and the World Facts dataset required special treatment within the CrisView prototype. The SHERFACS units, for example, contain substructures that are temporally related to each other and, hence, form a sequence. Similarly, some of the variables in SHERFACS and in World Facts have been given a list of values rather than a single value, and in some cases the value list is ordered. This additional information is often relevant for the later processing of the instances of the corresponding object classes or their values, and specific methods have to be defined to ensure the required behavior. Variables that associate their values with additional information, such as the unit of measurement, are a special feature of the World Facts data.

Since other datasets and their logical entities share one or the other of these characteristics, specialized classes and operations can be defined that determine the default behavior of the logical entities concerned. By way of illustration, the following paragraphs propose some specialized classes for representing the characteristics of the logical entities in a dataset.

Relationship Between Instances of a Class

Considering dataset-specific classes and, in particular, the classes defined for representing the logical entities of tree-structured data models, instances of a class may be related to each other in various ways. The relationships between instances (not necessarily of the same class) can be divided into what may be called *syntactic relationships* and *semantic relationships*. The former can be derived from the structure of the phenomenological data and mirrored in the structure of the corresponding classes. Semantic relationships are not depicted in the structure of the data. Rather, they are based on the specific role given to some of the logical entities in a dataset. An example of a semantic relationship in SHERFACS is the "side A," "side B" member relationship between the party-involvement-action feature vectors.

In CrisView, semantic relationships between instances of the same class have been tackled by methods specialized to dataset-specific classes. In order to provide this functionality for other datasets as well, classes have to be defined that account for the specific type of relationship between their instances and methods that determine the behavior of these instances.

Instance-sequence-class A specialized class called sequence-class is defined for instances of a class that form a sequence. The relationship between these instances can be specified by using two slots; a predecessor slot and a successor slot. For each slot an accessor method allows other classes and operations in the system to access the slot values in a uniform way. The definition of the sequence-class reads:

```
(defclass sequence-class ()
  ((predecessor :initform nil
                :accessor predecessor)
   (successor :initform nil
              :accessor successor))
  (:documentation "class sequence-class"))
```

Dataset-specific classes whose instances are ordered are defined as subclasses of the specialized class sequence-class. In SHERFACS, for example, the class phase-structure whose instances in a single unit form a chronological sequence can be defined as a subclass of sequence-class. The values of the predecessor and successor slots are added when a new instance of sequence-class is imported. This process is invoked by an import method specialized to the sequence-class. However, because the predecessor/successor relationship depends on dataset-specific characteristics, an additional method specialized to the subclass of sequence-class is called to accomplish the task. The following methods illustrate how the predecessor and successor slot values are determined for instances of the class phase-structure in SHERFACS:

```
(defmethod import :after ((ob sequence-class))
  (add-predecessor-successor ob))

(defmethod add-predecessor-successor ((ob phase-structure))
  (let* ((case (slot-value ob 'container))
         (phase-structure-fvs (phases case))
         (predecessor
           (find (- (phase-number ob) 1)
                 phase-structure-fvs :key #'phase-number)))
    (when predecessor
      (setf (slot-value ob 'predecessor) predecessor)
      (setf (slot-value predecessor 'successor) ob))))
```

Although the user needs to specify how the predecessor and successor of an instance are to be computed for each dataset-specific subclass of sequence-class, the advantage of using a specialized sequence-class is that subsequent operations on these values can be defined in a dataset-independent way.

Membership-class Another type of relationship between instances of the same class is the subset membership relation whereby two instances belong either to the same subset or to different subsets. An example is the relationship between the SHERFACS party-involvement-actions feature vectors that describe the actions of parties on side A or side B. This relationship is used by exploration techniques such as precedent-based reasoning. Like the sequence-class defined earlier, a specialized class membership-class is defined with a slot called "members." Each instance of the class stores in this slot the instances that belong to the same subset. Operations that need to work though all the instances of a subset can be given ready access to this information from any instance of the subset.

Additional Slot Information

A characteristic of the World Facts dataset is that some of the variables used to describe the properties of countries have been given a value as well as additional information about the value. The World Facts class "total-area," for example, provides a value for the size of a country and the unit of measurement, which is square kilometers. This additional information needs to be stored together with the value of the variable when the variable is represented as an instance of some class. However, the slots of standard-class metaobjects can be bound to one value only. A possible solution is, therefore, to define additional slots in the class of these variables and to store the information about the variable values in these slots. This was done to represent the World Facts data in CrisView. Alternatively, and due to the access to the metaobjects of CLOS, a new metaobject class can be defined whose instances are capable of storing *slot attributes*. Slot attributes are named locations, attached to slots, that can be used to store information about the value in the slot (Kiczales et al., 1991, 84).

It should be mentioned that the version of Macintosh Common LISP (MCL 2.0) that was used to implement the prototype did not support slot attributes. Given the necessary extension to the CLOS language (Kiczales et al., 1991, 83–89), it becomes possible, first, to define a new metaobject class (called slot-attribute-class) for those classes whose instances need to store slot attributes. Slot attribute inheritance and allocation of extra storage in each instance to store the values of the slot attributes are managed by methods specialized to this new metaobject class. Second, a new abstract class variable-attribute-class has to be defined to determine the default structure and behavior of these dataset-specific classes. This new abstract class is needed because the definition of the "content" slot has to be changed to include the option ":attributes." Subclasses of the abstract class variable-class, previously defined, assume this slot to be a standard CLOS slot.

```
(defclass variable-attribute-class ()
  ((content   :initarg :content
              :attributes (content-value content-value-specification))
   (container :initarg :container
              :accessor container))
  (:metaclass slot-attribute-class)
  (:documentation "abstract class variable-attribute-class"))
```

Third, the dataset-specific subclasses that correspond to the variables of a dataset carrying additional information about the variable values have to be defined as subclasses of variable-attribute-class. Finally, access operations for the slot attributes need to be specified in order to store and retrieve the particular attributes of the instances of the dataset-specific subclasses. Since it is desirable to provide a similar interface to the subclasses of both attribute-variable-class and variable-class, access functions for subclasses of attribute-variable-class are defined that have the same name as those used for the subclasses of variable-class. This means that an accessor method, called "content," is defined for accessing the slot attribute "content-value." The value of this attribute corresponds to the value of the "content" slot in the subclasses of variable-class and is used by exploration techniques or operations that need to compute the value of a variable (for example, compare operations). Another accessor method, called "content-specification," is defined for the attribute called "content-value-specification." This method provides the additional functionality required for processing the additional information associated with the variable value, for example, displaying the variable in a window of the user interface or printing it to a file.

Classes for Unstructured Textual Information

Some datasets in international relations contain unstructured textual data in addition to structured coded data. Although not part of the data imported into CrisView, many of the conflicts in SHERFACS are associated with a textual description of the development of the conflict (about 300 words). Similarly, the World Facts dataset provides short textual summaries for specific characteristics of a country (for example, economic overview, description of the flag). The current implementation of CrisView makes it possible to include textual data as the value of the content slot of a variable. However, CrisView does not provide operations that would allow the user to process the values of these variables.

As a first step toward the processing of variables whose values are unstructured textual data, a specialized class variable-text-class can be defined. This class is a subclass of variable-class since it shares the structure and behavior of the abstract class—that is, the container and the content slot—and methods such as import, export, and print. The data are imported into the document in the same way as the "ordinary" variable values (for example, numeric values or codes representing ordinal or nominal variable values). In addition to the method interface inherited from the abstract class, new methods are defined for the special class variable-text-class. These methods may support functionality such as simple key word or arbitrary string search or word counts. The user can add more sophisticated methods to this class such as those developed in the domain of information retrieval (Salton, 1990), or natural language processing (Gazdar and Mellish, 1989).

8.2.2 Specialized Classes for New Data-exploration Tasks

While the specialized classes of the previous section assist the user in dealing effectively with the particular characteristics found in international relations datasets, this section proposes a set of specialized classes for data exploration across different datasets. The reason for focusing on these classes lies in domain-relevant as well as methodological considerations.

Domain-relevant Considerations

The need to analyze phenomenological data across different collections of data has always been a strong reason in favor of developing a data exploration system. However, due to the different semantics associated with the logical entities in the datasets, it is difficult to define general classes and operations suitable for this type of analysis. What is more promising is the development of specialized classes or building blocks that can be customized by the user to meet either his or her analysis needs or specific restrictions imposed by the data. In particular, specialized classes are required to explicitly render the semantic connections between the logical entities of different datasets. Given these connections, it is possible to define operations that allow the user to compare the data from different datasets, to revise and possibly refine further the connections between logical entities, and to gain new information about the phenomena.

As part of a protocol for data exploration systems, these specialized classes offer new ways for users to integrate the data from different datasets. Data integration has been explicitly excluded from the CrisView prototype, the argument being that semantic knowledge is required if the logical entities used in different datasets are to be related. The specialized classes proposed in this section focus precisely on this kind of knowledge, yielding the kind of assistance that can realistically be provided in building, evaluating, and further refining a reference framework for the logical entities in different datasets as well as in the exploration of data across datasets.

Methodological Considerations

The CLOS metaobject protocol offers an elegant option for realizing the kind of functionality that is needed in data analysis across multiple datasets. Several steps are involved:

Definition of semantic connections on the level of object classes The semantic connections between the logical entities of different datasets have to be made explicit. For this purpose the user is offered a set of specialized classes that allow him or her to represent relevant relationships between those classes that correspond to the logical entities of different datasets. To work on the level of classes rather than instances is advantageous in that the user can concentrate fully on the semantics of the logical entities involved, without being distracted by the mass of individual occurrences of these entities. In addition, the classes that carry the information about the relationships between logical entities can easily be investigated, for example, by means of class browsers (see section 8.3). The definition of these classes is provided later. Once the dataset-specific classes have been related to each other, queries concerning the relationships of a class to other classes and classes involved in a particular relationship can be answered. In order to extend these queries to the instances of the classes and, thus, to initiate data analysis across multiple datasets, the specialized classes and their subclasses need control over their instances. This can be achieved by modifying the standard behavior of class metaobjects.

Control over the instances of a class Classes that keep track of their own instances have already been used for the definition of acceleration structures (section 8.1.3). It is even more important here, however, because it is the control over the instances of a class that enables the user to investigate the semantic connections between the data on the instance level. Modified class behavior has two major consequences:

Accumulation of instances The first consequence pertains to the instances that are stored with a class object (that is, the metaobject). As mentioned in section 8.1.2, these instances are not "garbage collected" when a document is closed because the class object contains a pointer to these instances. The classes themselves are not garbage collected in CLOS because they are primary objects and as such they are not affected by the built-in management of dynamic data structures. As a result, all the instances that are created during the time the user is working with his or her documents are accumulated in the corresponding class objects. This is generally considered a disadvantage: rather than benefiting from the automatic garbage collection, the user has to explicitly delete the value of the slot that stores the pointers to these instances. However, when exploring the data across different datasets or subsets thereof, the static nature of CLOS classes turns out to be a very useful characteristic.

Analysis across documents and/or datasets Since the instances of each class are stored with the class object, each class has access to its own instances—if there are any—as well as to the instances of its subclasses. In other words, the abstract classes unit-class, substructure-class, and variable-class have access to the instances in the core data of all the documents that have been activated or created in the course of a working session (that is, until the user leaves the application). If the instances that belong to a particular document are not explicitly deleted when the document is closed, the user can perform dataset analysis across documents and hence across datasets. The disadvantage mentioned earlier, caused by the static nature of the class objects in CLOS, becomes a significant advantage for this kind of analysis because it dispenses with the boundaries between individual documents. Instances are collected for classes not for documents (the classes that are shared by the instances of different documents) and hence the user can compare the instances of different datasets. Such a comparison is particularly interesting for datasets that store the same kind of data, yet employ different coding schemes.

The specialized classes proposed in this section enable the user to relate the logical entities of different datasets. Three types of relationship between pairs of logical entities are supported. They are the relationships most frequently used in the construction of a thesaurus. The first is the *synonym relationship*: logical entities of two different datasets are synonyms if their meaning is the same. For example, the logical entity "primary-party" (a variable in the SHERFACS dataset) may be considered a synonym of the logical entity "political-actor" in some other international relations dataset. The second type of relationship relevant for establishing semantic references between two datasets is the *hyponym relationship*. Two logical entities, A and B, are hyponyms if B is contained in A. For example, a conflict in SHERFACS may be described as a series of single events in some other datasets (typically, in an events dataset such as COPDAB). The third type of relationship is called *related-to relationship* that embraces semantically similar logical entities of two datasets. The GNP of a country collected in one dataset may be related to "economic-power" in another dataset. Clearly, it is the user's responsibility to specify these relationships.

Specialized Classes for Representing the Relationship Between Logical Entities

The classes for representing the three types of relationship between the logical entities of different datasets can be realized in two ways: as explicitly defined relationship classes referencing both classes involved in the relation or as superclasses of each dataset-specific class referencing the related class and specifying the type of relation between the two. The former is called *relationship-class solution*, the latter *mixin-class solution*. Each solution has a distinct advantage with respect to the analysis it can most effectively support.

Relationship-class solution Three specialized relationship classes are defined each of which corresponds to one of the relationships mentioned earlier (synonym, hyponym, or the related-to relationship). These classes serve as superclasses for user-defined relationship classes. Each subclass describes the relationship between two dataset-specific classes. The following code shows one of these specialized relationship classes:

```
(defclass synonym-relationship-class ()
  ((source :initarg :source)
   (target :initarg :target)
   (relationship :initform 'synonym
                 :allocation :class))
  (:documentation "abstract class for synonym relationships"))
```

Mixin-class solution The mixin-class solution involves defining a specialized class target-relationship-class that enables the user to specify for each dataset-specific class its relationship to the class or classes of a second dataset. The class-relationship-class is called a mixin-class because it is an abstract class that serves as a superclass for several other classes. Subclasses of this class are direct superclasses of the dataset-specific classes. Consequently, each dataset-specific class has two superclasses: an abstract class (unit-class, substructure-class, or variable-class) and a subclass of class-relationship-class representing the relationship between this dataset-specific class and the class corresponding to the logical entity of another dataset.

```
(defclass class-relationship-class ()
  ((target :initform nil
           :accessor target)
   (relationship :initform nil))
  (:documentation "mixin-class for all dataset-specific subclasses"))
```

The subclasses of the relationship-class and the subclasses of the mixin-class represent the semantic connections between the logical entities that have been used to describe the phenomena collected in different datasets. The reference framework established by these subclasses provides the necessary condition for carrying out data analysis across datasets. However, to connect the related classes to their instances and, hence, to assist the user in investigating and analyzing the differences and similarities between different datasets, access is needed from each dataset-specific classes to its instances. As in section 8.1.3, this new functionality is achieved by defining a metaobject class store-instance-class and a method initialize-instance that ensures that each of the instances of the metaobject class automatically stores its own instances.

Operations on Specialized Classes

The relationship-class solution and the mixin-class solution each support a different access to the semantic connections between the logical entities of datasets. While the former focuses on the relationship between the logical entities (their classes), the latter focuses on the classes involved in a relationship. Consequently, each solution promotes a different type of data analysis on the instances that are related by these classes. The relationship-class solution fosters operations that, for a particular type of relation, manipulate all the classes that are related to each other in this way. The mixin-class solution, on the other hand, suggests operations that, for a given class, examine the relationships between this class and the classes belonging to another dataset. Both solutions are necessary to cover and support the range of queries likely to be relevant. If only the relationship-class solution is supported, queries about the relationship of a particular class would be dealt with very inefficiently. They would require a search through all the relationship classes in order to find the relations in which the particular class is involved. Similarly, if the aim is to apply a particular operation to all the classes for which a given relation holds, the mixin-class solution is not appropriate. All the dataset-specific classes would have to be searched in order to find those for which a particular relationship holds.

Depending on the type of relationship between logical entities, different types of operations are meaningful for the relationship-class solution as well as the mixin-class solution. Clearly, the synonym relationship is the least problematic. Instances whose classes are synonyms can be subjected to the different exploration techniques supported in CrisView, and the results can easily be compared across documents or datasets. There are fewer operations suitable for exploiting hyponym relationships. Operations can be defined that seek to balance the level of specialization/generalization between the datasets. Instances of one dataset can be compared with the more specific instances in another dataset by condensing the information provided by the more specific instances. Alternatively, generalized information can be replaced by more specific information each time a hyponym relationship is encountered. Due to the unspecified nature of the relationship, the third type of relationship is the most difficult with regard to the definition of appropriate operations. It is always possible, however, simply to browse through and inspect the related data in each of the documents. More sophisticated operations may depend on the particular characteristics of the dataset involved.

8.3 Developing Introspective Classes

Part I introduced various operations to browse the core data of a document. Associated with the panels of the windows of the user interface, these operations create different views of the data by manipulating the logical entities and their values at every level of aggregation. They allow the user both to examine individually each logical entity of a dataset and to quickly have an overall view of the data (for example, size, frequency of values, distribution of values). These operations are called "data browsers" because their targets are the phenomenological data in a document. In contrast to these data browsers, the classes included in the third component of a protocol for data exploration systems focus on the application itself. These classes are called introspective classes or *class browsers* because they let the application inspect its own classes, generic functions, and methods.

The basis for defining class browsers is provided by the CLOS metaobject protocol. Kiczales and his colleagues discuss several access functions to metaobjects and the information associated with them (Kiczales et al., 1991, 47–70). Based on these access functions, class browsers can be written to query a class about its subclasses, its superclasses, its direct slots and the slots inherited from superior classes, and the methods specialized to the class. Generic functions can be browsed to find their methods and the number of required arguments. Finally, the methods can be queried about the classes they have been specialized to (their specializers), their qualifiers, and the generic function to which they belong.

With access to the CLOS metaobjects, a variety of class browsers can be built. However, it seems appropriate to place the definition of browsers in the context in which they are used. In particular, the browsing facilities need to be user-oriented, that is, related to the needs of the user who is working with an application. In CrisView, two types of users can be distinguished: those who work with the prototype without modifying or extending it and those who add new classes and new functionality or even build new versions of the prototype. The following sections consider the needs of the different users with respect to the introspective access to the application.

8.3.1 Introspective Access for End Users

Since CrisView is dedicated to the exploration of international relations data and data from related domains, the first type of potential users are domain experts. Rather than modify the CrisView prototype, these "end users" work with the current version of the prototype and the documents already available. To them, the classes, generic functions, and methods of the application are usually of little interest. Help facilities and, possibly, means to record their own exploration activities are more relevant.

Help Facilities

Most of the user interface in CrisView is self-explanatory: the names of buttons and menu items, as well as the titles of dialogs, indicate the kind of functionality these objects are associated with. Where this is not the case, the Macintosh *balloon helps* can be used to explain the operations and commands that are available to the user. Advocated by Macintosh user guidelines and supported by a high-level programming interface in MCL, the balloon help facility provides the possibility to associate help texts with individual windows, views, and controls. The effort to include this help facility in CrisView is only minor.

Recording User Activities

End users may wish to have a facility for reviewing and reexamining their previous exploration activities. Depending on the kind of activities they perform, different facilities are appropriate. In the case of a system embodying, for example, a densely linked data network whose exploration requires the user to navigate extensively through the different data items, a browsing tool that creates a *history tree* is most useful. A history tree records the steps a user has taken while exploring the data. The nodes along each path of the tree correspond to the actions that have been invoked. A history tree gradually evolves, because the user may go back to any previous node and embark from there on a different course of action.

To establish such a tree, the system has to store each stage before it is altered. CrisView does not fulfill this requirement. In particular, when new data are imported, the previous stage of the system is lost and cannot be restored (unless the user has been working with a document that has been saved earlier and, hence, can be activated again). Similarly, deleting operations such as deleting filters, subsets, and variables changes the status of a system without retaining a copy of the previous status. Nevertheless, CrisView incorporates the necessary mechanism for recording the relevant activities that surround the exploration of data. Exploration analyses, such as induction and precedent-based reasoning remain available while the user is working with the system. In the current version of CrisView, the windows the contents of which show the result of these analyses can be inspected by choosing the appropriate menu items from the induction and precedent menus. The results of inquiry methods are accumulated and can be reviewed by opening the windows of the inquiry dialogs. User activities such as the creation of filters, subsets, or new variables, which result in new views on the data, are stored as instances of the corresponding classes. In other words, the elements constituting the history of a user's exploration activities are available, albeit not in the form of a chronologically ordered sequence.

The sequence of activities carried out by a user can be recorded by changing the standard behavior of those window classes whose instances are associated with relevant exploration activities such as induction, precedent-based reasoning, comparison, and inquiries. Like the definition of class metaobjects, new method metaobjects can be created whose instances store a reference to the window they are operating upon and a time stamp in a variable called history. This variable, which is updated each time an exploration window is created or reopened, can be queried by the user, yielding a chronological list of the user's activities. By choosing an item on this list, the user can inspect the corresponding window and reexamine its contents. An additional modification is required if the activities surrounding the creation of filters, subsets, or new variables need to be recorded. The current CrisView version deletes the content of the corresponding windows after the user issues a save command. In order to retain not only the newly created instances (of filters, subsets, or variables) but also the corresponding windows, the save command, or more precisely the methods that implement the required behavior, can be extended. These extensions include saving the window and storing its reference in the history variable mentioned earlier. This facility is less sophisticated than the browsing tool that creates an exploration tree because it does not support the exploration of different paths from any previous stage. However, it allows the user to review the sequence of his or her actions and to reexamine each step.

8.3.2 Introspective Access for Specific User Groups

While end users basically work with the version of the CrisView prototype described in Part I and with documents that have been previously created, a second group of CrisView users actively engage in extending the prototype. Probably one of the most relevant extensions from a domain-oriented point of view is enlarging the system's data handling capacity. This task includes the definition of dataset-specific classes for the import of new data. It requires only limited introspective access to the classes of an application, namely access to the classes and operations affected by or affecting the import of new data. Other users of this second group may equally want to work on specific classes of the system and, hence, could benefit from a selective introspective access to the classes in question. This suggests to build browsers that are tailored to the needs of a specific user group by having them operate on selected parts of the systems.

Defining Semantic Aggregations

For the purpose of building browsers that provide a selective access to those classes that are relevant to a particular user group, user-defined classes and their method interface are associated with one or several *semantic aggregations.* A semantic aggregation is a subset of classes each related to the same aspect of an application. The choice of semantic aggregations as well as the membership of a class to a particular aggregation are left to the user. Since a single class may be a member of more than one aggregation, the resulting partitions overlap. Examples of possible semantic aggregations in CrisView are the aggregation "dataset," which spans all dataset-specific classes, their superclasses, and specialized metaobject classes; the aggregation "document," which embraces the classes of the core data and the supplementary data; and the aggregation "exploration techniques" that contains all the classes and operations involved in the exploration of phenomenological data. The advantage of these semantic aggregations is twofold. First, the membership information of each class can be exploited by class browsers. Depending on the requirements of a user group, the browsers can select the members of a particular semantic aggregation and limit the introspective access to the selected classes. Second, the partitions that are formed can be viewed as a high-level descriptive organization of classes. A user who is working with CrisView can examine this organization and achieve a good understanding of the classes that have been used.

Semantic aggregations can be implemented in several ways. First, the information about the membership of a class in a semantic aggregation can be stored in a global association list. Each entry consists of the name of the semantic aggregation and the list of its classes. Second, the information may be stored locally with each class. Metaobject classes can be defined for the classes, each with an additional slot to store the list of aggregations to which its instances belong. Although less elegant, the global approach can be justified by arguing that the task of establishing the network of relations between the classes and operations of the application and the semantic aggregations requires a global rather than a local perspective. For both approaches, different mechanisms can be used either to add the classes to the global list or to bind the corresponding slot values of the metaobjects. A solution here is to modify the "defclass," "defgeneric," and "defmethod" macros and to provide the information about the membership of each class as an argument to these macros.

Browsers Specialized to the Windows of the User Interface
Another type of semantic aggregation takes the windows of the user interface as the basis for selecting subsets of classes used in the system. The membership relation of the classes here may be defined as "accessed by." It refers to the subset of classes and operations that are used within and called from a window. Based on these subsets, class browsers can be defined that adapt to the context in which they are invoked: the individual window. These class browsers can be restricted further to cover only the operations that directly support the exploration technique associated with the window. For example, the browser invoked in the filter window would embrace the operations that serve to define Boolean combinations of variables and values and to apply and save the filter. It would also include the operations that allow the user to select the variables, specify the time intervals, and chose the chronological periods. Alternatively, the browsers may provide a more comprehensive coverage of elements, including all the elements that take a share in the window's functionality. In addition to the previously listed operations, these browsers include access operations for the units in the document's core data, access operations for the logical entities in each unit, operations for decoding variable values, and so on. In both cases, the selection is determined by the classes collected into the semantic aggregation.

Some programming environments offer similar functionality by providing cross-reference functions such as "caller" and "who-calls," listing the names of methods that a particular method calls or is called from, respectively. They also incorporate search functions such as "edit-definition" that enable the user to find the source code of a particular method. Macintosh Common LISP 3.0 is an example of a programming environment in which these functions are supported.

8.4 Generalizing the User Interface

As mentioned in section 8.1, many of the operations currently defined in CrisView and supported by the windows of the user interface assume that the data they process is structured into several types of logical entities. This is true for the operations that manipulate the objects that correspond to the logical entities of a dataset, the acceleration structures that are themselves a result of dealing with structured data, and the windows of the user interface that contain specific panels that display the different types of logical entities and support the operations that allow the user to browse and analyze these entities. Although the treatment of other than structured coded data is beyond the scope of this study, the following paragraphs introduce briefly a concept for generalizing the user interface in data exploration systems. The idea behind this concept is to provide different sets of windows and to make the selection of a particular set conditional on the type of data the user chooses to explore.

The Need for Diversified Windows

In CrisView, the only access to the core data of a document and hence to the domain-specific data is by means of the document-window. When a CrisView document is created, it is automatically associated with an instance of the document-window-class, and it is this instance that is presented to the user when he or she chooses to examine the core data of a document. All document-windows are instances of the same class. They have the same window panels and support the same kind of operations. The use of structurally and functionally identical document-windows in CrisView is justified because the data to be imported is supposed to be structured into units and variables and possibly substructures. However, if the restrictions on the data are released, the document-window as well as the other, equally customized, windows of the user interface are no longer appropriate.

By contrast, the definition of the document-class and the mechanism for importing the data are more general. This suggests that the potential of CrisView for the exploration of other types of data should be investigated. The examination of the classes affected by the import of data (section 8.1) has shown that new data can be stored in the slot unit-collection of a document regardless of their structure or content. The datasets that provide the data need only comply with CrisView's import/export format—that is, an arbitrarily structured list. This format is general enough to represent datasets that contain, for example, unstructured texts or pictures. However, to make the data of such datasets, or more precisely, the core data of the corresponding documents, available to the user, new windows are required. In particular, new document-window-classes are needed to associate the document with a window that is capable of accommodating the kind of data contained in the document and of supporting the operations to explore them.

Selection of an Appropriate User Interface

If the document-window—together with the other windows of the user interface—has to adapt to the data contained in a document, the appropriate window-class can be instantiated only *after* the user has chosen the data he or she wishes to explore. This requires a modification to the data import process in CrisView. In the current version, a document is associated with an instance of the document-window-class at the time it is created and hence before the user can choose the dataset from which the data are imported. There is only one document-window-class in CrisView. It determines the structure of each individual document-window, featuring all the panels and controls appropriate to the exploration of structured coded data. In the modified version of this process, the document-window is selected among different types of document-windows. The choice of the appropriate window depends on the data that are imported. For this purpose, new sets of windows are defined, consisting of a document-window and several windows for explorative data analysis. Each set constitutes a new user interface that is adapted to the requirements of the data that may be imported.

With new sets of window-classes available, the modified version of the import process involves the following steps. The user creates a new document by issuing the "new" command. Rather than an instance of the document-window-class whose structure and behavior suits structured coded data, an empty window is presented to the user. This empty window contains no panels and no controls. Next, the user selects the dataset whose data he or she wishes to import. Before the import process is started, the system selects from the document-window-classes the class that is specialized to the type of data the user has selected. The selection of an appropriate document-window-class can be based, for example, upon information provided by the file from which the data is imported. Once a document-window-class is selected and instantiated, the document is associated with the newly created instance. The data are imported into the system, and, depending on the structure and behavior of the document-window, some views of the data are displayed. The document-window controls the remaining windows that belong to the same set of windows and, hence, ensures that the user can work in an environment that is suitable for exploring the particular type of data.

Chapter 9
EVALUATION

Three related areas that have not received much attention in the sector of international relations research that is oriented toward formal modeling are (1) developing computational systems that allow domain experts to experiment with various techniques for analyzing phenomenological data; (2) providing systems that operate on multiple datasets and that, therefore, are capable of managing the different data models imposed by competing data collection traditions; and (3) investigating new techniques from computer science for their impact on solving domain-specific problems. The first and second areas are important because the amount of data on political events is steadily growing and so is the need of researchers in the field for systems and techniques that help systematically analyze these data. The third area is relevant to computer science because it exploits modern software engineering and programming techniques from an application-oriented perspective. Applying these techniques to specific problems helps to identify their strengths and weaknesses and to evaluate their potential for a given domain or research topic. It furthermore elucidates their influence on the kind of problem solving that can be undertaken. Focusing particularly on the third area, this study used object-oriented programming techniques for solving the domain-specific problems that surround the exploration of structured coded data.

While Part I presented an operational prototype, Part II further investigated the possibilities of object-oriented programming techniques for data exploration and, in particular, metaobject programming techniques of advanced object-oriented languages such as CLOS. Since no data exploration system can possibly satisfy all present or future needs of its users, it is desirable to let the user participate in the process of further developing and modifying a system. For this purpose, Part II proposed several classes and operations that provide the kind of functionality that enables the experienced user to extend the prototype and to customize a data exploration system to his or her analysis needs. Divided into three groups, these classes embrace general functionality that accounts for the basic behavior of any data exploration system (base classes), specialized functionality for tuning a system or parts thereof to the particular characteristics of the data to be explored, or for specifying analysis requirements (specialized classes), and introspective functionality for inspecting the elements of a data exploration system (introspective classes). Two reasons made the definition of the three groups of classes attractive. First, the definition of these classes can be seen as a step toward the development of a dedicated application framework for data exploration systems because it provides an operational specification for some of the key ingredients of an application framework. Second, the definition of these classes provided an excellent opportunity to examine the potential of metaobject programming. While not always necessary or even appropriate, the possibility to change the default behavior of the implementation language adds new alternatives to the problem-solving process and in some cases offers elegant solutions for implementing the desired functionality.

9.1 EVALUATION OF CRISVIEW

The CrisView system developed in Part I and extended in Part II is presented here as a prototype system that assists international relations analysts and political science scholars in exploring domain-specific data. Some of the major features will be summarized from the perspective of the user.

Employing Modern Software Engineering Techniques

There is no reason why a discipline such as international relations—and more specifically, the computational branch of international relations—should not benefit from the achievements of modern software engineering techniques. The CrisView prototype and its extensions are an attempt to bring modern techniques to bear on the design and the implementation of such interdisciplinary projects.

Easy access to data Researchers who want to make use of the carefully collected data in large datasets should have easy access to the data of the domain without having to deal with data structures, representation, and storage. The document concept that was realized in CrisView together with the object-oriented representation of the data has rendered this goal feasible.

Convenient user interface Another concern for the user is the way in that exploratory activities are supported. CrisView embodies many of the concepts underlying graphics-oriented, event-driven user interfaces; users can easily find their way through different sections of the data and switch freely back and forth between different analysis mechanisms without losing the place or getting stuck in a dead-end sequence of procedures.

Managing Data that is Complex in Structure

Almost all existing political research has concentrated on simple data structures, usually the rectangular case/variable data array. Regardless of whether or not the traditional use of statistical methods and the convenience of statistical packages such as SAS and SPSS have influenced the way in which many of the existing datasets are organized, datasets that exhibit more complex data structures have yet to receive adequate analytical processing despite their greater potential for substantive research.

CrisView's import/export operations and internal data representation are general enough to handle datasets whose data structure exceeds the traditional rectangular case-variable data array. Special relationships among logical entities can be readily explored and expressed by making use of the building blocks developed in Part II. The availability of data management facilities for data that is complex in structure may encourage data collectors to produce datasets that are richer in texture and hence closer to the phenomena that they aim to describe.

Operating on New Datasets

New datasets can be incorporated into the CrisView system with relatively little effort, allowing international relations scholars to extend their analysis and to compare results across different datasets. Most datasets in international relations are less complex in structure than, for example, the SHERFACS dataset and, hence, CrisView provides the basic mechanism for handling them. For example, Bercovitch's conflict management dataset, CONFMAN1 (Bercovitch, 1993) has recently been added to CrisView. The necessary tasks for this project included the definition of CONFMAN1-specific classes. Since the new classes can be defined as subclasses of already existing classes, many operations that are needed in order to work with the new data were already in place and were passed on to the new classes. In some instances, the method interface of the newly created classes had to be extended. New methods could be added locally without changing the methods already in operation.

Working with Different Analysis Techniques

Many researchers express skepticism regarding the use of structured coded data not only because such data give only a limited account of the real phenomena (Alker, 1975) but also because they can have low signal-to-noise ratio (Howell, 1983; Vincent 1983). Although they are aware of these problems, others believe that these data are still sufficiently close to the real phenomena that they describe to be used for theoretical and methodological development (Schrodt, 1991, 189). Rather than abandoning the use of such data altogether, these scholars suggest that more attention be paid to the special nature of the data by tuning the methods accordingly and by experimenting with new ways of extracting information from the available datasets (McClelland, 1983; King, 1989; Schrodt, 1991).

The CrisView system marks a step in this direction in that it provides two machine learning techniques and, in addition, allows the user to implement new techniques:

Employing machine learning techniques In addition to browsing, filtering, and comparing operations, CrisView's users can analyze their data with two powerful techniques from machine learning: induction and case-based reasoning. The implementations of these techniques are generally not applicable to data models that differ from the rectangular case/variable data array format, and hence their use for the analysis of international relations data is restricted. By extending the techniques to handle complex-structured data models, instead of forcing the data into the required format, CrisView makes these techniques available without losing potentially relevant information. As illustrated by Schrodt (1984a, 1987a, 1987b, 1989), other techniques from artificial intelligence and machine learning have great potential for the analysis of large datasets, though many of them must be modified in order to be applied to data that is complex in structure.

Extending the set of analysis techniques The observation that the results of some analyses are affected by the method used is neither novel nor unique to the domain of international relations. However, it underlines the importance of evaluating carefully and choosing selectively the methods that are to be applied to the data. Given the context of data exploration systems, users need to be able to experiment with a variety of different methods in order to choose those most suitable for the analysis of the data at hand. This is exactly what CrisView offers: it enables the user not only to experiment with the methods and techniques that are currently implemented in the prototype but also to add and test new ones in an incremental and modular fashion. Incremental and modular refinement and/or extension of functionality is one of the main characteristics of a well-designed object-oriented system and was an objective that guided the entire development cycle of CrisView. Although the CrisView prototype does not have the analysis capability desirable of a full-fledged data exploration system, its design enables users to add new techniques and methods and thus helps advance the methodological development deemed necessary in a domain such as international relations.

This last remarks leads us into the question of what CrisView offers international relations scholars apart from computational assistance. Indeed, easy access to different collections of domain-specific data together with the ready availability of techniques—including non-traditional ones—to explore them may be taken for granted by many, though it is more than most systems provide today.

CrisView's Role in the Field of International Relations Research

The major part of this study concentrated on software engineering and methodological aspects of data exploration for the purpose of developing a system that allows researchers to make better use of large bodies of carefully collected data. This objective may seem modest and unspectacular compared with what other systems and models in current artificial intelligence and international relations research aim to achieve (Hudson, 1991). Indeed, CrisView does not claim to replace domain expertise, simulate human performance, or model, for example, decision-making processes. Rather, it provides a basis for experts in the field of international relations to apply their knowledge and experience. Such a basis is needed if past and present data-collection efforts in international relations are still to be justified. Particularly when faced with the problems that surround the collections of structured coded data, including the bias of sources and the accompanied distortion effects that may lead to serious differences between datasets (Howell, 1983; Vincent, 1983), random as well as systematic coding errors, and the limitations inherent in the use of predefined coding categories for representing complex phenomena, researchers are well advised to spend some time evaluating the nature of the data and becoming aware of both the assumptions underlying the coding scheme and their own expectations about the data.

CrisView's role in the field of international relations research can thus be characterized as follows:

As a support tool it enables the user to examine the data across time, region, or parties involved, to uncover repeated patterns and regularities in a dataset, and to find similar instances of the phenomenon. The mechanisms and techniques that provide such findings have been described in Part I, section 3.4, and in Chapter 4.

As a basis for improving research based on structured coded data it enables the user to carry out preparatory studies for investigating, for example, the extent and interaction of variables, so that he or she can select those that are most useful for some analysis or to locate (by filtering, inductive generalization, comparing, or using statistical measurements) interesting constellations in the data that may warrant further analysis. As mentioned earlier, CrisView purports methodological considerations by letting the user experiment with different analysis techniques for the purpose of assessing their usefulness in the light of domain-specific data. Furthermore, CrisView encourages better data-collection efforts by, on the one hand, increasing the awareness of how different coding schemes affect the analyses of the phenomena and, on the other, by providing powerful data-management facilities that may influence and improve the way in which the data are collected.

9.2 The Use of Metaobject Programming

The most appropriate way of evaluating the impact of metaobject programming is from a software development perspective. Indeed, from the perspective of an end user, it makes no difference whether or not metaobject programming techniques were used, as long as a system provides the functionality he or she deems necessary. Users who wish to extend and modify the prototype with the help of the classes developed in Part II (Chapter 8) come into closer contact with the new techniques. Although the distinction between these users and a software engineer is somewhat blurred since the former need to have some knowledge about object-oriented programming and the metaobject protocol approach, the users' primary interests are the classes and operations that have been defined rather than the software engineering and development aspects that have been involved. These aspects, however, are crucial in assessing the relevance of metaobject programming and in evaluating critically the benefit it offers over the use of "conventional" object-oriented programming techniques.

Based on the experience gained from developing the classes in Part II, the following summary highlights some of the advantages and drawbacks of metaobject programming for developing and further extending an object-oriented application. It points out the kinds of problems or tasks that were addressed most successfully by metaobject programming techniques, and, on the other hand, it indicates some of the more problematic aspects surrounding the metaobject protocol approach.

Advantages

Adjusting the behavior of single classes and their instances One of the main characteristics of object-oriented programming is that for each class a specialized behavior can be defined. Metaobject programming further extends this capability to include not only the user-defined objects but also the metaobjects of the language. User-defined classes can be defined as instances of specialized metaobjects classes, thereby inheriting a behavior that deviates from the default behavior of standard CLOS classes. This additional capability can be best used in an application such as CrisView, where each logical entity imported from a dataset is defined as an instance of some class. Tasks that require that some logical entity should deviate from its standard behavior can be handled very elegantly and without affecting the behavior of other entities. An example is the construction of acceleration structure, especially those structures whose content depends on the choice of a specific variable—that is, the search criterion (section 8.1.3, specialized acceleration structures). By defining a new metaobject class for the class of such a variable and modifying its standard behavior, additional operations could be conditioned to the import of the instance of this class. These operations are not carried out for all other variables whose classes are not instances of the specialized metaobject class. Metaobject programming also allowed for adjusting the structure and behavior of specialized classes (building blocks) to the particularities found in the datasets of a domain (for example, variable values with additional attributes, section 8.2.1).

Adding new functionality Access to the standard generic functions and methods in CLOS makes it possible to associate additional functionality with these functions and methods. Most important are the generic functions operating on class metaobjects (for example, make-instance) and slot access functions (for example, setf slot-value-using-class). These functions can be modified for individual classes in order to yield additional information when these classes are processed. Counting the instances of a class and accumulating their values (section 8.1.2) as well as monitoring the access to specific exploration techniques (section 8.3.1) are examples of such modifications. In addition, metaobject programming can be used to give a class control over its instances. While storing instances with a class—that is, a metaobject—is not without its problems (as mentioned later), this capability proved to be extremely useful for the exploration of data across datasets (section 8.2.2).

Introspection What is indispensable is the access to the metaobjects of a language for the definition of class browsers (section 8.3). The access functions documented in the CLOS metaobject protocol yield information about the classes, generic functions, and methods of an application and, hence, provide the introspective access that is needed not only to navigate through the application but also to extract the information necessary in making modifications and extensions.

Drawbacks

Overriding of standard characteristics There is a danger that the flexibility provided by the access to the metaobjects of a language is used in such a way that some of its positive characteristics are lost. Since standard generic functions and methods can be overridden, it is the responsibility of the software engineer to ensure that the rest of the system—including all implementation and user-defined classes—remains unaffected. When necessary, explicit care has to be taken of undesired side effects. Side effects occur, for example, when metaobject programming techniques are used to store the instances with a class object. While this possibility offers new and often very attractive alternatives for solving a given problem, a coupling of classes and instances has some serious implications for garbage collection in a language such as CLOS, which distinguishes between classes and instances. Classes are primary objects and, hence, are not affected by the built-in management of dynamic data structures. Consequently, the instances that are stored in a class are not garbage collected until the pointer to these instances is explicitly removed. Moreover, if, as in CrisView, the same classes are used to represent the data from different datasets, instances that belong to different documents may be stored in the same class. Regardless of whether several documents are explored at the same time or sequentially, the instances of the corresponding classes are accumulated in their class metaobjects. This accumulation is precisely what is needed for exploring the data across different documents and datasets as discussed in section 8.2.2, but in general it is not desirable. The possibility of coupling the instances with their classes has to be exploited very carefully in order to avoid confusion, strain on memory, and errors or faulty results.

Complexity Object-oriented programming is an activity with many degrees of freedom. As mentioned previously, there are no clear guidelines as to how to proceed, and there is hardly ever one single solution to a given problem. The advent of metaobject protocols adds a new dimension to the development of object-oriented applications. The access to the elements of the language, and the possibilities available for modifying and adjusting them to the specific requirements of an application, extend the system engineer's scope of action to the so-called metaobject level—that is, the level of the elements of the programming language. Not surprisingly, the metaobject protocol also adds a level of complexity to the development of object-oriented applications. The use of metaobjects programming techniques often results in a tight coupling between the elements of an application, making it more difficult for the user and the software engineer to understand the system and its processes. A case in point is the connection between instances and classes that was mentioned earlier. Furthermore, the increase in structural and functional heterogeneity emerging from the use of specialized metaobjects for changing the default behavior of classes, generic functions, and methods seriously challenges the user or software engineer. Considerable knowledge is required to validate the performance of the system or to modify and extend its components. Comparisons can be drawn between the use of metaobject programming techniques and the use of semantic networks in the domain of databases. The idea of closely mapping the semantic relations that are found in the real world is a very intriguing one. However, experience with semantic networks showed that it became extremely difficult to understand the semantics of such a network and to define appropriate operations to proceed its data. Similar difficulties surround the use of metaobject programming techniques. A considerable amount of conceptual planning is required and a moderate use of these techniques is probably advisable.

Bearing in mind the drawbacks of metaobject programming such as the potential loss of desirable characteristics of the language and increased complexity it is clear that the benefits of these techniques for data exploration are undeniable. One important characteristic of the tasks that were addressed with metaobject programming techniques was that they were highly focused on the primary objective of the application: the exploration of structured coded data. This focus is essential because the metaobject programming techniques offer elegant solutions whenever minute adjustments have to be made; such adjustments are typical of the task of adapting a data exploration system to new kinds of data. Indeed, many tasks consist in making small changes to the standard behavior of individual classes without affecting other classes in the system.

One factor turned out to be of utmost importance for the effective use of metaobject programming techniques: the fully object-oriented implementation of the base prototype. The fact that each logical entity imported into the prototype was defined as an instance of some class meant that the extended protocol could rely on the standard functionality—including access to "meta-information"—provided by the class. Although the creation and maintenance of large numbers of objects is costly, the advantages gained justify the expense. Had only some of the logical entities of a dataset been defined as instances of classes, the metaobject programming techniques could not have been fully exploited. Evidently, the moderately sized datasets in the domain of international relations favor such a fully object-oriented representation.

Clearly, metaobject programming is not a panacea for the development or extension of object-oriented applications, even if the term *meta* is bound to raise euphoric expectations. However, it is not useless either: it offers the software engineer new and elegant solutions to the problem of addressing highly specialized tasks in carefully conceptualized applications.

REFERENCES

[Adler, 1989]
E. Adler, "Cognitive Evolution: A Dynamic Approach for the Study of International Relations and Their Progress," Working Paper No. 89–4, Center for Science and Int'l Affairs, John F. Kennedy School of Govt., Harvard Univ., 1989.

[Alker, 1969]
H.R. Alker, Jr., "Statistics and Politics: The Need for Causal Data Analysis," in *Politics and the Social Science*, S.M. Lipset, ed., Oxford Univ. Press, New York, 1969, pp. 244–313.

[Alker, 1975]
H.R. Alker, Jr., "Polimetrics: Its Descriptive Foundations," in *Handbook of Political Science*, Polsby and Greenstein, eds., Addison-Wesley, Reading, Mass., 1975, pp. 139–210.

[Alker, 1985a]
H.R. Alker, Jr., "International Disputes Data: A Comparison of Approaches and Products, with Some Recommendations for the Future," *Int'l Studies Quarterly Notes*, Vol. 12, No. 1, 1985.

[Alker, 1985b]
H.R. Alker, Jr., "Global Modeling Alternatives: The First Twenty Years," in *Theories, Models, and Simulations in International Relations*, M.D. Ward, ed., Essays in Honor of Harold Guetzkow, Westview Press, Boulder, 1985.

[Alker and Christensen, 1972]
H.R. Alker, Jr., and C. Christensen, "From Causal Modeling to Artificial Intelligence: The Evolution of a UN Peace-Making Simulation," in *Experimentation and Simulation in Political Science*, J.A. Laponce and P. Smoker, eds., Univ. of Toronto Press, Toronto, 1972.

[Alker and Greenberg, 1971, 1977]
H.R. Alker, Jr., and W.J. Greenberg, "On Simulating Collective Security Regime Alternatives," in *Thought and Action in Foreign Policy*, G.M. Bonham and M.L. Shapiro, eds., Birkhaeuser Verlag, Basel, 1977; reprinted from *The United Nations: Problems and Prospects*, E.H. Feder, ed., St. Louis, 1971.

[Alker and Sherman, 1982]
H.R. Alker, Jr., and F. Sherman, "Collective Security-Seeking Practice Since 1945," in *Managing International Crises*, D. Frei, ed., Sage, Beverly Hills, Calif., 1982, pp. 113–145.

[Alker et al., 1980]
H.R. Alker, Jr., J. Bennett, and D. Mefford, "Generalized Precedent Logics for Resolving Insecurity Dilemmas," *Int'l Interactions*, Vol. 7, 1980, pp. 165–206.

[Alvarado, 1990]
S.J. Alvarado, *Understanding Editorial Text: A Computer Model of Argument Comprehension*, Kluwer Academic Publishers, Boston, 1990.

[Andriole and Young, 1977]
S.J. Andriole and R.A. Young, "Toward the Development of an Integrated Crisis Warning System," *Int'l Studies Quarterly*, Vol. 21, Mar. 1977, pp. 107–150.

[Azar, 1980]
E. Azar, "The Conflict and Peace Data Bank (COPDAB) Project," *J. of Conflict Resolution*, No. 24, 1980, pp. 143–152.

[Bareiss et al., 1987]
E.R. Bareiss, B.W. Porter, and C.C. Wier, "Protos: An Exemplar-Based Learning Apprentice," *Proc. 4th Int'l Workshop on Machine Learning*, Irvine, Calif., 1987.

[Barletta and Mark, 1988]
R. Barletta and W. Mark, "Explanation-Based Indexing of Cases," *AAAI Proc.*, 1988, pp. 541–546.

[Bercovitch, 1993]
J. Bercovitch, "International Conflict Management, 1945–1992," *Official Codebook for the International Conflict Management Dataset (CONFMAN1)*, Dept. of Political Science, Univ. of Canterbury, New Zealand, Dec. 1993.

[Bloomfield, 1986]
L.P. Bloomfield, "Analytical Rigor and Real-World Conflicts: The Death and Life of CASCON," paper presented at the Annual Meeting of the Int'l Studies Assoc., Anaheim, 1986.

[Bloomfield and Beattie, 1971]
L.P. Bloomfield and R. Beattie, "Computers and Policy-Making: The CASCON Experiment," *J. of Conflict Resolution*, Vol. 15, Mar. 1971, pp. 33–46.

[Bloomfield and Leiss, 1969]
L.P. Bloomfield and A. Leiss, *Controlling Small Wars: A Strategy for the 1970's*, Knopf, New York, 1969.

[Bloomfield and Moulton, 1989]
L.P. Bloomfield and A. Moulton, *CASCON III User Manual*, Center for Int'l Studies, MIT, Cambridge, 1989.

[Bobrow and Sylvan, 1988]
D. Bobrow and Donald A. Sylvan, "Computational Models for Foreign Policy Decision Making: Purpose, Politics, and Information," paper presented at the Annual Meeting of the Int'l Soc. of Political Psychology, Secaucus, N.J., 1988.

[Booch, 1994]
G. Booch, *Object-Oriented Analysis and Design with Applications*, 2nd ed, Benjamin/Cummings Publishing, Redwood City, Calif., 1994.

[Boynton and Dozark, 1992]
G.R. Boynton and P. Dozark, "Looking Forward by Looking Back. Deliberations in the Senate Foreign Relations Committee," paper presented at the Annual Meeting of the Int'l Soc. of Political Psychology, Atlanta, 1992.

[Breiman et al., 1984]
L. Breiman et al., "Classification and Regression Trees," Belmont Wadsworth Int'l Group, Belmont, Calif., 1984.

[Budd, 1991]
T. Budd, *Introduction to Object-Oriented Programming*, Addison-Wesley, Reading, Mass., 1991.

[Buntine, 1990]
W. Buntine, "Myth and Legends in Learning Classification Rules," *AAAI Conf. Proc.*, 1990, pp. 736–742.

[Butterworth with Scranton, 1976]
R.L Butterworth with M.E. Scranton, "Managing Interstate Conflict, 1945–1974: Data with Synopses," Univ. Center for Int'l Studies, Pittsburgh, 1976.

[Bylander et al., 1991]
T. Bylander et al., "The Computational Complexity of Abduction," *Artificial Intelligence*, Vol. 49, Nos. 1–3, May 1991, pp. 25–60.

[Choucri, 1974]
N. Choucri, "Key Issues in International Relations Forecasting," in *Population, Dynamics, and International Violence: Propositions, Insights, and Evidence*, N. Choucri, ed., D.C. Health, Lexington, Mass., 1974, pp. 3–72.

[Cimbala, 1987]
S.J. Cimbala, ed., *Artificial Intelligence and National Security*, Lexington Books, Lexington, Mass., 1987.

[Clark and Niblett, 1988]
P. Clark and T. Niblett, "The CN2 Induction Algorithm," *Machine Learning*, No. 3, 1988, pp. 261–283.

[Davies, 1991]
J.L. Davies, *The Global Event Data System: Coder's Manual*, Center for Int'l Development and Conflict Management, Dept. of Govt. and Politics, Univ. of Maryland, August 1991.

[Davies and McDaniel, 1991]
J.L. Davies and C.K. McDaniel, "The Global Event Data System," paper presented at the Annual Meeting of the Int'l Studies Assoc., Vancouver, 1991.

[Duffy, 1987]
G. Duffy, *Language, Politics, and Method: Grounding a Computational Hermeneutic*, doctoral dissertation, Dept. of Political Science, MIT, Cambridge, August 1987.

[Duffy, 1991]
G. Duffy, "Time Space: Representing Historical Time for Efficient Event Retrieval," in *Artificial Intelligence and International Politics*, V. Hudson, ed., Westview Press, Boulder, 1991, pp. 386–405.

[Duffy and Mallery, 1986]
G. Duffy and J.C. Mallery, "RELATUS: An Artificial Intelligence Tool for Natural Language Modeling," paper presented to the panel on Artificial Intelligence Models of International Politics at the Annual Meeting of the Int'l Studies Assoc., Anaheim, 1986.

[Dupuy, 1988]
T. Dupuy, "History and Case-based Reasoning," in *Proc. DARPA Workshop on Case-Based Reasoning*, Vol. 1, J.L. Kolodner, ed., Morgan Kaufmann, San Mateo, Calif., 1988.

[Farrell, 1987]
R. Farrell, "Intelligent Case Selection and Presentation," *Proc. Int'l Joint Conf. Artificial Intelligence*, Morgan Kaufmann, Los Altos, Calif., 1987.

[Farris et al., 1980]
L. Farris et al., "Phase-Actor Disaggregated Butterworth-Scranton Codebook," working paper, Center for International Studies, MIT, Cambridge, 1980.

[Finney et al., 1963]
D.J. Finney et al., *Tables for Testing Significances in a 2 x 2 Contingency Table*, Cambridge University Press, Cambridge, Mass, 1972.

[Fisher and Langley, 1986]
D. Fisher and P. Langley, "Conceptual Clustering and Its Relation to Numerical Taxonomy," in *Artificial Intelligence and Statistics*, W.A. Gale, ed., Addison-Wesley, Reading, Mass., 1986, pp. 77–116.

[Gale, 1986]
W.A. Gale, ed., *Artificial Intelligence and Statistics*, Addison-Wesley, Reading, Mass., 1986.

[Gamma et al., 1995]
E. Gamma et al., *Design Patterns*, Addison-Wesley, Reading, Mass., 1995.

[Ganzel and Meyer-Stamer, 1986]
K.J. Ganzel and J. Meyer-Stamer, eds., *Die Kriege nach dem Zweiten Weltkrieg bis 1984: Daten und erste Analysen [The Wars after the Second World War until 1984: Data and Analyses]*, Köln: Weltforum Verlag, 1986.

[Garson, 1987]
D. Garson, "The Role of Inductive Expert Systems Generators in the Social Science Research Process," *Social Science Microcomputer Rev.*, Vol. 5, No. 1, Spring 1987, pp. 11–21.

[Gazdar and Mellish, 1989]
G. Gazdar and C. Mellish, eds., *Natural Language Processing in LISP: An Introduction to Computation Linguistics*, Addison-Wesley, Wokingham, England, 1989.

[Genter, 1989]
D. Genter, "Finding the Needle: Accessing and Reasoning from Prior Cases," in *Proc. DARPA Workshop on Case-Based Reasoning*, Vol. 2, K.J. Hammond, ed., Morgan Kaufmann, San Mateo, Calif., 1989, pp. 137–143.

[Gochman and Maoz, 1984]
C.S. Gochman and Z. Maoz, "Militarized Interstate Disputes, 1816–1917: Procedures, Patterns, and Insights," *J. of Conflict Resolution*, No. 26, 1984.

[Goel and Chandrasekaran, 1989]
A. Goel and B. Chandrasekaran, "Use of Device Models in Adaption of Design Cases," in *Hammond,* 1989b, pp. 100–109.

[Goodman, 1989]
M. Goodman, "CBR in Battle Planning," in *Hammond, 1989b*, pp. 246–269.

[Haas, 1968]
E.B. Haas, *Collective Security and the Future International System*, Vol. 5, Monograph No. 1, Monograph Series in World Affairs, Univ. of Denver, 1968.

[Haas et al., 1972]
E.B. Haas, R.L. Butterworth, and J.S. Nye, *Conflict Management by International Organizations*, General Learning Press, Morristown, N.J., 1972.

[Hammond, 1987]
K.J. Hammond, "Explaining and Repairing Plans That Fail," *Proc. Int'l Joint Conf. Artificial Intelligence*, Vol. 1, Morgan Kaufmann, San Mateo, Calif., 1987, pp. 109–114.

[Hammond, 1989a]
K.J. Hammond, *Case-Based Planning: Viewing Planning as a Memory Task*, Academic Press, Boston, 1989.

[Hammond, 1989b]
K.J. Hammond, ed., *Proc. DARPA Workshop on Case-Based Reasoning*, Vol. 2, Morgan Kaufmann, San Mateo, Calif., 1989.

[Harman, 1965]
G. Harman, "The Inference to the Best Explanation," *Philosophical Rev.*, No. 74, 1965, pp. 88–95.

[Haussler, 1990]
D. Haussler, "Probably Approximately Correct Learning," *AAAI Proc.*, 1990, pp. 1101–1108.

[Hermann et al., 1973]
C.F. Hermann et al., *CREON: A Foreign Events Data Set*, Sage Professional Papers in International Studies, Vol. 1, Series No. 02-024, Sage Publications, Beverly Hills, Calif., 1973.

[Holland et al., 1989]
J.H. Holland et al., *Induction: Process of Inference, Learning, and Discovery*, MIT Press, Cambridge, 1989.

[Howell, 1983]
L.D. Howell, "A Comparative Study of the WEIS and COPDAB Data Sets," *Int'l Studies Quarterly*, Vol. 27, No. 2, 1983, pp. 149–159.

[Howell et al., 1986]
L.D. Howell et al., "Changing Priorities: Putting the Data Back onto Events Data Analysis," paper presented at the 1986 Meeting of the Int'l Studies Assoc., Anaheim, 1986.

[Hudson, 1991]
V.M. Hudson, *Artificial Intelligence and International Politics*, Westview Press, Boulder, 1991.

[Hull and Nie, 1981]
C.H. Hull and N.H. Nie, *SPSS*, 2nd ed., McGraw Hill, New York, 1981.

[Hunt et al., 1966]
E.B. Hunt, J. Marin, and P.J. Stone, *Experiments in Induction*, Academic Press, New York, 1966.

[ISO-8879, 1986]
ISO-8879, *Information Processing—Text and Office Systems—Standard Generalized Markup Language (SGML)*, ISO, Geneva, 1986.

[Iawayama et al., 1990]
M. Iawayama, T. Tokunaga, and H. Tanaka, "A Method of Calculating the Measure of Salience in Understanding Metaphors," *AAAI Conf. Proc.*, 1990, pp. 298–303.

[Job and Johnson, 1991]
B.L. Job and D. Johnson, "UNCLESAM: The Application of a Rule-Based Model of U.S. Foreign Policy Making," in *Artificial Intelligence and International Politics*, V.M. Hudson, Westview Press, Boulder, 1991, pp. 221–244.

[Josephson et al., 1987]
J.R. Josephson et al., "A Mechansim for Forming Composite Explanatory Hypotheses," *IEEE Trans. Systems, Man, and Cybernetics*, Vol. 17, No. 3, 1987, pp. 445–454.

[Keene, 1989]
S.E. Keene, *Object-Oriented Programming in Common LISP: A Programmer's Guide to CLOS*, Addison-Wesley, Reading, Mass., 1989.

[Kende, 1978]
I. Kende, "Wars of Ten Years (1967–1976)," *J. of Peace Research*, No. 3, Vol. XV 178, 1978, pp. 227–241.

[Kernighan and Pike, 1984]
B.W. Kernighan and R. Pike, *The UNIX Programming Environment*, Prentice Hall, Englewood Cliffs, N.J., 1984.

[Kiczales et al., 1991]
G. Kiczales, J. de Rivieres, and D.G. Bobrow, *The Art of the Metaobject Protocol*, MIT Press, Cambridge, 1991.

[King, 1989]
G. King, "Event Count Models for International Relations: Generalizations and Applications," *Int'l Studies Quarterly*, Vol. 33, No. 2, June 1989.

[Kolodner, 1983]
J.L. Kolodner, "Reconstructive Memory: A Computer Model," *Cognitive Science*, Vol. 7, 1983, pp. 280–328.

[Kolodner, 1988]
J.L. Kolodner, ed., *Proc. DARPA Workshop on Case-Based Reasoning*, Vol. 1, Morgan Kaufmann, San Mateo, Calif., 1988.

[Kolodner, 1991]
J.L. Kolodner, "Improving Human Decision Making through Case-Based Decision Aiding," *AI Magazine*, Summer 1991, pp. 52–68.

[Kolodner and Simpson, 1988]
J.L. Kolodner and R.L. Simpson, "The MEDIATOR: A Case Study of Cased-Based Problem Solver," Tech. Report GIT-ICS-88/11, Georgia Inst. of Technology, 1988.

[Kononenko et al., 1984]
I. Kononenko, I. Bratko, and P. Stone, "Experiments in Automatic Learning of Medical Diagnostic Rules," tech. report, Josef Stephan Inst., Ljubljana, Yugoslavia, 1984.

[Jacobson et al., 1992]
I. Jacobson et al., *Object-Oriented Software Engineering: A Use Case Driven Approach*, Addison-Wesley, Wokingham, England, 1992.

[Leng, 1987]
R.J. Leng, "Behavioral Correlates of War: User's Manual and Data Handbook," Middlebury College, Vermont, 1987, mimeo.

[Leng, 1988]
R.J. Leng, "Militarized Interstate Crisis: The BCOW Typology and Its Applications," *Int'l Studies Quarterly*, 1988.

[Lopez De Mantaras, 1991]
R. Lopez De Mantaras, "A Distance-Based Attribute Selection Measure for Decision Tree Induction," *Machine Learning*, No. 6, 1991, pp. 81–92.

[Lutherbacher and Ward, 1985]
U. Lutherbacher and M.D. Ward, eds., *Dynamic Models of International Conflict*, Lynn Rienner Publishers, Boulder, 1985.

[Macintosh, 1985]
Inside Macintosh, Vol. 1, Addison-Wesley, Reading, Mass., 1985.

[Mallery, 1988a]
J.C. Mallery, *Thinking about Foreign Policy: Finding an Appropriate Role for Artificial Intelligent Computers*, master's thesis, Dept. of Political Science, MIT, Cambridge, 1988.

[Mallery, 1988b]
J.C. Mallery, "Beyond Correlation: Reconstructing the Relational Structure of Conflict Processes from SHERFACS Data," paper presented to the Panel on "International Conflict Management Since 1945: New Computational Possibilities," at the Annual Meeting of the Int'l Studies Assoc., St. Louis, 1988.

[Mallery, 1994]
J.C. Mallery, "Beyond Correlation: Bringing Artificial Intelligence to Events Data," *Int'l Interactions*, 20 (1–2), 1994, pp. 101–145.

[Mallery and Hurwitz, 1987]
J.C. Mallery and R. Hurwitz, "Analogy and Precedent in Strategic Decision-Making: A Computational Approach," paper presented at the Meeting of the Am. Political Science Assoc., Chicago, 1987.

[McClelland, 1976]
C.A. McClelland, *World Event/Interaction Survey Codebook. (ICPSR 5211)*, Inter-Univ. Consortium for Political and Social Research, Ann Arbor, Mich., 1976.

[McClelland, 1983]
C.A. McClelland, "Let the User Beware," *Int'l Studies Quarterly*, Vol. 27, No. 2, June 1983, pp. 169–177.

[McClelland et al., 1971]
C.A. McClelland et al., "The Management and Analysis of International Event Data: A Computerized System for Monitoring and Projecting Event Flows," School of International Relations, Univ. of Southern California, Los Angeles, 1971, mimeo.

[Mefford, 1984]
D. Mefford, "Formulating Foreign Policy on the Basis of Historical Analogies: An Application of Developments in Artificial Intelligence," paper presented at the Annual Meeting of the Int'l Studies Assoc., Atlanta, March 1984.

[Mefford, 1987]
D. Mefford, "The Policy Process and the Evolution of Argument. A Theory in the Form of a Series of Computer Programs," paper prepared for the Annual Meeting of the Int'l Studies Assoc., Washington, D.C., April 1987.

[Mefford, 1988]
D. Mefford, "Case-Based Reasoning, Legal Reasoning, and the Study of Politics," working paper, Dept. of Political Science, Ohio State Univ., 1988.

[Meyer, 1988]
B. Meyer, *Object-Oriented Software Construction*, Series in Computer Science, Prentice-Hall, Englewood Cliffs, N.J., 1988.

[Mingers, 1989a]
J. Mingers, "An Empirical Comparison of Selection Measures for Decision Tree Induction," *Machine Learning*, No. 3, 1989, pp. 319–342.

[Mingers, 1989b]
J. Mingers, "An Empirical Comparison of Pruning Methods for Decision Tree Induction," *Machine Learning*, No. 4, 1989, pp. 227–243.

[Morgan and Sonquist, 1963]
J.M. Morgan and J.A. Sonquist, "Some Problems in the Analysis of Surveys and a Proposal," *J. of the Am. Statistical Assoc.*, Vol. 58, 1963, pp. 415–434.

[Newell and Simon, 1972]
A. Newell and H. Simon, *Human Problem Solving*, Prentice-Hall, Englewood Cliffs, N.J., 1972.

[Niblett, 1987]
T. Niblett, "Constructing Decision Trees in Noisy Domains," *Proc. 2nd European Working Session on Learning*, Sigma Press, Bled, Yugoslavia, 1987, pp. 67–78.

[Norvig, 1992]
P. Norvig, *Paradigms of Artificial Intelligence Programming: Case Studies in Common LISP*, Morgan Kaufmann, San Mateo, Calif., 1992.

[Onishi, 1986]
A. Onishi, "A New Generation of FUGI Model — A Global Early Warning System for National and International Conflicts," in *Proc. IFAC Working Group on Supplemental Ways for Improving International Stability (SWIIS)*, H. Chestnut and Y. Haimes, eds., Cleveland, 1986.

[OTT]
Open Text Corporation, Suite #559, 180 King Street South, Waterloo, Ontario, Canada.

[Panagos, 1985]
F.N. Panagos, *A Knowledge Based Approach to the CASCON Decision-Making System*, master's thesis, Political Science Dept., MIT, Cambridge, 1985.

[Patterson and Niblett, 1983]
A. Patterson and T. Niblett, *ACLS User Manual*, Intelligent Terminals Ltd., Glasgow, 1983.

[Peirce, 1950]
C.S. Peirce, "Abduction and Induction," in *The Philosophy of Peirce: Selected Writings*, J. Bucher, ed., Hartcourt, Brace and World, New York, 1950.

[Punch et al., 1990]
W.F. Punch et al., "Peirce: A Tool for Experimenting with Abduction," *IEEE Expert*, Vol. 5, No. 5, Oct. 1990, pp. 34–44.

[Quinlan, 1979]
J.R. Quinlan, "Induction Over Large Data Bases," Heuristic Programming Project Report HPP-79-14, Computer Science Dept., Stanford Univ., 1979.

[Quinlan, 1983]
J.R. Quinlan, "Learning Efficient Classification Procedures and Their Application to Chess End Games," in *Machine Learning*, R.S. Michalski, J.G. Carbonell, and T.M. Mitchell, eds., Tioga Press, Palo Alto, Calif., 1983.

[Quinlan, 1985]
J.R. Quinlan, "Decision Trees and Multi-Valued Attributes," in *Machine Intelligence*, Vol. 2, J. Hayes and D. Michie, eds., Ellis Horwood, Chichester, 1985, pp. 305–318.

[Quinlan, 1986a]
J.R. Quinlan, "Simplifying Decision Trees," AI Memo No. 930, Artificial Intelligence Laboratory, MIT, Cambridge, 1986.

[Quinlan, 1986b]
J.R. Quinlan, "Induction of Decision Trees," *Machine Learning*, No. 1, 1986, pp. 81–106.

[Redmond, 1989]
M. Redmond, "Combining Explanation Types for Learning by Understanding Instructional Examples," *Proc. 11th Annual Conf. Cognitive Science Society*, Lawrence Earlbaum, Hillsdale, N.J., 1989, pp. 147–154.

[ReMind, 1990]
ReMind™ Development Version 1.0, Cognitive Systems, Boston, 1990.

[Rissland and Ashley, 1987]
E.L. Rissland and K.D. Ashley, "A Case-Based System for Trade Secret Laws," *Proc. 1st Int'l Conf. Artificial Intelligence and Law*, 1987.

[Rivest, 1987]
R.L. Rivest, "Learning Decision Lists," *Machine Learning*, No. 2, 1987, pp. 229–246.

[Rumbaugh et al., 1991]
J. Rumbaugh et al., *Object-Oriented Modeling and Design*, Prentice Hall, Englewood Cliffs, N.J., 1991.

[Salton, 1986]
G. Salton, "Another Look at Automatic Text-retrieval Systems," *Communications of the ACM*, Vol. 29, No. 7, July 1986, pp. 648–656.

[Salton, 1990]
G. Salton, *Automatic Text Processing: The Transformation, Analysis, and Retrieval of Information by Computer*, Addison-Wesley, Reading, Mass., 1990.

[Sankoff and Kruskal, 1983]
D. Sankoff and J.B. Kruskal, *Time Warps, String Edits, and Macromolecules: The Theory and Practice of Sequence Comparison*, Addison-Wesley, New York, 1983.

[Schank and Abelson, 1977]
R.C. Schank and R.P. Abelson, *Script, Plans, Goals, and Understanding*, Lawrence Earlbaum, Hillsdale, N. J., 1977.

[Schank and Childers, 1984]
R.C. Schank and P.G. Childers, *The Cognitive Computer: On Language, Learning, and Artificial Intelligence*, Addison-Wesley, Reading, Mass., 1984.

[Schrodt, 1984a]
P.A. Schrodt, "Artificial Intelligence and International Crisis: An Application of Pattern Recognition to the Analysis of Event Sequences," meeting of the Am. Political Science Assoc., Washington, D.C., 1984.

[Schrodt, 1984b]
P.A. Schrodt, "Artificial Intelligence and the State of Mathematical Modeling in International Relations: A Survey," paper presented at the Conf. on Dynamic Models of International Conflict, Boulder, 1984.

[Schrodt, 1985]
P.A. Schrodt, "Precedent-Based Logic and Rational Choice: A Comparison," in *Dynamic Models of International Conflict*, U. Lutherbacher and M.D. Ward, eds., Lynn Rienner Publishers, Boulder, 1985, pp. 373–400.

[Schrodt, 1987a]
P.A. Schrodt, "Classification of Interstate Conflict Outcome Using a Bootstrapped CLS Algorithm," paper at the Annual Meeting of the Int'l Studies Assoc., Washington, D. C., 1987.

[Schrodt, 1987b]
P.A. Schrodt, "Pattern Matching, Set Prediction, and Foreign Policy Analysis," in *Artificial Intelligence and National Security*, S.J. Cimbala, ed., Lexington Books, Lexington, Mass., 1987, pp. 89–108.

[Schrodt, 1988]
P.A. Schrodt, "The Statistical Characteristics of Events Data," paper prepared for the Annual Meeting of the Int'l Studies Assoc., St. Louis, 1988.

[Schrodt, 1989]
P.A. Schrodt, "Short-Term Prediction of International Behavior Using a Holland Classifier," *Math. Computational Modeling*, Vol. 12, No. 4/5, Pergamon Press, 1989, pp. 589–600.

[Schrodt, 1991]

P.A. Schrodt, "Pattern Recognition in International Events Sequences," in *Artificial Intelligence and International Politics*, V.M. Hudson, Westview Press, Boulder, 1991, pp. 166–193.

[Schrodt et al., 1992]

P.A. Schrodt et al., "Machine Coding of Event Data Using International and Regional Sources," paper presented at the Meeting of the Int'l Studies Assoc., Atlanta, 1992.

[Sherman, 1987a]

F.L. Sherman, *Partway to Peace: The United Nations and the Road to Nowhere?* Ph.D thesis in political science, Pennsylvania State Univ., May 1987.

[Sherman, 1987b]

F.L. Sherman, "Four Major Traditions of Historical Events Research," distribution paper at the MIT/Center for International Studies — Data Directions in International Revelations Conf. on "New Technologies for Storing, Indexing, Retrieving, Coding, and Analyzing Information on International Events," Cambridge, 1987.

[Sherman, 1988]

F.L. Sherman, "SHERFACS: A New Cross-Paradigm, International Conflict Data Set," paper presented at the Annual Meeting of the Int'l Studies Assoc., St. Louis, 1988.

[Sherman et al., 1992]

F.L. Sherman et al., "Grammars of Conflict and Cooperation in the Post-War International System," paper presented at the Meeting of the Int'l Studies Assoc., Atlanta, 1992.

[Shriver and Wegner, 1987]

B. Shriver and P. Wegner, *Research Directions in Object-Oriented Programming*, MIT Press, Cambridge, 1987.

[Skalak and Rissland, 1990]

D.B. Skalak and E.L. Rissland, "Inductive Learning in a Mixed Paradigm Setting," *AAAI Conf. Proc.*, 1990, pp. 840–847.

[Slade, 1991]

S. Slade, "Case-Based Reasoning: A Research Paradigm," *AI Magazine*, Spring 1991, pp. 42–55.

[Small and Singer, 1982]

M. Small and J.D. Singer, *Resort to Arms: International and Civil Wars, 1861–1980*, Sage Publications, Beverly Hills, Calif., 1982.

[Smoker, 1985]

P. Smoker, "Towards a Systems Perspective: Directions for the Eighties," in *Dynamic Models of International Conflict*, U. Lutherbacher and M.D. Ward, eds., Lynn Rienner Publishers, Boulder, 1985, pp. 101–114.

[Sonquist et al., 1971]
J.A. Sonquist, E.L. Baker, and J.M. Morgan, "Searching for Structures (ALIAS - AID - II)," Survey Research Center, Inst. for Social Research, Univ. of Michigan, Ann Arbor, 1971.

[Steele, 1990]
G.L. Steele, Jr., *Common LISP: The Language*, 2nd ed., Digital Press, Bedford, Mass., 1990.

[Sylvan and Chan, 1984]
D.A. Sylvan and S. Chan, *Foreign Policy Decision Making: Perception, Cognition, and Artificial Intelligence*, Praeger, New York, 1984.

[Sylvan et al., 1991a]
D.A. Sylvan, A. Goel, and B. Chandrasekaran, "Modeling Foreign Policy Decision Making as Knowledge-Based Reasoning," in *Artificial Intelligence and International Politics*, V.M. Hudson, Westview Press, Boulder, 1991, pp. 245–273.

[Sylvan and Majeski, 1992]
D.J. Sylvan and S.J. Majeski, "Modeling Theories of Constititive Relations in Politics," research paper, Univ. of Colorado and Univ. of Minnesota, 1992.

[Sylvan et al., 1991b]
D.J. Sylvan, S.J. Majeski, and J.L. Milliken, "Theoretical Categories and Data Construction in Computational Models of Foreign Policy," in *Artificial Intelligence and International Politics*, V.M. Hudson, Westview Press, Boulder, 1991, pp. 327–346.

[Tanaka, 1984]
A. Tanaka, "China, China Watching, and CHINA-WATCHER," in *Foreign Policy Decision Making: Perception, Cognition, and Artificial Intelligence*, D.A. Sylvan and S. Chan, Praeger, New York, 1984, pp. 310–344.

[Taylor and Joice, 1983]
C.F. Taylor and D.A. Joice, *World Handbook of Political and Social Indicators*, 3rd ed., Yale Univ. Press, New Haven, 1983.

[Thagard, 1988]
P. Thagard, *Computational Philosophy of Science*, MIT Press, Cambridge, 1988.

[Thorson and Sylvan, 1982]
S.T. Thorson and D.A. Sylvan, "Counterfactuals and the Cuban Missile Crisis," *Int'l Studies Quarterly*, Vol. 26, No. 4, 1982, pp. 539–571.

[Trappl, 1986]
R. Trappl, "Reducing International Tension through Artificial Intelligence: 3 Potential Approaches," in *Power Autonomy Utopia: New Approaches Towards Complex Systems*, R. Trappl, ed., Plenum, New York, 1986, pp. 97–103.

[Trappl, 1992]
R. Trappl, "The Role of Artificial Intelligence in the Avoidance of War," in *Cybernetics and Systems '92*, R. Trappl, ed., World Scientific Publishing, Singapore, 1992, pp. 1667–1672.

[Trappl and Miksch, 1991]
R. Trappl and S. Miksch, "Can Artificial Intelligence Contribute to Peacefar," paper presented at the Conf. on Artificial Intelligence, Prague, 1991.

[Trappl and Unseld, 1993]
R. Trappl and S.D. Unseld, "Artificial Intelligence und die moegliche Vermeidung von Krisen und Kriegen [Artificial Intelligence and its Potential for Avoiding Crises and Wars]," *Wiener Infomations-Technology-Tagung*, Wien, April 1993.

[Unseld, 1990]
S.D. Unseld, "A Formal Framework for Political Analyses," Memorandum, The Graduate Inst. of Int'l Studies, Geneva, 1990.

[Unseld and Mallery, 1992]
S.D. Unseld and J.C. Mallery, "Interaction Detection in Complex Data models," A.I. Memo No. 1298, Artificial Intelligence Laboratory, MIT, Cambridge, May 1992.

[Vincent, 1983]
J.E. Vincent, "WEIS vs. COPDAB: Correspondence Problems," *Int'l Studies Quarterly,* Vol. 27, No. 2, 1983, pp. 161–168.

[Utgoff, 1988]
P.E. Utgoff, "ID5, "An Incremental ID3," *Proc. 5th Int'l Conf. Machine Learning*, Morgan Kaufmann, Ann Arbor, Mich., 1988, pp. 107–120.

[Weber, 1985]
R.P. Weber, *Basic Content Analysis*, Sage, Beverly Hills, Calif., 1985.

[Weiner, 1985]
E.J. Weiner, "A Knowledge Representation Approach to Understanding Metaphors," *Computational Linguistics*, Vol. 10, No. 1, 1985, pp. 1–14.

[Winston, 1975]
P.H. Winston, ed., *The Psychology of Computer Vision*, McGraw Hill, New York, 1975.

[Winston, 1982]
P.H. Winston, "Learning New Principles from Precedents and Exercises," *Artificial Intelligence*, Vol. 19, 1982, pp. 321–350.

[Wirfs-Brock et al., 1990]
R. Wirfs-Brock, B. Wilkerson, and L. Wiener, *Designing Object-Oriented Software*, Prentice Hall, Englewood Cliffs, N.J., 1990.

[Young, 1970]
R.A. Young, *Prediction and Forecasting in International Relations: An Exploratory Analysis*, Ph.D dissertation, Univ. of Southern California, Los Angeles, Calif., 1970.

INDEX

D

E

F